Best Wildflower
Hikes Colorado

Best Wildflower Hikes Colorado

A Guide to the Area's Greatest Wildflower Hiking Adventures

Chris Kassar

Guilford, Connecticut

FALCONGUIDES

GUILFORD, CONNECTICUT

An imprint of Globe Pequot
Falcon and Falcon Guides are registered trademarks and Make Adventure Your Story is a trademark of Rowman & Littlefield.

Distributed by NATIONAL BOOK NETWORK

Copyright © 2017 by Rowman & Littlefield

Maps by Melissa Baker © Rowman & Littlefield
All photos by Chris Kassar unless noted otherwise.

British Library Cataloguing-in-Publication Information available

Library of Congress Cataloging-in-Publication Data available

ISBN 978-1-4930-2259-5 (paperback)
ISBN 978-1-4930-2260-1 (e-book)

∞™ The paper used in this publication meets the minimum requirements of American National Standard for Information Sciences–Permanence of Paper for Printed Library Materials, ANSI/NISO Z39.48-1992.

The author and Rowman & Littlefield assume no liability for accidents happening to, or injuries sustained by, readers who engage in the activities described in this book.

Dedicated to
My wonderful sisters, Angele and Helen
and
My incredible Aunt Aggie
Because I promised I would.

Written in loving memory of
Dan Sidles and Jason Lawrence—you are loved and missed.

Contents

The Hikes

Overview

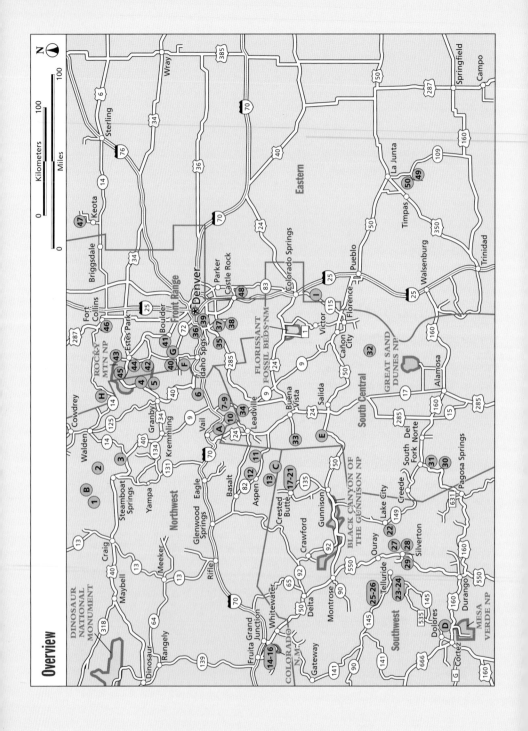

Acknowledgments

Many thanks to all who helped me write this book. For their suggestions and guidance, I would like to thank the Colorado Native Plant Society, Jan and Charlie Turner, Mary Dubler, Steve Olson, Scott Smith, Ed Biery, Hugh Mackay, Irene Shonle, Jill Handwerk, Dave Van Manen, Megan Bowes, Megan Ronda Koski, Melissa Islam, Sarada Krishnan, Cindy Newlander, Barbara Doe Fahey, and Carol English for taking the time to suggest hikes, hike with me, and for connecting me with so many wildflower enthusiasts.

I am very grateful to the National Park Service, Katy Sykes of Rocky Mountain National Park, Molly Murphy, and Kim Hartwig at Colorado National Monument and Amy Stevens from RMNA for their recommendations and expert advice. I appreciate the Rocky Mountain Nature Association for the great work it does and its continued support of my efforts in creating and distributing this guide. Extreme gratitude to David Legere, Melissa Baker, Joe Novosad, and Ellen Urban who directed the efforts at Falcon Guides.

I would like to express my heartfelt appreciation to my family and friends for their support and encouragement in this overwhelming undertaking. Thanks to Nathan Perrault (aka "tall Nate") for providing great hike suggestions and flower updates from the field, to my parents and siblings for constantly offering reassurance, and to Nick Watson for living with me while I hunkered down to complete this project.

Lastly, I would like to express my gratitude to Mother Nature and to the flowers for making me slow down and take more notice of the infinite and intense beauty that is all around us.

—*Chris Kassar*

Rocky Mountain Conservancy

Founded in 1931, the nonprofit Rocky Mountain Conservancy (formerly Rocky Mountain Nature Association/RMNA) promotes stewardship of Rocky Mountain National Park and similar lands through education and philanthropy. Rocky Mountain Conservancy is a major contributor to improvement projects, educational programs, research efforts, and critical land acquisitions. For more, visit: rmconservancy.org or call (970) 586-0108.

Introduction

Days lengthen. Mercury rises. Rivers swell. Winter concedes defeat and snow pours off hillsides with wild abandon. With each passing day, the sun hangs in the sky for a few minutes longer. Tiny bursts of color surge through the soil, heralding spring's return. After a long, frigid season, the hillsides, forests, and mountaintops beckon once again. You heed their call and return to the mountains, meandering through sweet-smelling pines, strolling along striking tundra, and squishing through patches of mud and persistent snow. Some old friends reward your efforts and welcome you back by slowly revealing themselves in hidden blooms of blue, pink, yellow, white, and red. Time moves on and summer takes hold. Sporadic blossoms give way to grand wild-flower displays as nature generously cloaks Colorado in a dazzling gown of colors.

These changes excite the senses, and if you love flowers like I do, spring and summer unearth an irresistible inner urge that drives you to explore. But, where should you go and when, in order to catch the peak bloom? In a state overflowing with striking trails that meander through canyon country, rugged mountain ranges, and wild plains dappled with ancient buttes, this can be a challenging question to answer.

Fear not! This user-friendly book guides you to fifty of my favorite wildflower hikes—some classics, some lesser known, all delightful. The Centennial State is amazingly diverse, with many joys awaiting the ardent adventurer. Among our gems are the

diamond-shaped east face of Longs Peak in Rocky Mountain National Park, brilliant blue alpine lakes of the San Juans, red rock canyons rife with ancestral artifacts, other-worldly buttes rising from plains, and world-famous meadows of neck-high flowers framing Gothic Mountain near Crested Butte. In an attempt to encourage you to sample the range of Colorado's varied terrain and experience its fascinating geology, flora and fauna, and human history, I've chosen hikes scattered across the state that vary in difficulty and explore a range of habitats.

This region boasts many of the highest mountains in the lower 48, with fifty-eight summits over 14,000 feet and hundreds over 13,000 feet. Glaciers have given rise to some of these mountains, while erosion, wind, water, and ice have joined forces with time to sculpt other peaks. As a result, summits vary greatly from jagged crests to rounded knobs to massive wide expanses. Tiny trickles of water begin high in the hills, flowing downward and turning into some of the continent's largest rivers, while the mountainous spine of the Continental Divide dictates which way this water flows. Four of the nation's major rivers, the Colorado, the Rio Grande, the Arkansas, and the Platte, begin within the state's borders.

Substantial swaths of wild and remote lands remain relatively untouched in Colorado, allowing an array of ecosystems—alpine tundra, woodlands, shrub-lands, grasslands, wetlands, lakes, riparian corridors, and forests—to thrive. This rich landscape provides habitat for an abundance of charismatic wildlife like elk, black bears, bighorn sheep, and mountain lions as well as lesser-known critters like the Clark's nutcracker, sphinx moth, broad-tailed hummingbird, the Phoebus Parnassian butterfly, and numerous species of bees and bats. Many of these animals, big and small, depend on a diverse community of plants and flowers for their survival.

Botanists estimate that there are more than 3,000 species of flowering plants in Colorado alone. Wildflowers range in size from the ground-hugging moss campion (*Silene acaulis* var. *subacaulescens)* to towering 13-foot-high annual sunflowers (*Helianthus annuus)*. Numerous shapes and flower types grace hillsides, and the colors are as wide-ranging as the paints on an artist's palette.

Flora and Fauna

Colorado ranges in elevation from 3,337 feet at its lowest point in the northeastern plains to 14,433 feet at the top of Mount Elbert near Leadville. In the rain shadow of the Rocky Mountains, the Eastern Plains are high and dry, with less than 15 inches of annual precipitation. Wolf Creek Pass on the Continental Divide often receives over 300 inches of snow annually. Just east of Wolf Creek Pass, the San Luis Valley is a true desert, receiving less than 8 inches of moisture per year. It is these environmental extremes and the unique range in elevation, latitude, and climate that give rise to Colorado's incredible diversity.

Other factors, including variation in rock and soil type, moisture, and changes in temperature greatly affect growing season and species distribution, thus creating regions commonly referred to as ecosystems or life zones. An ecosystem is a recognizable community of living organisms existing together in a particular area; the plants, animals, and microorganisms within a zone interact with each other and local environmental factors like elevation, wind, temperature, precipitation, sunlight, soil type, and slope.

Climate plays an important role in delineating life zones. This factor is extremely variable, susceptible to localized shifts, and influenced largely by changes in altitude and latitude. For instance, temperatures typically drop as elevation increases. On average, the temperature drops 3°F for every 1,000 feet gained. As elevations rise and

temperatures cool, precipitation generally increases. In addition, gaining 1,000 feet in elevation is similar to traveling 600 miles north, meaning climatic conditions and plants encountered on the highest peaks resemble those found in the Arctic. This is why, as you make your way through the various life zones, you will notice obvious shifts in plant life. Certain plants are adapted to living in cooler, windier spots while others need shelter and warmth to survive. Monsoon moisture, drought, fires, and other environmental events can also add to plant variation.

On drives or hikes, you have probably observed that certain species of flowers and trees grow within a certain range of elevations. At the lowest elevations, short-grass prairie dominates the Eastern Plains, while semidesert scrub and sagebrush shrublands populate the west side of the Rockies. Prairie dogs, mule deer, white-tailed deer, coyotes, and pronghorn antelope rule these areas. Coyotes, foxes, eagles, hawks, and great horned owls feed on little critters. As elevation and precipitation increase, you pass from mountain shrublands into pinyon-juniper forest, then ponderosa pine and Douglas fir forests. Mule deer browse on bushes, elk munch grasses, and black bears roam the forest in search of food, while mountain lions prowl rocky rises. Continue to climb through lodgepole pine and aspen forests into forests of spruce-fir and limber and bristlecone pine. Mountain grasslands and wetlands punctuate the forest blanket. Mountain goats and Rocky Mountain bighorn sheep thrive on cliffs and rocky steeps towering overhead.

As you gain elevation, animals and plants show their adaptations to shorter summers, less oxygen, and colder temperatures. In the high country, alpine tundra supports miniature vegetation on wind-blown slopes or in the crevices of sheltering rocks. Above tree line, pikas scurry around with mouthfuls of grasses and flowers, while lazy marmots sun themselves on rocks. Across ecosystems, you can easily spot crows, magpies, blue Steller's jays with their black crowns, and pesky Clark's nutcrackers and gray jays (nicknamed "camp robbers").

The altitude at which a plant grows is an important clue in plant identification. Thus, it's useful to have a basic understanding of Colorado's five broad-based life zones, which are characterized by different temperatures and moisture conditions that give rise to unique communities of plants and animals. These noticeable belts of vegetation demonstrate the power that altitude has to shape the environment. Each hike outlined here travels through one or more of the following distinct life zones: grassland/semidesert (below 6,000 feet), foothills (6,000–8,000 feet), montane (8,000–9,500 feet), subalpine (9,500–11,400 feet), and alpine (above 11,400 feet). (See sidebars for more information about each life zone.)

These life zones help us know what to expect, but remember that nature varies. Although we discuss these ecosystems by elevational boundaries, don't be surprised when you notice variation and overlap.

Weather

Quick to change and challenging to forecast, Colorado's weather is as varied as the state itself. On the plains, afternoon thunderstorms offer a respite from hot summer days. Mountainous areas tend to stay cool and comfortable due to low humidity, but the mountains often create their own weather, bringing thunderstorms and rain up high in summer. Rains may drench the Front Range and Eastern Plains, while western mountains and canyons remain sunny and warm.

Spring and summer bring unpredictable weather. One day can be warm and dry, while the next can be wet and chilly. Snow in the high country typically begins melting in May, causing runoff and thus river levels to peak in mid-June. On Colorado's Eastern Plains, wildflowers begin to blossom in April and May, while the high country remains snowed in until mid-June or later. Exact timing depends on snowfall and summer temperatures, but expect an abundant and concentrated late season dose of color in the subalpine and alpine environs, often peaking in early to mid-July. Be ready for persistent patches of snow through July or even all year in certain areas.

Stay tuned to thunderstorms, which are quite prevalent in the plains and mountains during spring and summer. As the sun heats the ground, warm air rises, cools, and releases moisture that condenses into clouds. Thunderstorms can become quite severe, bringing a multitude of problems, including dangerous lightning, flash floods that roar into mountains and desert canyons, and cold rain or hail which can lead to hypothermia in unprepared hikers. The monsoon season, which lasts from mid-July to early September, brings occasional gray, rainy days and increased thunderstorms, so start early in the day and be prepared for anything.

Whatever the season, always be prepared for an array of conditions. Weather often changes on a dime, and temperature drops of 10°F to 20°F in an hour are regular occurrences. No matter the forecast or the weather at the start of a hike, bring clothing layers and rain (or snow) gear.

Wilderness Restrictions/Regulations

Opportunities for adventure and discovery abound on Colorado's public lands. With two national grasslands, eight national wildlife refuges, twelve National Forests, forty-three

Wilderness areas (not counting Wilderness study areas), three national conservation areas, four National Parks, forty-two state parks, various open space areas, and several National Monuments, there are endless chances to explore many different settings and ecosystems.

In the following chapters, we strive to give you the most accurate, thorough, and up-to-date information on regulations. However, because regulations change, we include contact information so you can check with the responsible agency for up-to-date restrictions and regulations. In general, each Wilderness area has specific group-size limitations and some have designated campsites in heavily used areas.

National Parks and Monuments charge entrance fees and require backcountry permits for camping and sometimes for hiking. State parks charge entrance fees and separate camping fees. Each county and city open space or mountain park area has its own regulations.

As you take advantage of this spectacular region, remember that our planet is very dear and fragile. Regardless of regulations, we can help keep it healthy by using common sense, following Leave No Trace principles and employing the Green Tips found throughout the text.

How to Use This Guide

Anyone with an interest in discovering more about Colorado and its unique tapestry of plants can use this guide as a tool. Using this book requires no specialized knowledge, just a curious nature, perceptive skills, and an eye for detail.

This remarkable region is home to thousands of incredible wildflower hikes, and a book this size cannot cover every one. It would have been easy to write solely about hikes in the Crested Butte area, which is the wildflower capital of Colorado. However, to create a geographically diverse book, we included a range of hikes—some with less dazzling but equally worthy flower displays—that span a range of interesting ecosystems and landscapes. We not only chose many classic flower hikes, but also included a handful of less common hikes that we felt filled in the gaps. We did this to ensure that this guide accurately highlights the diversity of flora found in Colorado by including a broad range of flowers, habitats, and altitudes. Included here are photographs, maps, and descriptions of over fifty day hikes throughout Colorado.

Each region begins with a section introduction, where you're given a sweeping look at the lay of the land. After this overview, we describe specific hikes within that region.

Each hike starts with a short summary of the hike's highlights. These quick overviews give you a taste of the adventure to follow.

Next, you'll find the quick, nitty-gritty details of the hike: trailhead location, nearest town(s), hike distance, approximate hiking time, difficulty rating, best season for wildflowers, peak bloom, common flowers, type of terrain, and what other trail users you may encounter.

Most are self-explanatory, but here are details on others:

Distance: The total distance of the recommended route: one-way for loops, round-trip for out and back or lollipops, point-to-point for shuttles. Options are additional.

Difficulty: Each hike received a level of difficulty rating: easy, moderate, strenuous. Difficulty varies greatly based on your fitness level, distance, terrain, elevation gain, and altitude. In the high country especially, altitude and elevation gain can make short hikes much more challenging than usual. Thus, you will find these rankings are largely subjective and vary greatly based on steepness of climbs and altitude. Use these as guidelines only; trails may prove easier or harder depending on you.

Flowers Commonly Found: List of flowers commonly found; not a comprehensive list of all flowers you might encounter.

Finding the Trailhead: Gives you dependable directions from a nearby town to where you'll want to park. (GPS coordinates are in WGS 84 datum.)

Hike: This is the meat of the chapter. Detailed and honest, this is the author's carefully researched impression of the trail. While it's impossible to cover everything, we do our best to include what's important and to discuss natural history and wildflowers commonly encountered along the way. Keep in mind that flowers will vary from year to year depending on snowfall, temperatures, and the date you hike the trail. Flower blooms can happen and disappear quickly depending on conditions. At times in the description, we mention historical or medicinal uses or mention edibility. This is meant solely for educational purposes and not as a definitive guide for plant use. Many plants, including those used medicinally or historically, are toxic and can cause harm or death. In addition, countless edible plants have poisonous counterparts that look similar. Because of the difficulties and uncertainties associated with plant identification, do not eat, use or attempt to create medicine out of any of the plants or fruits you find.

Miles and Directions: Mileage cues identify turns, intersections, and trail name changes, as well as points of interest.

Hike Information: Provides details about local events and attractions, hiking tours, and hiking organizations.

Honorable Mentions: Describes some hikes that didn't make the cut, for whatever reason; in many cases it's not because they aren't great hikes, but because they're crowded or environmentally sensitive to heavy traffic.

How to Use the Maps

Overview Map

This map shows the location of each hike in the state by hike number.

Route Map

Your primary guide to each hike, it shows roads, trails, points of interest, water, land-marks, and geographical features. We have highlighted the selected route, and directional arrows point the way. Shaded topographic relief in the background gives you an accurate representation of the terrain and landscape in the hike area.

Final Note: Leave Only Footprints, Take Only Photographs

There is a great deal to discover within each of the ecosystems in this remarkable state. Here charismatic wildlife roam free, rare plants thrive, and humans have untouched space in which to wander—an unusual delight in our burgeoning world. Please remember that as an adventurer, you have a duty to leave things as you found them, or even better. Be aware of all regulations in the areas you visit and please do not pick wildflowers. It harms nature's handiwork and in some instances is illegal. Always be sure to carry a camera and a notepad. Taking photographs or keeping a journal will provide memories that long outlast even the most colorful blooms.

Trail Finder

Hike #	Region	Hike Name	Water Lovers (Waterfall, Streams)	Geology Lover	Dinosaur Lovers	Children/ Families	Peak Baggers	Great Views	Lake Lovers	Canyons	History Lovers	Anglers	Solitude	Wildlife Lovers
1	Northwest	Mad Creek	●			●				●	●			
2	Northwest	Spring Creek	●											
3	Northwest	Rabbit Ears Peak	●											
4	Northwest	Green Mountain-Onahu Loop					●	●					●	●
5	Northwest	East Inlet/ Adams Falls	●			●		●	●					
6	Northwest	Upper Straight Creek	●					●					●	
7	Northwest	McCullough Gulch to White Falls	●			●		●				●		
8	Northwest	Lower Mohawk Lake	●					●			●	●		
9	Northwest	Monte Cristo Gulch	●					●			●			

Hike #	Region	Hike Name	Water Lovers (Waterfall, Streams)	Geology Lover	Dinosaur Lovers	Children/ Families	Peak Baggers	Great Views	Lake Lovers	Canyons	History Lovers	Anglers	Solitude	Wildlife Lovers
10	Northwest	Mayflower Gulch				●		●			●		●	
11	Northwest	Linkins Lake	●					●	●			●	●	
12	Northwest	Cathedral Lakes	●					●	●			●		
13	Northwest	Aspen to Crested Butte via West Maroon Pass	●					●	●			●	●	●
14	Northwest	Monument Canyon		●				●		●			●	
15	Northwest	CCC Trail		●		●		●					●	
16	Northwest	Pollock Bench		●				●		●			●	
17	Southwest	Rustler Gulch	●					●					●	●
18	Southwest	Judd Falls	●			●		●						

Hike #	Region	Hike Name	Water Lovers (Waterfall, Streams)	Geology Lover	Dinosaur Lovers	Children/ Families	Peak Baggers	Great Views	Lake Lovers	Canyons	History Lovers	Anglers	Solitude	Wildlife Lovers
19	Southwest	Long lake				•		•	•			•		
20	Southwest	Copley lake	•					•	•			•	•	
21	Southwest	East River	•			•		•					•	•
22	Southwest	American Basin	•					•					•	
23	Southwest	Bear Creek Falls	•			•		•		•				
24	Southwest	Blue Lake	•					•	•		•		•	
25	Southwest	Lake Hope	•					•	•			•		
26	Southwest	Cross Mountain		•				•					•	•
27	Southwest	Lower Highland Mary Lakes	•					•	•			•	•	

Hike #	Region	Hike Name	Water Lovers (Waterfall, Streams)	Geology Lover	Dinosaur Lovers	Children/ Families	Peak Baggers	Great Views	Lake Lovers	Canyons	History Lovers	Anglers	Solitude	Wildlife Lovers
28	Southwest	Ice Lakes	●					●	●			●		●
29	Southwest	Pass Creek Trail		●			●	●						
30	South Central	Continental Divide Trail North				●		●					●	
31	South Central	Big Meadows Loop	●			●			●			●		●
32	South Central	Dry Lakes	●					●	●				●	
33	South Central	Lost Lake	●			●		●	●			●	●	
34	South Central	Crystal Lake via Hoosier Pass		●		●		●	●				●	
35	Front Range	Staunton Ranch/Davis Ponds Loop				●					●		●	
36	Front Range	Mount Falcon Loop				●		●			●			●

Hike #	Region	Hike Name	Water Lovers (Waterfall, Streams)	Geology Lover	Dinosaur Lovers	Children/ Families	Peak Baggers	Great Views	Lake Lovers	Canyons	History Lovers	Anglers	Solitude	Wildlife Lovers
37	Front Range	Fountain Valley		●		●		●			●			
38	Front Range	Willow Creek-South Rim Loop	●	●				●					●	
39	Front Range	Green Mountain-Hayden Loop				●		●					●	
40	Front Range	Caribou Ranch Loop	●			●		●			●		●	●
41	Front Range	Lichen Loop				●					●			●
42	Front Range	Ouzel Falls Trail	●							●			●	●
43	Front Range	Gem Lake		●		●		●	●	●				
44	Front Range	Cub Lake Loop	●					●	●	●				●
45	Front Range	Tundra Communities Trail		●		●		●						●

Hike #	Region	Hike Name	Water Lovers (Waterfall, Streams)	Geology Lover	Dinosaur Lovers	Children/ Families	Peak Baggers	Great Views	Lake Lovers	Canyons	History Lovers	Anglers	Solitude	Wildlife Lovers
46	Front Range	Well Gulch Loop	●			●		●		●				
47	Eastern	Pawnee Buttes	●	●		●		●					●	●
48	Eastern	Castlewood Canyon Loop	●	●		●				●			●	
49	Eastern	Picket Wire Canyon	●	●	●					●	●		●	
50	Eastern	Vogel Canyon	●	●		●				●	●		●	

Map Legend

Municipal

≡70≡ Interstate Highway

≡285≡ US Highway

≡145≡ State Highway

≡311≡ Local/County/Forest Road

= = = Unpaved Road

Trails

------ Featured Trail

- - - - - Trail

——— Paved Trail/Bike path

Water Features

Body of Water

River/Creek

Intermittent Stream

Waterfall/Cascade

Land Management

National Park/Forest

State/County Park

Wilderness Area

Symbols

Bench

Bridge

Building/Point of Interest

Campground

Campsite

Dam

Gate

Parking

Pass

Peak/Mountain

Picnic Area

Ranger Station

Restroom

Scenic View/Lookout

Tower

Town

Trailhead

Tunnel

Visitor/Information Center

Northwest

D ramatic forested peaks and high mountain passes dotting the mighty Continental Divide lie in stark contrast to the sage-covered mesas and deep red rock canyons of the Western Slope. Adding to the region's diversity, where the Colorado Plateau meets the Rocky Mountains, are stunning cliffs, huge alpine lakes, world-renowned ski resorts, iconic rocky crags like Aspen's Maroon Bells, dinosaur footprints, and the Yampa and Green rivers, whose gushing whitewater careens through narrowly carved sandstone chasms.

Steamboat Springs, boasting a ski resort, hot springs, and premier mountain biking, straddles two worlds where ranching and tourism play a role in sustained growth. Further north, nestled between the Medicine Bow, Rabbit Ears, and Park mountain ranges and the Mount Zirkel and Flat Tops Wildernesses, a huge valley called North Park harbors elk, pronghorn, moose, mule deer, and sage grouse. To the south, the region's lifeblood—the mighty Colorado River—flows through Grand Junction and Fruita, two towns punctuated by Grand Mesa, the world's highest flattop mountain, and the exquisite rock formations and canyons of the Colorado National Monument and the Black Ridge Canyon Wilderness, home to the second largest assembly of arches in the country (second only to Arches National Park). East on I-70, the paved artery road cutting across Colorado, numerous peaks tower overhead while world-renowned ski resorts like Breckenridge and Vail—which are now year-round destinations—await. The eastern part of the region holds the more remote and less trammeled west side of Rocky Mountain National Park, which you can access from Grand Lake. Home to the headwaters of the Colorado River and the wildlife-rich Kawuneechee Valley, this side of Rocky is typically cooler, wetter, and more lushly vegetated than its eastern counterpart.

1 Mad Creek

Accompanied by the invigorating sound of rushing water, stroll through a steep, peaceful canyon high above a rugged forested riparian corridor harboring a range of species and offering fabulous views. Nestled adjacent to the Zirkel Wilderness, this relatively easy walk winds through aspen groves and meanders across open meadows to reach the Mad Barn, a piece of history harkening back to homesteading days.

Start: From the Mad Creek Trailhead kiosk at the north edge of the parking lot (6,760 feet)
Distance: 3.8 miles out and back
Hiking time: 2-3 hours
Difficulty: Easy due to smooth terrain and minimal elevation gain
Trail surface: Dirt, forested trail
Best season: July to October
Peak bloom: mid-June to mid-July
Flowers commonly found: mountain harebell, wild rose, Rocky Mountain penstemon, Wyoming paintbrush, stemless evening primrose, sticky geranium, chokecherry dogbane, wax currant, heartleaf arnica, false Solomon's seal, yarrow, serviceberry, silvery lupine, scorpionweed, sulphur flower, mule's ears, aspen sunflower, golden aster, nettle-leaf giant-hyssop, beautiful cinquefoil, smooth woodland star, Geyer's onion

Other trail users: Equestrians, mountain bikers
Canine compatibility: Dogs permitted
Land status: National Forest
Nearest town: Steamboat Springs
Fees and permits: No fees or permits required
Schedule: Open all year, but often covered in snow from fall to summer
Maps: USGS Rocky Peak; Trails Illustrated 117: Clark, Buffalo Pass
Trail contacts: Medicine Bow-Routt National Forest, Hahns Peak/Bears Ears Ranger District, 925 Weiss Dr., Steamboat Springs; (970) 870-2299; www.fs.usda.gov/mbr

Finding the trailhead: From Steamboat Springs, drive west on US 40 for 2 miles. Turn north (right) onto CR 129/Elk River Road and follow it for 5 miles. Park in the large lot on the right. **GPS: N40 34.034'/W106 53.206'**

The Hike

From the trailhead kiosk, pick up Trail #1100 (Swamp Park Trail). Begin meandering along this angled trail as it cuts across a dry slope to rise above Mad Creek. Notice mountain harebell, wild rose, Rocky Mountain penstemon, and Wyoming paintbrush blooming along the open hillsides. This exposed route flanked by gravelly soil provides perfect habitat for stemless evening primrose, whose showy white fragrant flowers bloom low to the ground. The flowers usually bloom in the late afternoon or evening only to wither from the heat and sun by the following afternoon at which point the blossoms turn pink and close. Continue walking high above the lush riparian corridor passing sticky geranium and chokecherry and reveling in the powerful sound of the raging water below. Be sure to look back often to absorb the gorgeous scene below: A roaring creek cuts through an expansive valley as mountains rise in every direction.

Weave along the rim of this rugged, water-carved canyon as you pass through deep green scrub oaks and Douglas firs complemented by bursts of color from dogbane, wax currant, geranium, and heartleaf arnica. Delicate purple mountain harebells flourish amidst rocky outcrops while false Solomon's seal blooms from the shady undergrowth. Yarrow, purple asters, and serviceberry bloom here too.

Continue climbing to find silvery lupine, harebells, and Rocky Mountain penstemon adorning the trail in a flurry of purple. Look closely for scorpionweed, an interesting plant that might escape discovery since its white flowers blooming in a curved scorpion tail begin as tight green spheres. Across the river, towering cliffs draw your eyes upward; observe keenly to spy small cascades tumbling over vertical rock walls high overhead.

Tightly hugging the canyon rim, the trail lures your eyes back to the ground where sulphur flower, mule's ears, aspen sunflower, and golden aster light up the forest in various shades of sunshine. The trail levels high above the brook to pass another unique bloom, nettle-leaf giant-hyssop, a member of the mint family with a dense, pungent pinkish-purple spire of flowers sitting atop a square stem.

Descend along the narrow, rocky trail to catch a better glimpse of the creek and the black chunky rocks making up its bank. A tranquil aspen grove delivers you to the remnants of an old gate and a fence-lined portion of trail. Beautiful cinquefoil, smooth woodland star, and towering specimens of corn lily bloom in this cool corridor. Just a few steps beyond, massive numbers of mule's ears, dappled with geranium and fragrant Geyer's onion, bloom exuberantly in a sandy, open area where social trails head down toward the water.

Stay on the main trail and continue straight. The canyon yields to an emerald meadow where you'll discover the historic Mad Barn, an original US Forest Service homestead built in 1906. Enjoy a moment's rest on shaded rocks nearby or explore the inside of the cabin where a ladder brings you to the second floor for a spectacular vantage point. Absorb the creek's soothing rhythm and vistas before retracing your steps to the trailhead.

Options: Near the barn, pick up the Saddle Trail (#1140), which passes through a lush environment to hook up with the Red Dirt Trail (#1171), a route that descends through a drier environment and affords the opportunity to explore different flowers. This option, a 3.4-mile loop, requires a car shuttle or an additional 1.2-mile walk along Elk River Road since you end at the Red Dirt Trailhead.

Mule's ears on Mad Creek

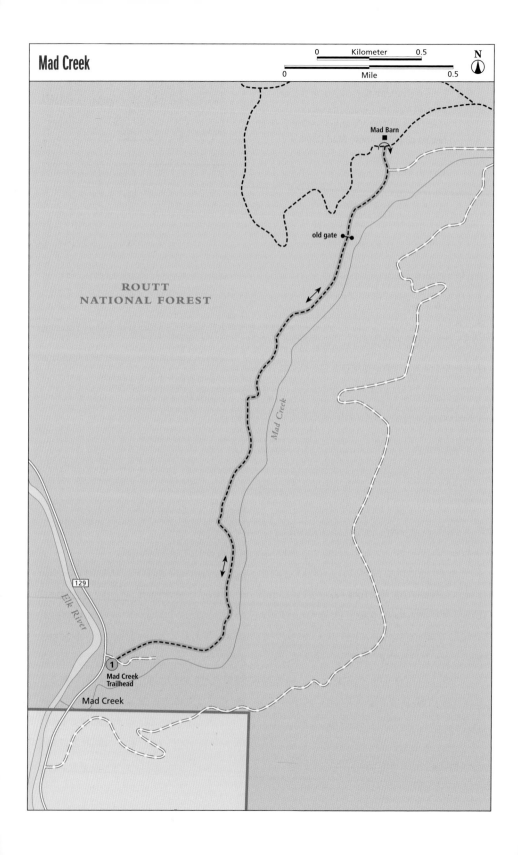

0   Kilometer   0.5

0   Mile   0.5

N

ROUTT
NATIONAL FOREST

Mad Barn

old gate

Mad Creek

Elk River

129

1
Mad Creek
Trailhead

Mad Creek

Miles and Directions

0.0 From the informational kiosk at the well-marked trailhead, cross the service road to reach Trail #1100 (Swamp Park Trail), which begins climbing above Mad Creek.

1.5 Reach an old gate and fence-lined portion of trail. Continue straight.

1.9 Leave the constricted canyon to reach the restored Mad Barn sitting in a large open meadow.

3.8 Arrive back at the trailhead.

Hike Information

Local Information

Steamboat Springs Chamber: Steamboat; (970) 879-0880; steamboatchamber.com

Local Events/Attractions

Hot Air Balloon Rodeo: Steamboat; (970) 875-7006; hotairballoonrodeo.com

Organizations

Yampatika: Steamboat Springs; (970) 871-9151; www.yampatika.org

Nettleleaf hyssop

DISCOVERING THE FOOTHILLS (6,000–8,000 FEET)

Grassy, flower-dotted plains creep into the lower edges of this region, quickly giving way to the more characteristic dry, rocky sagebrush shrublands and open woodlands. At lower elevations, pinyon pine, Rocky Mountain juniper, and Gambel's oak form the backbone of this ecosystem. Wildlife like western scrub jays, chipmunks, and mule deer thrive on the seeds of these trees and utilize various shrubs, including serviceberry, mountain mahogany, rabbitbrush, and sagebrush for food and shelter. In the higher foothills, ponderosa pines and Douglas fir invade from the montane ecosystem above. Depending on winter snowfall and early season rains, spring can come to the foothills as early as March, when the first delicate lavender pasqueflower pokes through the snow. Before long, other species, such as the white, star-like sand lily and the yellow-centered Easter daisy take the stage.

Foothills

2 Spring Creek

Explore a lush montane riparian ecosystem on a lovely walk that undulates between open spots offering cliff views and jungle-like sections where the path resembles a slender hallway carved into thriving ferns. Dropping through this shady chasm lined with a rainbow of colors, expect to cross the creek ten times or more, but don't fret—most of these crossings are aided by a bridge and none are formidable. Remember that returning to the trailhead requires you to regain any altitude lost on the outbound journey.

Start: From the Dry Lake Trailhead (8,300 feet)
Distance: 5.4 miles out and back
Hiking time: 2–4 hours
Difficulty: Moderate due to length and elevation gain
Trail surface: Dirt, forested trail
Best season: July to October
Peak bloom: mid-June to mid-July
Flowers commonly found: mule's ears, Richardson's geranium, wild rose, nettle-leaf giant-hyssop, wax currant, aspen sunflower, silvery lupine, serviceberry, sulphur flower, cow parsnip, salsify, bracted lousewort, corn lily, scarlet paintbrush, chokecherry, mountain bluebells, monkshood, thimbleberry, white bog orchid, twisted stalk, Colorado columbine, Canada violet, heartleaf arnica, beautiful cinquefoil, tall larkspur, loveroot, false Solomon's seal, lambstongue groundsel, red elderberry, northern bedstraw, ball-head waterleaf, rosy pussytoes

Other trail users: Equestrians, mountain bikers
Canine compatibility: Dogs permitted
Land status: National Forest and city property
Nearest town: Steamboat Springs
Fees and permits: No fees or permits required
Schedule: Open all year
Maps: USGS Rocky Peak; Trails Illustrated 118: Steamboat Springs, Rabbit Ears Pass; Routt National Forest Map
Trail contacts: Medicine Bow–Routt National Forest, Hahns Peak/Bears Ears Ranger District, 925 Weiss Dr., Steamboat Springs; (970) 870-2299; www.fs.usda.gov/mbr. City of Steamboat Springs, 137 10th St., Steamboat Springs; (970) 879-2060; steamboatsprings.net
Special considerations: We started from the upper trailhead for optimal flower viewing. This trail is popular with mountain bikers so keep an eye out for descending traffic.

Finding the trailhead: From Steamboat Springs, travel 4 miles north on CR 36 (Strawberry Park Road). Turn right onto CR 38 (Buffalo Pass Road) and continue for 3.5 miles until you reach the trailhead on the south (right) side of the road. **GPS: N40 32.065'/W106 47.062'**

The Hike

Leave the parking area to enter an aspen-filled wonderland bursting with brilliant-yellow mule's ears, white Richardson's geranium, deep pink wild rose, and nettle-leaf giant-hyssop, whose long tight cluster of pink flowers stands on a long stem with triangular leaves. The narrow trail abruptly spits you out into the open where scrub oak, sunshine, and blue sky prevail. As a result, the hillside above and below overflows with a dramatic display of yellow mule's ears, wax currant, aspen sunflowers, silvery

Mule's ears on Spring Creek

lupine, hyssop, geranium, rose, serviceberry, and sulphur flower. Continue dropping down through outstanding meadows teeming with purple, pink, yellow, red, white, and deep green. Enjoy the soothing sound of the creek as you flow through the rainbow of colors and oscillate between aspens and open meadows.

The trail curves west (right) passing cow parsnip, salsify, geranium, bracted lousewort, corn lily, and scarlet paintbrush before heading into a more lush area where ferns and chokecherry flowers thrive. Reach the brook and pause a moment on the bridge to notice mountain bluebells, cow parsnip, monkshood, corn lily, thimbleberry, and rose. You may have to leave the bridge and get down to creek level to see smaller, but equally stunning, blooms like white bog orchid, twisted stalk, and Colorado columbine.

Continue walking through head-high ferns where Canada violet, heartleaf arnica, beautiful cinquefoil, and columbine hide. Reach a second water crossing where tall larkspur, monkshood, geranium, thimbleberry, wild rose, and loveroot bloom exuberantly. Nearby, false Solomon's seal and Canada violets color the trailside.

Soon, reach the creek to find a thicket of thimbleberry dappled with scarlet paintbrush, aspen sunflower, and lambstongue groundsel. Red elderberry, scarlet paintbrush, and geranium adorn the forest floor with

▶ GREEN TIP—Carry a reusable water container that you can fill with tap water. Bottled water is not only expensive, but also a lot of petroleum goes into making plastic bottles and they create a disposal nightmare.

Thimbleberry

sparkles of color. Cross the stream and look for beautiful cinquefoil and northern bed-straw thriving in the shade of aspens. Just after you cruise through a lush area with mountain bluebells and corn lily, another bridge carries you across the water followed immediately by another crossing where heartleaf bittercress and an array of violets thrive. After this fifth crossing, quaking aspens and head-high ferns create a thin corridor colored with lupine, geranium, thimbleberry, cow parsnip, and loveroot. The lush vegetation, sound of the creek, and buzzing birds and insects momentarily transform this mountain adventure into a jungle-like journey.

Cross a sixth time, passing similar flowers including salsify, geranium, cow parsnip, and lambstongue groundsel. As you meander along this shady, tranquil trail, rejoice in the fact that the soothing sound of the creek accompanies you for the entire adventure. Look up and to your right for glimpses of the lovely red, brown, and black cliff walls comprising the canyon.

Navigate slowly through a steep, rocky descent past plentiful geranium, rose, and thimbleberry. Climb a bit only to descend again, this time even more steeply past ball-head waterleaf and heartleaf arnica to reach another water crossing. Threading through giant boulders, the trail descends once more cruising by rosy pussytoes, arnica, and false Solomon's seal. The next bridge brings you to a muddy section of trail ripe with white bog orchids. Descend through another lush section of quaking aspens and giant wildflowers to reach two creek crossings in quick succession. Take a break in the shade near the last bridge, and then retrace your steps (uphill!) to return to the trailhead.

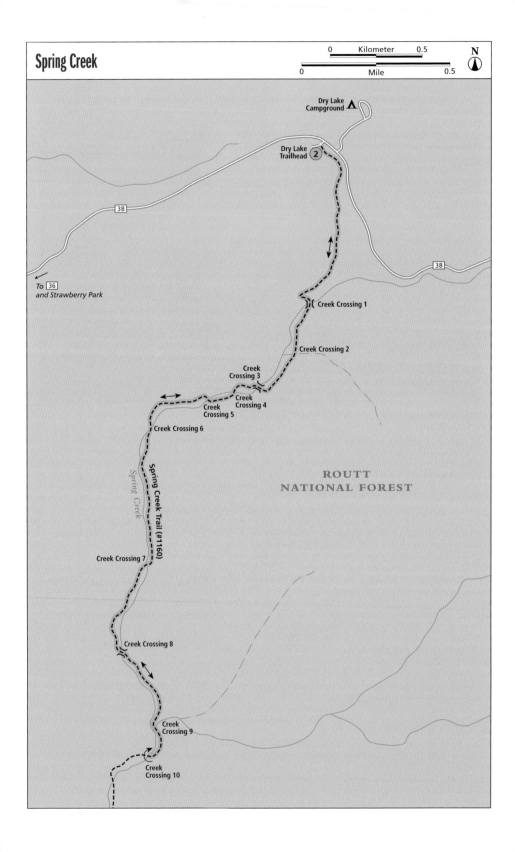

Spring Creek

0 Kilometer 0.5
0 Mile 0.5

N

Dry Lake
Campground ▲

Dry Lake
Trailhead ②

38

To 36
and Strawberry Park

Creek Crossing 1

Creek Crossing 2

Creek
Crossing 3

Creek
Crossing 4

Creek
Crossing 5

Creek Crossing 6

ROUTT
NATIONAL FOREST

Spring Creek

Spring Creek Trail (#1160)

Creek Crossing 7

Creek Crossing 8

Creek
Crossing 9

Creek
Crossing 10

Miles and Directions

0.0   Start from the Dry Lake Trailhead. Follow the Spring Creek Trail (#1160) south through the forest.

0.6   Drop downhill to reach a small bridge that crosses the creek for the first time.

0.8   Follow the trail across the water for the second time. Continue downhill.

1.0   Come to a bridge that brings you across the creek for the third time.

1.1   Cross the brook for the fourth time.

1.2   Reach the fifth creek crossing and then pass through a narrow corridor of head-high ferns.

1.5   Come to the sixth water crossing.

1.9   The trail descends steeply over rocky terrain to reach your seventh creek crossing.

2.3   Continue descending to reach another bridge that carries you over the roaring creek for the eighth time of the day.

2.6   Pass through a lush section to reach the creek again.

2.7   Rest in the shade at your final water crossing.

5.4   Arrive back at the trailhead.

Options: Use two cars and hike the entire length (~4 miles) from top to bottom.

Hike Information

Local Information
Steamboat Springs Chamber: Steamboat; (970) 879-0880; steamboatchamber.com

Local Events/Attractions
Hot Air Balloon Rodeo: Steamboat; (970) 875-7006; hotairballoonrodeo.com

Organizations
Yampatika: Steamboat Springs; (970) 871-9151; www.yampatika.org

3 Rabbit Ears Peak

A short drive from Steamboat Springs, this moderately challenging 5-mile adventure follows an old winding road through pine forest and open meadows to reach the base of Rabbit Ears Peak (10,550 feet). Though steep in sections, the tough climbs are short-lived, while plentiful and varied blossoms and spectacular views reward hikers with each step.

Start: From the small parking area at the intersection of FR 291 and 311 (9,600 feet)
Distance: 5.4 miles out and back
Hiking time: 2–4 hours
Difficulty: Strenuous due to rocky terrain and steep sections
Trail surface: Dirt road
Best season: July to October
Peak bloom: mid-June to mid-July
Flowers commonly found: loveroot, silvery lupine, yarrow, beautiful cinquefoil, scarlet paintbrush, northern goldenrod, golden aster, showy daisy, pearly everlasting, heartleaf bittercress, white bog orchid, marsh marigold, heartleaf arnica, mountain bluebells, cow parsnip, aspen sunflower, triangularleaf senecio, Fremont geranium, elephant heads, Colorado columbine, tall larkspur, corn lily, twinberry, Coulter's daisy, beautiful daisy, Richardson's geranium, Fendler's meadowrue, wild rose, Whipple's penstemon, sulphur flower, red elderberry, mule's ears, glacier lilies, globeflower, brook saxifrage, tall valerian, yellow violet, subalpine Jacob's ladder, American vetch, peavine, mountain parsley, wax currant, yarrow, parrot's beak, wild candytuft, wild raspberry, Nuttall's gilia, cutleaf daisy, tall larkspur

Other trail users: Equestrians, mountain bikers
Canine compatibility: Dogs permitted
Land status: National Forest
Nearest town: Steamboat Springs
Fees and permits: No fees or permits required
Schedule: Open all year
Maps: USGS Rabbit Ears; Trails Illustrated 118: Steamboat Springs, Rabbit Ears Pass; Routt National Forest Map.
Trail contacts: Medicine Bow–Routt National Forest, Hahns Peak/Bears Ears Ranger District, 925 Weiss Dr., Steamboat Springs; (970) 870-2299; www.fs.usda.gov/mbr
Special considerations: Though many people tackle the 4th class summit pitch to the top of the west tower (10,654 feet) or a technical route to the top out on the east tower (10,657 feet), our description ends at the base of the peak. The towers were formed from the remnants of pyroclastic materials, or volcanic rock and ash, which means the rock crumbles in your hand and can be dangerous to climb.

Finding the trailhead: From Steamboat, head east on US 40 for 19 miles. Climb past Rabbit Ears Pass Summit (9,426 feet) to the signed Dumont Lake Campground turnoff. Turn north (left) onto FR 315 and follow it for 1.5 miles until you reach an old stone monument. Turn north (left) at the monument onto FR 311. Continue on the main road past an information kiosk. After a quarter mile, reach FR 291. Turn right and immediately park in a small lot on the right.
GPS: N40 24.235'/W106 37.133'

The Hike

Follow the pine-lined route northeast to find loveroot, silvery lupine, yarrow, beautiful cinquefoil, and scarlet paintbrush just steps from the trailhead. Turn a corner and get your first glimpse of the Rabbit Ears, slender monoliths in the distance. Erosion has ensured they no longer exactly resemble their namesakes—a change more defined years ago when part of the east tower toppled over. Though nature continues reshaping this volcanic plug, Rabbit Ears Peak remains an iconic, popular summit with wildflower lovers, hikers, and bikers

Continue along the level road through a dry, open area where northern goldenrod, golden aster, showy daisy, lupine, and pearly everlasting add bits of color to the scene. Continue gradually climbing to reach a creek lined with lush vegetation that gives rise to heartleaf bittercress, white bog orchid, marsh marigold, heartleaf arnica, mountain bluebells, loveroot, and cow parsnip. This spot is truly a flower gold mine!

Cross the brook to find aspen sunflower, triangularleaf senecio, Fremont geranium, elephant heads, and Colorado columbine painting the trailside in a dazzling display of color. Heading upslope away from the trickle, peavine, lupine, tall larkspur, and paintbrush line both sides. Leveling, the trail continues its journey through verdant pastures teeming with corn lily, twin-berry, Coulter's daisy, and beautiful daisy. In the distance, the Rabbit Ears stand like sentinels calling you toward them.

Heading straight for the Ears, huge fields of corn lily speckled with Richardson's geranium, Fendler's meadow rue, Colorado columbine, aspen sunflower, beautiful cinquefoil, larkspur, and bluebells create a wavy sea of deep green bursting with bits of yellow, purple, red, and white.

Follow the road back into the forest to find wild rose and Whipple's penstemon. When you pop out into the open again, sulphur flower, lupine, corn lily, red elderberry, mule's ears, paintbrush, and bluebells await.

Shortly after you drop down into a wet seep where you spy glacier lilies, columbine, and loveroot, cross a tranquil tributary. Here

Columbine with Rabbit Ears in back

Nuttall's gilia

marsh marigolds and globeflower thrive side by side. Bluebells, heartleaf bittercress, brook saxifrage, senecio, larkspur, and cow parsnip flourish.

Hop across the seep and follow the road as it ascends steadily through impressive stands of spruce where tall valerian, lupine, and Whipple's penstemon take shelter. Alternating between open meadows and forested stands of spruce, the road travels upward, a bit more steeply now. In the forested spots, notice tiny yellow violets, subalpine Jacob's ladder, and larkspur while columbine, scarlet paintbrush, Richardson's geranium, and loveroot burst from meadows. Periodically you pass an impressive display of glacier lilies, exquisite bright yellow blossoms dangling from slender stems and often blooming at the edge of snow banks. Continue climbing past American vetch, peavine, mountain parsley, wax currant, yarrow, and yellow violets. parrot's beak and wild candytuft hide amid the undergrowth of the trees as well.

At the bottom of a short descent, the trail ascends very steeply to reach a giant pine in the middle of the trail where you can find mats of Nuttall's gilia and impressive clumps of Onesided penstemon. A small adjacent open area bursting with blooms offers views back across the valley and toward the rocky outcrops leading up to the Ears.

The route increases in verticality offering a very challenging but short lung-busting climb. Push through to reach the base of the Ears where you will find various social trails meandering across the stone formations. Explore to find wild raspberry,

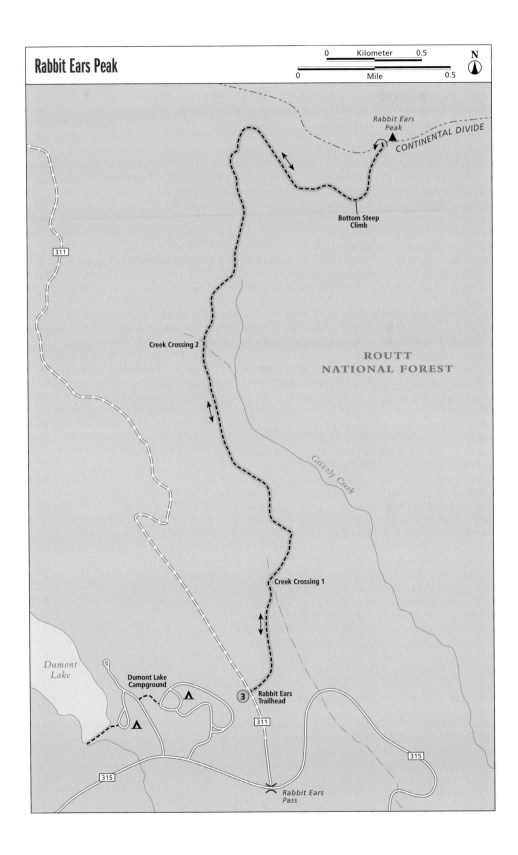

Nuttall's gilia, cutleaf daisy, and larkspur, but take care since loose rocks and slippery, narrow trails make this a potentially dangerous spot. Rest for a bit, soak in the vistas, refuel, and then retrace your steps back to the trailhead.

Miles and Directions

0.0 From the trailhead, follow the old jeep road (FR 291) northeast.

0.4 Head north and continue climbing to reach the creek lined with lush vegetation. Cross and climb gradually through an open meadow heading straight toward the Ears.

1.3 Cross a tranquil tributary that trickles across the road. Follow the road as it ascends.

2.4 Reach the bottom of a rocky, steep descent and climb sharply to reach a giant pine in the middle of the trail. Continue climbing even more steeply from here.

2.5 Explore the base of the peak and soak in the views, but be careful as you do. Retrace your steps back to the trailhead.

5.4 Arrive back at the trailhead.

Hike Information

Local Information
Steamboat Springs Chamber: Steamboat; (970) 879-0880; steamboatchamber.com

Local Events/Attractions
Hot Air Balloon Rodeo: Steamboat; (970) 875-7006; hotairballoonrodeo.com

Organizations
Yampatika: Steamboat Springs; (970) 871-9151; www.yampatika.org

WHAT'S IN A NAME?

Plant lovers—from botanists with PhDs to wildflower enthusiasts—spend a lot of time talking about plant and flower names. Those just joining the game might wonder, "What's so important about what we call each plant?" As Juliet famously said, "That which we call a rose by any other name would smell as sweet." Well, in the world of botany this isn't exactly true. Unless we agree on the name of a plant, we could be talking about two entirely different species. The whole idea of naming can cause confusion, even among those of us with years of experience. Here's a simple primer that will give you some insight and make things clearer.

Common names: Common names are unreliable. Most plants have several common names, and a common name used in one region may apply elsewhere to a totally unrelated plant.

Scientific names: Because of the confusion surrounding common names, the scientific name of the plant is necessary to label a species accurately. These names, rendered in Latin or Greek, are a more stable and universal means of referring to a particular plant; scientists across the planet usually use and accept the same scientific name. The scientific name consists of two words. The first word, the *genus*, is the name of a group of plants with similar general characteristics. The second part of the scientific name is the "specific epithet" or *species name*, which identifies the particular species of a plant and distinguishes this plant from all others in that genus. Thus, there are many species found within a single genus. In a few cases, the scientific name for a plant will have a third part, preceded by the word "variety," abbreviated "var.," or "subspecies," abbreviated "ssp." These plants differ slightly but consistently from other plants of the same species and often have distinct ranges.

Besides being consistent, scientific names can describe a characteristic of the plant (hairy, short, twin seeds), honor a place or person, or may be derived from history (an ancient use or the name of an ancient country where the plant was first recorded). Perhaps most importantly, scientific names show relationships by identifying species in the same genus. For example, *Mertensia ciliata*, the scientific name for mountain bluebells, identifies it as the species *ciliata* and part of the larger genus *Mertensia*. This gives you a clue that it shares DNA and characteristics with *Mertensia lanceolata* (lanceleaf chiming bells).

How This Guide Handles Naming: To make this guide easier to read and more user-friendly, we use common names of plants within the text and narrative. To avoid confusion and ensure we accurately label each species, we have included a list of corresponding scientific names for reference in appendix A.

Mountain bluebells

Although scientific names apply more universally than common names, botanists and plant taxonomists do not always agree on the best system of classification or which scientific name is appropriate. As research progresses and scientists learn more about plant DNA, they are constantly reevaluating what they know about plant genetics and relationships. If research reveals that a plant was classified incorrectly, families may shift, genera may transform, and names may change. In addition, if a botanist discovers an older name for a plant, its scientific name may revert to the oldest name on record.

Most of the scientific names used in this book reflect the name accepted by Dr. John Kartesz' *Synthesis of the Flora of North America*, which describes thousands of plants, provides over 150,000 photographs, and gives county-by-county records of every plant in North America. We chose Dr. Kartesz, who is also the Director of the Biota of North America Program (BONAP; www.bonap.org), as our authority for naming in order to provide a consistent, accurate, research-based naming system that would cover the entire region. His *Synthesis* provides a uniquely comprehensive source of nomenclature and taxonomy for all known native and naturalized vascular plants and serves as an international standard for multiple agencies, educational institutions, and private conservation groups.

There are many exceptional scientists studying and naming plants in Colorado. For instance, William Weber & Ronald C. Wittmann's outstanding *Colorado Flora* is widely used by biologists and botanists to identify plants. In 2015, Jennifer Ackerfield, who has been studying the Colorado plants for twenty years, released *Flora of Colorado*, a comprehensive guide to all the state's plant species. Because changes are happening so rapidly and our guide is used by readers with a wide range of experience who may be familiar with the above-mentioned works, we have done our best to assist in identification by including scientific synonyms in appendix A when appropriate.

4 Green Mountain-Onahu Loop

Starting on Rocky Mountain National Park's quieter west side, this moderate 8.0-mile loop meanders along a mountain stream and through lush, tranquil forest teeming with wildflowers. One highlight—a visit to Big Meadows—offers exquisite peak views, plentiful blossoms, and opportunities to spy moose, elk, and deer. With many worthwhile side trips and extensions, this journey allows you to explore the park while enjoying solitude.

Start: From the Green Mountain Trailhead (8,794 feet)
Distance: 8.0-mile loop
Hiking time: 3–5 hours
Difficulty: Moderate due to length and altitude gain
Trail Surface: Dirt, forested trail
Best season: July to October
Peak bloom: late June to July
Flowers commonly found: cow parsnip, wild rose, Fremont geranium, beautiful cinquefoil, mountain bluebells, heartleaf arnica, monkshood, aspen sunflower, Colorado columbine, silvery lupine, twinflower, white bog orchid, heartleaf bittercress, twisted stalk, Richardson's geranium, American speedwell, fairy slippers, bog pyrola, green mitrewort, parrot's beak, elephant heads, pond lily, wild strawberry, fireweed, western yellow paintbrush, spotted coral root orchid, Parry's lousewort, brownie ladyslipper, rosy pussytoes, wild rose, greenflower pyrola, wax currant, yarrow, northern bedstraw, Rocky Mountain pussytoes, shrubby cinquefoil, Geyer's onion, shooting stars, marsh marigold, American bistort, subalpine Jacob's ladder

Other trail users: Equestrians
Canine compatibility: Dogs prohibited
Land status: National Park
Nearest town: Grand Lake
Fees and permits: Entrance fee, required. Wilderness permits are required for overnight wilderness camping (970-586-1242); a fee is charged. Download the Wilderness Camping Guide from the park website.
Schedule: Open all year
Maps: USGS Grand Lake; Nat Geo Trails Illustrated 200 Rocky Mountain National Park; Latitude 40 Front Range Trails; Rocky National Park Map
Trail contacts: Rocky Mountain National Park; Kawuneeche Visitor Center, Grand Lake; (970) 586-1206; www.nps.gov/romo
Special considerations: You can hike in either direction, but we start at the Green Mountain Trailhead, only 2 miles from Big Meadows. If you decide to cut your day short, you will still reach Big Meadows, see a host of flowers, and possibly glimpse wildlife.

Finding the trailhead: From Grand Lake, drive 1.8 miles north on US 34 to the park entrance station and pay the fee. Drive another 2.8 miles to reach the signed Green Mountain Trailhead on the right. **GPS: N40 18.438'/W105 50.466'**

Note: Do not pick flowers at Rocky Mountain National Park.

The Hike

Cross a tiny footbridge where cow parsnip, wild rose, Fremont geranium, and beautiful cinquefoil greet you immediately. Begin ascending steadily through a creekside conifer forest supporting hearty clusters of mountain bluebells interspersed with heartleaf arnica and monkshood. Continue past aspen sunflower, cinquefoil, Colorado columbine, silvery lupine, and twinflower to reach an opening on the bank that reveals delicate white bog orchid, heartleaf bittercress, and twisted stalk.

Single delight, wild strawberry, lupine, Richardson's geranium, cow parsnip, and wild rose reveal themselves amid the pines. Leveling near the water again, heartleaf bittercress lines the verdant creekside while American speedwell, a tiny bluish-purple flower that favors streams and bogs, pushes forth from damp soil. Cross a plank bridge to find fairy slippers, bog pyrola, and twinflower hiding in the undergrowth. Periodically, short steep inclines slow your pace, but overall the moderate grade carries you upward past more arnica, geranium, monkshood, bluebells, fairy slippers, and new blooms like green mitrewort and parrot's beak. The trail levels to pass a few small meadows bursting with elephant heads, clover, pond lily, parrot's beak, and geranium.

Passing wild strawberry, arnica, bluebells, and fireweed, the trail arrives at Tonahutu Creek Trail junction. Head downhill toward the hitch rack to reach the edge of Big Meadow, an open area enveloped by Nakai Peak (12,216 feet), Snowdrift

Big meadows

Fairy slipper

Peak (12,274 feet), and Mount Patterson (11,424 feet). Tonahutu Creek flows on the eastern edge of the aptly named spot—the largest montane meadow in the park—which comprises optimal deer, elk, and moose habitat. Western yellow paintbrush and elephant heads add waves of brilliant pink and gold to a sea of green. Looking across the meadow, note that pine beetle infestation, an epidemic in forests across the west, has killed many of the trees you see. (See sidebar The Power of a Tiny Insect.)

Returning to the junction, pick up the Tonahutu Creek Trail, which skirts the western edge of the meadow. This level shady section of trail gives rise to heartleaf arnica, spotted coral root orchid, elephant heads, strawberry, Parry's lousewort, cinquefoil, columbine, parrot's beak, and parsley. Nearby, the elusive brownie ladyslipper, an unusual orchid with a bottom petal forming a yellowish green sac with reddish brown or dark purple markings, makes an occasional appearance.

After meandering along the meadow's edge, come to Onahu Creek Trail junction where Tonahutu Creek Trail heads east (right) to Granite Falls. Continue toward the Onahu Creek Trailhead on a narrow trail that turns steeper and rugged as it passes rosy pussytoes, bog pyrola, twinflower, wild rose, and green-flower pyrola.

A long ascent brings you to a gentle descent where the vegetation turns lusher. Cross a boulder field and descend switchbacks to intersect Timber Creek/Long Meadows Trail. Stay straight to cross a bridge over Onahu Creek where you find huge clumps of mountain bluebells mixed in with parsley, false dandelion, wax currant, yarrow, northern bedstraw, goldenrod, heartleaf arnica, and rosy and Rocky Mountain pussytoes.

Passing signed backcountry campsites proceed along the main trail that parallels sweet-sounding water and passes several meadows offering excellent moose- and elk-spotting opportunities. Rolling terrain crosses a bridge spanning a small tributary harboring heartleaf bittercress.

▶ **TIDBIT—Tonahutu is the Arapaho word for "big meadows."**

Continue straight into a thicket of flowers including Colorado columbine, shrubby and beautiful cinquefoil, wild rose, parsley, and Geyer's onion. Nearing the road, break into an open area where shooting stars cinquefoil, Geyer's onion, marsh marigold, American bistort, death camas, and subalpine Jacob's

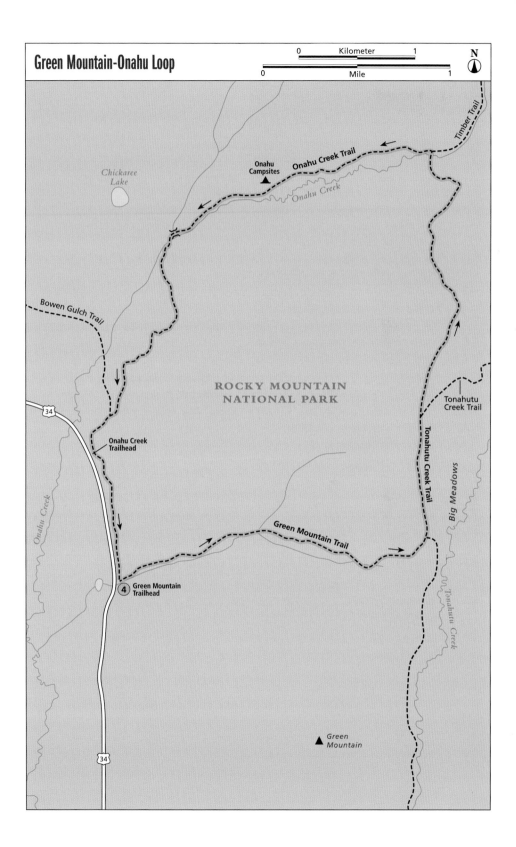

Green Mountain-Onahu Loop

Kilometer

0   1

Mile

0   1

N

Timber Trail

Onahu Campsites

Onahu Creek Trail

Onahu Creek

Chickaree Lake

Bowen Gulch Trail

Tonahutu Creek Trail

ROCKY MOUNTAIN NATIONAL PARK

Tonahutu Creek Trail

Onahu Creek Trailhead

34

Onahu Creek

Big Meadows

Green Mountain Trail

Green Mountain Trail

Tonahutu Creek

Green Mountain Trailhead

4

Green Mountain

34

ladder bloom. Though this final section of the loop lacks tranquility, an impressive array of flowers more than make up for the noise.

Follow the path veering into the forest. Stands of pines adorned with brilliant clusters of lupine guide you back to the Green Mountain Trailhead.

Miles and Directions

0.0 From the Green Mountain Trailhead, head east along a well-defined path that climbs steadily through the forest.

2.0 Just after passing a signed spur leading to Green Mountain campsites, the trail drops down, passes a hitch rack, and reaches Big Meadows. After exploring, return to the trail and head north skirting the west edge of the meadow.

2.7 At a signed junction with the Tonahutu Creek Trail, stay straight to remain on the Onahu Creek Trail, which climbs gradually through the forest.

4.3 Reach a signed trail junction with the Timber Creek Trail. Stay straight on the Onahu Creek Trail and cross a bridge over Onahu Creek.

5.3 Pass the Onahu Bridge Wilderness Campsite and the Upper Onahu Wilderness Campsite to proceed along the main Onahu Creek Trail.

6.7 Continue over rolling terrain to cross a bridge spanning the creek.

7.1 Undulating through the forest, the trail drops down to pass an intersection with Bowen Gulch Trail. Continue southeast (straight) through an open meadow.

7.3 Reach the Onahu Creek Trailhead. Take the left fork to follow a path that veers away from the parking area and into the forest.

8.0 Arrive back at the trailhead.

Options: Hike to Big Meadow and back.

Hike Information

General Information

Grand Lake Chamber of Commerce: Grand Lake; (800) 531-1019 or (970) 627-3402; grandlakechamber.com

Local Events/Attractions

Annual Buffalo BBQ Weekend: Grand Lake; (970) 627-3402; grandlakechamber.com
Rocky Mountain Repertory Theatre: Grand Lake; (970) 627-3421; rockymountainrep.com

Clubs and Organizations

Rocky Mountain Conservancy: Estes Park; (970) 586-0108 or rmconservancy.org

Hike Tours

Rocky Mountain Conservancy: Estes Park; (970) 586-0108; rmconservancy.org
Rocky Mountain National Park: Kawuneeche Visitor Center (offers hikes to various locations on the west side); Grand Lake; (970) 586-1206; www.nps.gov/romo

THE POWER OF A TINY INSECT

Throughout many parts of Colorado, including sections of Rocky Mountain National Park like Big Meadows, you will notice huge swaths of dead or dying trees amid thick strands of forest. This noticeable change is largely due to a dramatic increase in the number of bark beetles, a tiny insect the size of a pencil eraser that has been ravaging forests throughout the west. Bark beetles are part of the natural forest cycle; however, since the mid-1990s a series of factors including changing climate and warmer temperatures has boosted the beetles' population and expanded their range. Warmer winters also allowed many more than usual to live on while drought-weakened trees that might otherwise be able to withstand attacks were unable to survive. In combination, these events have created the perfect storm for the desecration of millions of trees, which are now hazards since they add fuel to wildfires and are prone to toppling over especially in high winds. Take precautions while hiking and camping since they present a risk to hikers, tents, and cars.

Moose roam in Big Meadows, an open area in Rocky Mountain National Park that is surrounded by beetle killed trees.

5 East Inlet/Adams Falls

Red, yellow, and purple come together in a vibrant explosion along this short but worthwhile trail to reach a raging cascade in Rocky Mountain National Park. If you are limited on time or energy, this jaunt through the forest offers an excellent introduction to the montane accompanied by pleasant scenery and an alluring stream. Culminating near the confluence of two waterways and a vast meadow where moose, deer, and elk often wander, this hike has it all.

Start: From the East Inlet Trailhead (8,400 feet)

Distance: 1.7 miles out and back including a loop to the falls

Hiking time: 1–2 hours

Difficulty: Easy due to distance, minimal elevation gain, and smooth terrain

Trail surface: Dirt trail

Best season: July to October

Peak bloom: late June to July

Flowers commonly found: showy locoweed, Rocky Mountain loco, yellow stonecrop, wild rose, beautiful cinquefoil, rosy pussytoes, wild strawberry, northern bedstraw, kinnikinnick, shrubby cinquefoil, Rydberg's penstemon, dotted saxifrage, red columbine, Colorado columbine, twinflower, mountain harebell, Wyoming paintbrush, sulphur flower, northern goldenrod, northern bedstraw, twinberry, heartleaf arnica, cow parsnip, elephant heads, alpine sorrel, mountain parsley, spotted coralroot orchids, bog pyrola, mariposa lily

Other trail users: Equestrians

Canine compatibility: Dogs prohibited

Land status: National Park

Nearest town: Grand Lake

Fees and permits: Entrance fee, required. Wilderness permits are required for overnight camping (970-586-1242); a fee is charged. Download the Wilderness Camping Guide from the park website.

Schedule: Open all year

Maps: USGS Grand Lake; Nat Geo Trails Illustrated 200 Rocky Mountain National Park; Latitude 40 Front Range Trails; Rocky National Park Map

Trail contacts: Rocky Mountain National Park; Kawuneeche Visitor Center, Grand Lake; (970) 586-1206; www.nps.gov/romo

Finding the trailhead: From Grand Lake, head east on West Portal Road (CO 278) and follow signs for the boat launch for 2.5 miles to the East Inlet Trailhead, located on the eastern shore of Grand Lake, opposite the boat launch. This is a popular area which can be very busy and congested. Plan ahead for a more enjoyable visit. In summer, the park's busiest times are between 9 a.m. and 3 p.m. Expect congestion, including full parking lots, busy roads, and crowded trails. **GPS: N40 14.355'/W105 47.985'**

The Hike

The East Inlet Trail starts on the edge of Grand Lake, a tiny town set on a lake of the same name. Before setting out, take a moment to appreciate Colorado's largest natural body of water, Grand Lake, which is located directly across from the trailhead. Head south on the wide, level trail that immediately passes an open area adorned with showy locoweed, Rocky mountain loco, yellow stonecrop, and wild rose. The trail crosses a stream and proceeds through a mixed forest of conifers and aspens where Fremont geranium, beautiful cinquefoil, and pussytoes bloom brightly. Continue past a rocky outcrop where yellow stonecrop breaks through crevices. Enjoy this short, easy, but delightful introduction

▶ GREEN TIP—Observe wildlife from a distance. Don't interfere in their lives—both of you will be better for it.

to the montane ecosystem as you continue gradually weaving your way through the forest passing wild strawberry, wild rose, northern bedstraw, and kinnikinnick.

After just one-third of a mile, reach a junction with the Adams Falls Trail, a semicircle loop that reconnects with the East Inlet Trail in two-tenths of a mile. Go southwest (right) at the junction toward the thundering sound of roaring water. This section of trail comes alive with shrubby cinquefoil, wild rose, Rydberg's penstemon, and dotted saxifrage. When you reach the Adams Falls Overlook, pause and enjoy the grandeur and power of this 55-foot torrent that drops over a series of rock steps through a constricted gorge.

From the overlook, follow the trail southeast as it climbs slightly next to the water to reach the top of the falls. Look back for a spectacular view of the powerful cascade and Grand Lake off in the distance. The trail turns north (left) into a treed section of trail paralleling the roaring East Inlet. Rosy pussytoes, wild strawberry, twinflower, harebell, and stonecrop color this tranquil path on its way to rejoining the main trail.

Turn left at the signed junction if you want to return to the parking area. If you have energy and time, turn east (right) to explore more of the East Inlet Trail, which slopes gradually uphill passing harebell, Wyoming paintbrush, shrubby cinquefoil, sulphur flower, northern goldenrod, northern bedstraw, Rydberg's penstemon, and twinberry.

Leveling, the trail reaches the confluence of East Inlet Creek and Echo Creek, where water, mountains, evergreens, and an emerald meadow collide to create a remarkable scene. Fremont geranium, heartleaf arnica, twinberry, cow parsnip, harebell, and rose bloom at the edge of this lush area. Continue walking around this large open area ablaze with wildflowers including elephant heads, sunflowers, and alpine sorrel in midsummer. Stay observant because deer, moose, and elk frequent this rich spot.

Skirting the north edge of this open expanse cut by slow-moving water, head back into the forest where single delights hide in the underbrush. Look closely to find mountain parsley, spotted coralroot orchids, red columbine, and Colorado columbine growing in the shade of pines. At the edge of the meadow, also find twinflower and bog pyrola peeking through in bits of pink. Drink in the vistas and scan for moose wandering through the meadow. Turn around here and enjoy the hike back down to the trailhead being sure to look up near Adams Falls so you don't miss the barely perceptible snow-capped mountains and blue waters of Grand Lake.

Options: Continue all the way to Lone Pine Lake for a hardy 11-mile round-trip adventure.

East meadow

Miles and Directions

0.0 From the trailhead, head south on the wide, level trail that passes through an open area, crosses a stream and proceeds through a mixed forest of conifers and aspens.

0.3 Reach a junction with the Adams Falls Trail and turn southwest (right).

0.35 Arrive at the Adams Falls overlook, a wonderful spot to pause and absorb the grandeur.

0.5 Turn east (right) to explore more of the East Inlet Trail.

0.7 Leveling, the trail reaches a striking view of the confluence of the East Inlet Creek and Echo Creek.

1.0 Turn around at the edge of the meadow and make your way back to the trailhead.

1.7 Arrive back at the trailhead.

Hike Information

General Information

Grand Lake Chamber of Commerce: Grand Lake; (800) 531-1019 or (970) 627-3402; grandlakechamber.com

Local Events/Attractions

Annual Buffalo BBQ Weekend: Grand Lake; (970) 627-3402; grandlakechamber.com

East Inlet/Adams Falls

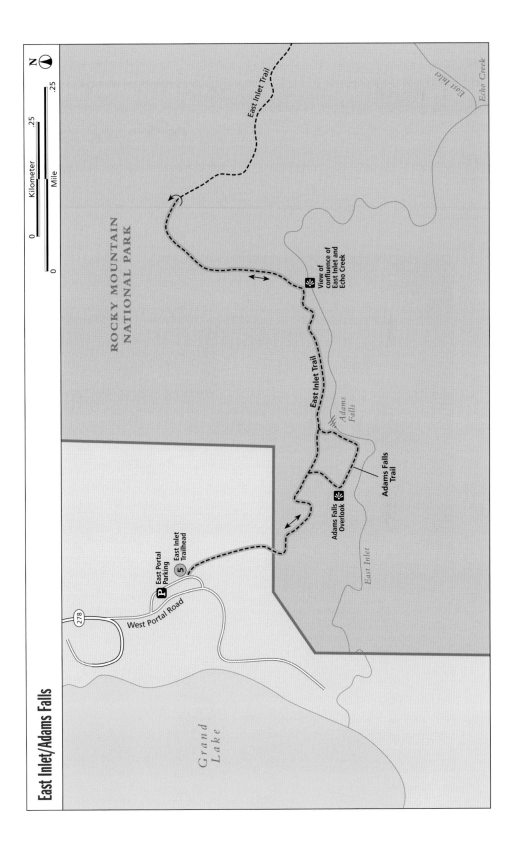

Rocky Mountain Repertory Theatre: Grand Lake; (970) 627-3421; rockymountainrep.com

Clubs and Organizations

Rocky Mountain Conservancy: Estes Park; (970) 586-0108; rmconservancy.org

Hike Tours

Rocky Mountain Conservancy: Estes Park; (970) 586-0108; rmconservancy.org

Rocky Mountain National Park: ranger-led hikes to various locations on the west side); Grand Lake; (970) 586-1206; www.nps.gov/romo

Red columbine

6 Upper Straight Creek

Splendid blossoms carpet a deep, verdant valley nestled directly below the Continental Divide. Walk along a gentle stream through a dazzling wildflower display and then climb gradually through the blossom-filled tundra to reach jaw-dropping views. This moderate, well-defined, half-day hike begins and ends above tree line and is worth every bit of effort and sweat. Bonus feature: If you are short on energy or time, this hike delivers a splendid flower spectacle from the moment you leave the car, so even just a quick jaunt will deliver huge payoffs.

Start: From the north side of the west portal of the Eisenhower Tunnel (11,120 feet)

Distance: 4.2 miles out and back

Hiking time: 2–4 hours

Difficulty: Moderate due to altitude and elevation gain. *Note:* The entire hike is above 11,000 feet, which could make it more challenging.

Trail surface: Dirt two-track and trail

Best season: July to October

Peak bloom: mid-July to early August

Flowers commonly found: Colorado columbine, glacial daisy, elephant heads, mountain bluebells, tall larkspur, Gray's angelica, cowbane, Whipple's penstemon, king's crown, yellow monkeyflower, heartleaf bittercress, brook saxifrage, Parry clover, snowball saxifrage, showy ragwort, northern bedstraw, king's crown, alpine thistle, Parry primrose, marsh marigold, bog saxifrage, lanceleaf chiming bells, beautiful cinquefoil, western yellow, rosy and scarlet paintbrush, alpine avens, sky pilot, silky phacelia, pygmy gentian, snow buttercup, alpine clover, pygmy bitterroot, alpine bistort, alpine chiming bells, moss campion, alpine sandwort, black-headed daisy, old man of the mountains, alpine harebell, alpine thistle

Other trail users: Equestrians and mountain bikers

Canine compatibility: Dogs permitted

Land status: National Forest

Nearest town: Dillon

Fees and permits: No fees or permits required

Schedule: Open all year, but often covered in snow from fall to summer

Maps: USGS Loveland Pass; Trails Illustrated Idaho Springs, Georgetown, Loveland Pass; Latitude 40 Summit County Colorado Trails

Trail contacts: White River National Forest, Dillon Ranger District, 680 Blue River Pkwy., Silverthorne, 80498; (970) 468-5400; www.fs.usda.gov/whiteriver

Special considerations: Don't confuse this hike with the route up Lower Straight Creek (FR 48) that begins from Straight Creek Road (CR 51), meanders through lodge pole pine forest, and parallels I-70 all the way up to the Eisenhower Tunnel. Both are often referred to as "Straight Creek," so it is easy to mix them up.

Finding the trailhead: Take I-70 west through the Eisenhower Tunnel. Immediately after you pass through the tunnel, veer right off the highway and park near a green Truck Break Check sign. Walk a short distance uphill to the trail. **GPS: N39 40.723'/W105 56.275'**

The Hike

It seems counterintuitive, but one of the most stunning hikes begins from I-70, the busy 2,100-mile paved artery bisecting the country. Fields of flowers overwhelm every sense as you pass fields thick with scarlet paintbrush and Colorado columbine. Heading up Straight Creek, a gentle stream that cuts down the middle of a lush valley, take note of the unmatched and impressive meadows of red, yellow, white, and blue lining the way even before you leave behind the concrete and thundering noise of the highway.

The pavement gives way to a gravel two-track enveloped in scarlet paintbrush, glacial daisy, elephant heads, mountain bluebells, tall larkspur, Gray's angelica, cowbane, and purple and white variations of Whipple's penstemon. Climbing up the gulch toward the spiny headwall rising from the northern edge of the basin, tiny seeps flow across the road giving life to verdant vegetation like king's crown, yellow monkeyflower, heartleaf bittercress, brook saxifrage, and Parry clover. With each step, the soothing sound of rushing water and the boisterous calls of songbirds on the wing replace the noise of semis crashing past. Looming large on the western skyline, find jagged crags shaped—by wind and water—into castle-like turrets and rugged steeples. Snowball saxifrage, Gray's angelica, scarlet paintbrush, Whipple's penstemon, showy ragwort, and elephant heads create a palette of oranges, pinks, and reds. Continue along the gentle trail through a wetter area where Colorado columbine, northern bedstraw, ruby-colored king's crown, and alpine thistle grace the route. As you meander even deeper into the gulch, arnica and paintbrush join forces to create an amazing combination of yellow and red confetti littered across deep green hillsides. Colorado columbines are thick and bushy on the down slope.

View from Continental Divide

Soon, a solid creek crosses the trail from the north (straight). In this true riparian area, Parry primrose, elephant heads, heartleaf bittercress, marsh marigold, snowball and bog saxifrage, Whipple's penstemon, and willows thrive. The trail starts to climb more steadily through a total wildflower explosion of all colors, shapes, and sizes, including lanceleaf chiming bells, beautiful cinquefoil, western yellow and scarlet paintbrush, alpine avens, and elephant heads.

Reach a junction where an unnamed trail heading into a huge back bowl calls your name. Instead of answering, turn right to follow the main trail toward the Great Divide. Leave the subalpine meadows behind and break into the alpine where fuchsia-colored rosy paintbrush, alpine avens, sky pilot, and silky phacelia decorate the tundra. The delicate, tiny blue blossoms of pygmy gentian reveal themselves as you climb.

Marmots scamper across the tundra, leaving countless digs in their wake. The trail crisscrosses an incline dappled with impressive clusters of Colorado columbine, snow buttercup, alpine clover, alpine avens, pygmy bitterroot, sky pilot, western yellow paintbrush, alpine bistort, alpine chiming bells, and silky phacelia. With each step, outstanding vistas reward your efforts: The wild, barely explored Gore Range riddled with dramatic ridges and twisted, fin-like spires emerges to the west while Mount Holy Cross (14,005 feet) reveals itself to the southwest.

Sky pilot

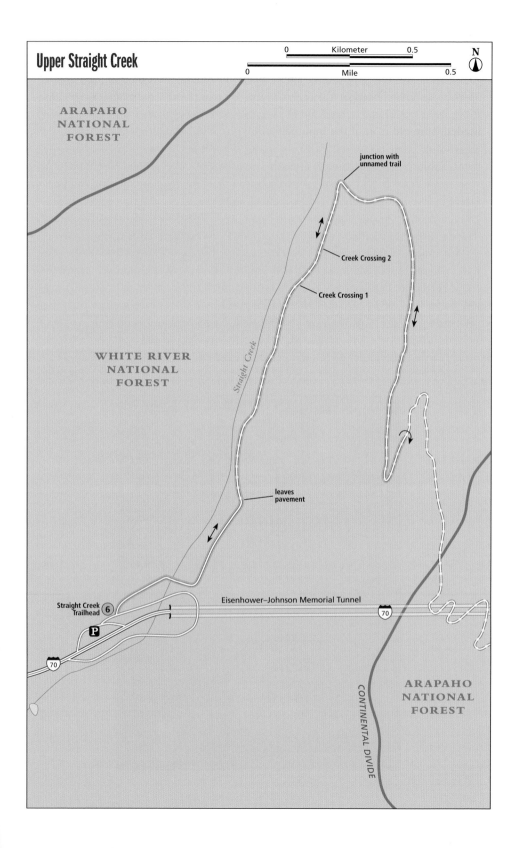

Leveling, the trail continues south along a rolling ridge frequented by mountain goats. Amid the rocks, note tiny alpine plants including brilliant pink cushions of moss campion and mats of alpine sandwort. Revel in superb views of Loveland Ski Area, the Gore Range, Ten Mile Range, and the Holy Cross Wilderness. Black-headed daisy, old man of the mountain, silky phacelia, alpine harebell, sky pilot, and alpine thistle join forces to create an impressive foreground for these magnificent vistas. Explore the high country for as long as you'd like and then retrace your steps back to the trailhead.

Miles and Directions

0.0 From the trailhead, head west on a paved service road. Stay left past the air intake drums to pick up the route that travels north up Straight Creek.

0.4 Reach a generator shack and a road closure gate where the pavement ends and gives way to a gravel two-track continuing north up the gulch.

1.0 Hop across the brook coming in from the north to continue along the trail.

1.1 Cross the small creek again and start climbing more steadily.

1.3 Reach an intersection with an unnamed social trail heading north. Turn sharply east (right); stay on the main trail.

2.1 Climb a series of switchbacks and traverse the ridge to reach the turnaround near Continental Divide (or for as long as you desire).

4.2 Arrive back at the trailhead.

Options: For a shorter adventure that still provides magnificent vistas and a range of flowers, walk as far up the trail as you want. Choose your turnaround point based on available energy and time. Those looking for a longer hike can reach the Divide and hike north to Hagar Mountain or south along the ridgeline.

Hike Information

Local Information

Copper Mountain Resort Chamber: Copper Mountain; (970) 968-2318 or (970) 968-6477; visitcoppermountain.com

Frisco/Copper Visitor Information Center: Frisco; (800) 424-1554; townoffrisco .com—with knowledgeable staff who provide a variety of information including maps and advice on activities and dining options.

Summit County Chamber of Commerce: Frisco; (970) 668-2051; summitchamber.org

Local Events/Attractions

Town of Frisco: Frisco; (970) 668-5276 or (800) 424-1554; townoffrisco.com

Organizations

Friends of the Dillon Ranger District: (970) 262-3449; fdrd.org

7 McCullough Gulch to White Falls

Journey through spruce-fir forest in a rugged canyon to reach White Falls, a sparkling ribbon of water cascading forcefully over dark granite. This quintessential Colorado hike meanders through meadows, crosses streams, traverses gardens of boulders, and passes mining remnants. Rainbow-colored clusters of wildflowers line the trail as it travels in the shadow of snow-capped peaks and provides dramatic views in all directions.

Start: From the McCullough Gulch Trailhead (11,105 feet)
Distance: 2.8 miles out and back
Hiking time: 1.5-3 hours
Difficulty: Short, but moderate due to altitude, steep sections, and rocky terrain
Trail surface: Forested, rocky dirt trail
Best season: June to October
Peak bloom: late July to mid-August
Flowers commonly found: monkshood, tall larkspur, mountain bluebells, shrubby and beautiful cinquefoil, American bistort, bracted lousewort, subalpine arnica, Gray's angelica, elephant heads, queen's crown, rosy pussytoes, marsh marigold, cowbane, globeflower, northern bedstraw, fireweed, Parry primrose, Colorado columbine, heartleaf bittercress, yarrow, black-tip senecio, death camas, bog pyrola, heartleaf arnica, scarlet, western yellow and rosy paintbrush, edible valerian, dotted saxifrage, subalpine Jacob's ladder, brook saxifrage, triangularleaf senecio
Other trail users: Equestrians, mountain bikers
Canine compatibility: Dogs permitted
Land status: National Forest
Nearest town: Breckenridge
Fees and permits: No fees or permits required
Schedule: Open all year, but often obstructed by snow from fall to early summer
Maps: USGS Breckenridge, CO; Trails Illustrated 109 Breckenridge, Tennessee Pass; Latitude 40 Summit County Colorado Trails
Trail contacts: White River National Forest, Dillon Ranger District, 680 Blue River Pkwy., Silverthorne, 80498; (970) 468-5400; www.fs.usda.gov/whiteriver
Special considerations: To secure parking and avoid crowds, arrive early to this very popular trail. Take care near the falls where steep, wet terrain can be tricky. Please respect the private property you pass through along the way.

Finding the trailhead: From the last traffic light in Breckenridge (Boreas Road), drive south on Hwy. CO 9 for 7.6 miles. Turn west (right) onto Blue Lakes Road (FR 850). After 0.1 mile, turn north (right) onto McCullough Gulch Road (FR 851), an improved dirt road that continues past the Quandary Peak Trailhead and curves around the peak's east end. After 1.7 miles, stay south (left) at the fork in the road. Continue for another 0.5 mile to a parking area. Please do not block the gate. **GPS: N39 24.061'/W106 04.738'**

The Hike

From the start, rejoice in the impressive vistas—which only improve—and the lovely sound of McCullough Creek roaring with intensity in a ravine on the right. Ascending McCullough Gulch, mountain bluebells, triangular leaf senecio, and scarlet paintbrush greet you immediately. Pace yourself by enjoying the delicate blossoms of brook saxifrage and heartleaf bittercress inhabiting this moist territory. A small wooden bridge offers a perch for spotting hot-pink Parry primrose, cowbane, and blue-lavender subalpine Jacob's ladder. Continue climbing more steeply along the rough road to pass multicolored rocky outcrops that harbor Colorado columbine and ground-hugging mats of dotted saxifrage.

The inclined trail passes the Last Dollar Mine, a claim first developed in the 1800s known to have confirmed gold deposits. Notice elephant heads, fireweed, scarlet, and western yellow paintbrush lingering around the small log cabin perched on a shelf above the trail's south (left) side. As you pass through private property, please respect the many No Trespassing signs. The rugged road, lined with creamy western yellow paintbrush, tall larkspur, and edible valerian, rises along the creek. As you creep along the north side of Quandary Peak (14,256 feet), glimpses down-canyon provide fantastic views of water roaring below and peaks like Quandary and Pacific (13,998 feet).

At the signed fork, a rocky, rooted singletrack path dives deep into the trees and passes another dilapidated mining building. Black-tip senecio, beautiful cinquefoil, heartleaf arnica, yarrow, and scarlet, western yellow, and rosy paintbrush add color to forest openings. Now the trail climbs at a steady but mellower grade through lodgepole pines and aspen where death camas and bog pyrola peek out from the undergrowth.

Pick your way across a boulder garden where fireweed, elephant heads, and black-tip senecio explode in pinks and yellows while heartleaf bittercress and yarrow peek out of cracks and crevices. Crossing a small bridge, proceed over rocky terrain dappled with several small stream crossings that bring you closer to the falls cascading over cliffs ahead. These seeps support an array of amazing blooms including American bistort, northern bedstraw, fireweed, queens' crown, mountain bluebells, Parry primrose, and Colorado columbine.

Cross an open talus field with astounding vistas of the snow-covered peaks lining the valley. Listen for the falls thundering in the distance. Periodic breaks in the forest provide tiny glimpses of the cascade ahead from small but lush meadows bursting with Gray's angelica, elephant heads, American bistort, queen's crown, monkshood, rosy pussytoes, marsh marigold, mountain bluebells, cowbane, globeflower, and a multicolored collection of paintbrush.

Head down into the gorge even further to reach a signed trail junction. The McCullough Gulch Trail (#43) continues uphill to the right while the White Falls Loop goes west (left). Turn left on the White Falls Loop heading through the forest toward an increasingly deafening falls. Take your time and wander along the curvy loop trail that winds through the forest brimming with bistort, bracted lousewort, subalpine arnica, and vocal chipmunks and marmots.

> **GREEN TIP**—When hiking in a group, walk single file on established trails to avoid widening them. If you come upon a sensitive area, spread out so you don't cut one path through the landscape. Don't create new trails where there were none before.

Monkshood with White Falls

After a short jaunt through a peaceful forest, the trail spits you out onto giant rocky slabs overflowing with shrubby cinquefoil at the base of White Falls, which sends sparkling water flowing in glittering bands over several hundred feet of black granite. Climb up to explore the falls from different angles, but beware of slippery wet rock. Huge stands of monkshood, tall larkspur, mountain bluebells, and bright yellow, magenta, red, and orange paintbrush of all types flank this waterfall.

Take a cooling dip in the water, enjoy a snack, and then retrace your steps back to the trailhead.

Miles and Directions

0.0 Start from the McCullough Gulch Diversion Dam. Skirt to the left of the locked gate and ascend via an old mining road.

0.2 Cross the raging creek on a small wooden bridge. Climb steeply to head northwest on the rugged road rising above the creek.

0.7 At a signed fork, veer northwest (left) onto a path that dives deep into the trees and passes another dilapidated mining building.

0.8 Pick your way across a small boulder garden to reach a tiny footbridge preceded by a few wooden steps. Cross the bridge and continue northwest and downhill.

0.9 Stay straight to cross a talus field.

1.2 Head down into the gorge to reach a signed trail junction. Follow the White Falls Loop west (left).

1.6 Reach the base of White Falls and explore.

2.8 Arrive back at the trailhead.

Options: Return to the signed trail junction and take the McCullough Gulch Trail (#43) upward for another 1.2 miles past a series of bubbling rivulets to reach Upper Blue Reservoir. Continue even further to explore the expansive alpine meadows and six additional lakes and tarns hiding in the upper valley. Navigation skills and topographic maps are required to explore this trail-less cirque ringed by Quandary Peak (14,265 feet), Fletcher Mountain (13,951 feet), and Atlantic Peak (13,841 feet).

Tall larkspur

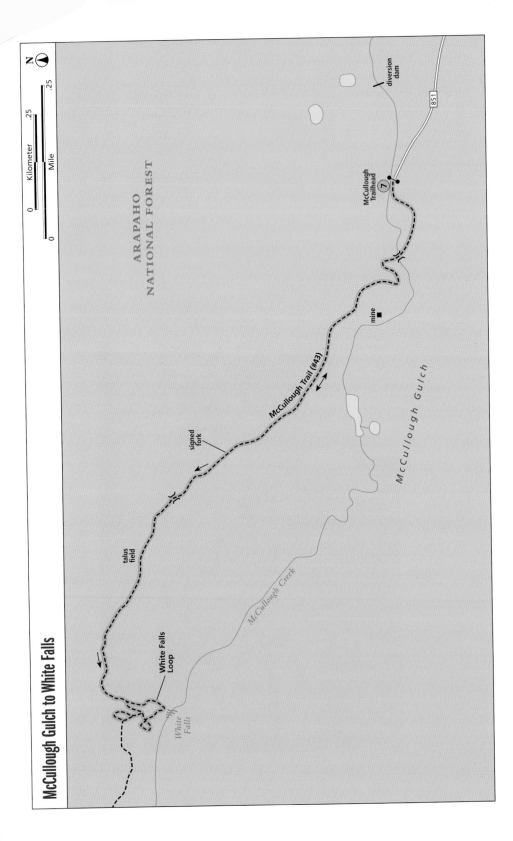

McCullough Gulch to White Falls

ARAPAHO
NATIONAL FOREST

talus
field

White Falls
Loop

signed
fork

McCullough Trail (#43)

mine

McCullough Gulch

McCullough Creek

White
Falls

McCullough
Trailhead

7

851

diversion
dam

N

Kilometer

0   .25

Mile

0   .25

Hike Information

Local Information

Breckenridge Resort Chamber: Breckenridge; (970) 453-2918 or (888) 251-2417; gobreck.com

Local Events/Attractions

Country Boy Mine: 0542 French Gulch Rd., Breckenridge; (970) 453-4405; countryboymine.com

    Town of Frisco: Frisco; (970) 668-5276 or (800) 424-1554; townoffrisco.com

    Historic Walking Tour; (970) 453-9767; breckheritage.com/historic-walking-tour

Hike Tours

Guided Hiking Tours: Breckenridge; (970) 453-5000; breckenridge.com/summer-breck-treks.aspx; townofbreckenridge.com/index

Organizations

Friends of the Dillon Ranger District: (970) 262-3449; fdrd.org

8 Lower Mohawk Lake

Complete with superb mountain views, a high alpine lake, and gulches and meadows teeming with colorful blossoms, this 2.4-mile hike is a perpetual favorite of locals and visitors alike. This absolute must-do adventure that parallels a huge, furious waterfall offers numerous chances to explore unique relics from the area's gold mining days and provides many opportunities for beautiful and worthwhile side trips.

Start: From the Upper Mohawk Lakes Trailhead (10,390 feet) at the Spruce Creek Diversion
Distance: 2.4 miles out and back
Hiking time: 2–4 hours
Difficulty: Short, but moderate due to altitude, elevation gain, and rocky terrain
Trail surface: Forested and dirt trail
Best season: June to September
Peak bloom: mid-July to mid-August
Flowers commonly found: heartleaf arnica, beautiful daisy, beautiful cinquefoil, yarrow, mountain bluebells, Whipple's penstemon, scarlet and rosy paintbrush, monkshood, triangularleaf senecio, bracted lousewort, subalpine arnica, northern goldenrod, elephant heads, globeflower, narcissus anemone, American bistort, subalpine Jacob's ladder, Colorado columbine, tall larkspur, Parry clover, Gray's angelica, yellow stonecrop, mountain harebells, dotted saxifrage, fringed sagewort, corn lily,
marsh marigold, heartleaf bittercress, brook saxifrage, Parry's lousewort, queen's crown, star gentian, fireweed, Parry primrose
Other trail users: Equestrians, mountain bikers
Canine compatibility: Dogs permitted
Land status: National Forest
Nearest town: Breckenridge
Fees and permits: No fees or permits required
Schedule: Open all year, but often obstructed by snow from fall to early summer
Maps: USGS Breckenridge, CO; Trails Illustrated 109 Breckenridge, Tennessee Pass; Latitude 40 Summit County Colorado Trails
Trail contacts: White River National Forest, Dillon Ranger District, 680 Blue River Pkwy., Silverthorne, 80498; (970) 468-5400; www.fs.usda.gov/whiteriver
Special considerations: This hike is very popular, so arrive early to secure parking and avoid crowds.

Finding the trailhead: From the last traffic light in Breckenridge (Boreas Road), drive south on Hwy. 9 for 2.1 miles. Turn west (right) onto Spruce Creek Road (CR 800), opposite of the Goose Pasture Tarn, and continue straight for 0.1 mile uphill on a dirt road. Bear left to stay on the main road through the intersection and continue 1.8 miles to reach the Spruce Creek Trailhead and a large parking lot. Two-wheel-drive vehicles should park here. Those with high clearance and four-wheel drive can continue upward, veering southwest (left) at the intersection with Crystal Lake Road (CR 803) to stay on the extremely rough, rocky Spruce Creek Road for another 1.5 miles to reach the upper trailhead. **GPS: N39 25.284'/W106 04.516'**

Note: This description begins from the upper trailhead, which requires four-wheel drive and high clearance. If you choose not to drive all the way, there are a few roadside parking spots you can use en route to the trailhead. Right before you reach the trailhead, a very steep section of road offers a formidable challenge for any vehicle. We highly recommend parking and hiking up this short, steep section regardless of your vehicle.

The Hike

Grab a glimpse of Mount Helen (13,164 feet) towering to the north before you follow the narrow trail into the dense forest dominated by spruce and fir where heartleaf arnica, beautiful daisy, beautiful cinquefoil, and yarrow greet you. Climb slowly to discover mountain bluebells, Whipple's penstemon, a colorful array of scarlet paintbrush, and an overlook offering a glimpse of Continental Falls' cascading white ribbons. Along the trail monkshood, cinquefoil, triangularleaf senecio, bracted lousewort, subalpine arnica, and northern goldenrod erupt in a sparkling array of gold and purple.

Just after the Mayflower junction, cross Spruce Creek and curve through a wet area where elephant heads, marsh marigold, globeflower, narcissus-flowered anemone, and American bistort linger. A dilapidated cabin hides in the forest, while the surrounding meadow flourishes with scarlet and rosy paintbrush and subalpine Jacob's ladder. Moose and elk frequent this lush area teeming with willows.

Wander past giant meadows of red, hot-pink, and orange paintbrush blooms and twist steeply up a rocky, rooted section. At the top, stone and brick remains of a mill greet you. Move west over big rock slabs to reach another trail junction and historic cabin ruins. A remarkable amount of flowers, including beautiful cinquefoil, Colorado columbine, subalpine arnica, tall larkspur, Parry clover, Gray's angelica, and rosy and scarlet paintbrush occupy this clearing. Head west (left) toward the lake, but not before checking out "Continental Cabin," a fully restored structure you can explore.

Mount Helen looms large ahead and the trail winds across raw rocky slopes. At a signed junction with a spur trail heading north (right) to the falls, go left to navigate

Lower Mohawk Lake

Falls at Lower Mohawk

switchbacks that sweep and flow over the hillside. Yellow stonecrop's flat clusters of golden, star-shaped flowers atop fleshy stems peek out from outcrops. Mountain hare-bells, dotted saxifrage, beautiful daisy, Whipple's penstemon, and fringed sagewort appear.

Grassy gulches lining the trail overflow with corn lily, bistort, bluebells, triangular-leaf senecio, marsh marigold, and subalpine arnica. Small seeps give life to clusters of Colorado columbine, heartleaf bittercress, and brook saxifrage. Near the top, the trail moves over streamside bedrock slabs. Perched at the top, an intact wooden structure with thick cables used to move ore up and down the mountain awaits. Views of distant peaks and the valley below will drop your jaw.

Continue climbing to enter an expansive, lush basin dappled with grand pine trees and luxurious vegetation. The stunning, multitiered chute known as Continental Falls pours from its outlet to welcome you into a willowy oasis where Parry's lousewort hides. Skirt the south (left) edge of Lower Mohawk Lake, a sparkling shallow pool resting in the shadow of Mount Helen (13,164 feet). At your feet, queen's crown, marsh marigold, bistort, Gray's angelica, star gentian, fireweed, and subalpine Jacob's ladder adorn the lakeshore.

Take in the amazing scenery. Peer across the lake to discover that another old cabin rests halfway up the rocky face holding the elegant cascade. Enjoy a snack, explore the flower-lined shores, and scan the ridges above for mountain goats before retracing your steps to the trailhead.

Star gentian

Miles and Directions

0.0 From the diversion dam, follow signs for the trail, which heads west (right) into the trees.

0.3 Reach the Mayflower Lakes split. Go southwest (straight) to continue climbing toward Mohawk Lakes.

0.5 Pass over big rock slabs to reach a clearing with a signed trail junction and historic cabin ruins. A sign points hikers left (west) to Lower Mohawk Lake and right (east) to the Lower Continental Falls vista, which we suggest you visit on the descent (see Options). Head west (left) toward the lake.

0.6 Reach a signed junction, where a spur trail heads north (right) to the falls. Follow the arrow left and continue climbing up rocky switchbacks to traverse the hillside.

0.9 After climbing a series of switchbacks, the trail levels and reaches an intact wooden mining structure with thick cables.

1.0 Climb up a steep rocky section to enter an expansive basin where Continental Falls welcomes you.

1.2 Explore the south (left) edge of Lower Mohawk Lake, a sparkling shallow pool resting in the shadow of Mount Helen (13,164 feet).

2.4 Arrive back at the trailhead.

Options: Continue around the south side of Lower Mohawk Lake to pick up the steep, twisty trail that climbs another 0.4 mile to reach Upper Mohawk Lake (12,073 feet), which offers breathtaking vistas and angling opportunities. On your return trip, two side trip options await: (1) experience Continental Falls up close and personal by taking the spur trail and take one of the turnoffs to Continental Falls and (2) visit Mayflower Lake by turning at the signed junction. Walk partially around the lakeshore for a view of the falls feeding the lake. As you return to the main path, look carefully for the ruins of at least six cabins. Though most of the ruins have walls just one to three logs high, you can still imagine the miners and others who lived here years ago.

Lower Mohawk Lake

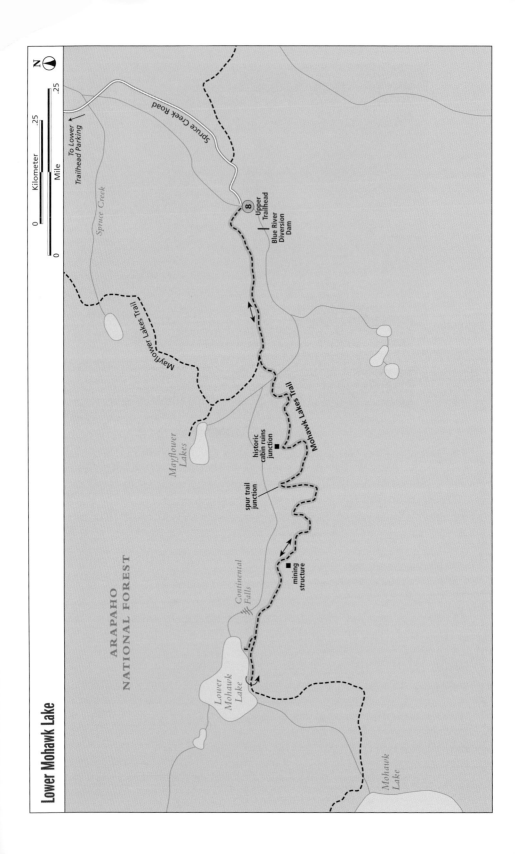

Lower Mohawk Lake

Hike Information

Local Information

Breckenridge Resort Chamber: Breckenridge; (970) 453-2918 or (888) 251-2417; gobreck.com

Local Events/Attractions

Country Boy Mine: 0542 French Gulch Rd., Breckenridge; (970) 453-4405; countryboymine.com

  Town of Frisco: Frisco; (970) 668-5276 or (800) 424-1554; townoffrisco.com

  Historic Walking Tour; (970) 453-9767; breckheritage.com/historic-walking-tour

Hike Tours

Guided Hiking Tours: Breckenridge; (970) 453-5000; breckenridge.com/summer-breck-treks.aspx; townofbreckenridge.com/index.

Organizations

Friends of the Dillon Ranger District: (970) 262-3449; fdrd.org

SUBLIME SUBALPINE (9,500–11,400 FEET)

This zone extends from the upper edge of the montane forest to the tree line. Dense forests of coniferous trees, largely Engelmann spruce and subalpine fir, cover the upper reaches of the Colorado mountains. They hold precious moisture and promote lush growth in this harsh environment. The narrow, pointy shape of the trees easily sheds heavy snows that would break the branches of broader species. Groves of quaking aspen dot the subalpine ecosystem. Stream sides and sodden ground, damp from recently melted snow, overflow with lush wildflowers. Tall larkspur and monkshood burst from moist meadows while bog pyrola, Parry's lousewort, and brilliant red and yellow paintbrush grow along trails and on the forest floor. Mule deer, elk, Canada lynx, and black bear share this zone with the American marten, snowshoe hare, red-tailed hawk, and white-tailed ptarmigan.

On ridges, limber pines bend in the strong winds. Small stands of bristlecone pines, among the earth's oldest living things, may be more than 1,000 years old. At the upper limits of the sub-alpine ecosystem, high winds blow over the mountaintops forming stands of stunted and twisted trees known as *krummholz*, a German term meaning crooked wood that is further explained in a sidebar for the Linkins Lake hike.

Subalpine

9 Monte Cristo Gulch

Walk above the trees on a delightful hike through a high alpine wonderland rich with mining history. Though short, this trail climbs steeply in spots as it meanders along a rushing creek, rife with colorful blooms, to reach a lush basin enveloped by jagged cliffs. Perched at the end of the trail, a shimmering tarn and cascading falls await your arrival. Expect sublime views, multiple easy stream crossings, and the opportunity to see a range of wildlife from mountain goats to marmots.

Start: From the north end of the dam (11,700 feet)
Distance: 2.5 miles out and back
Hiking time: 2–4 hours
Difficulty: Short, but moderate due to altitude, a few steep sections, and rocky terrain
Trail surface: Rocky and dirt trail
Best season: June to September
Peak bloom: late July to mid-August
Flowers commonly found: black-tip senecio, American bistort, Colorado columbine, yellow stonecrop, mountain harebell, silky phacelia, moss campion, rosy, scarlet and western yellow paintbrush, alpine clover, alpine spring beauty, shrubby cinquefoil, mountain blue-bells, Parry gentian, yarrow, Parry primrose, elephant heads, narcissus anemone, beautiful cinquefoil, fringed gentian, king's crown, marsh marigold, alpine thistle, heartleaf

bittercress, queen's crown, alpine avens, star gentian, alpine harebell, mountain parsley, beautiful daisy, alpine thistle, old man of the mountains, moss campion, alpine sandwort
Other trail users: Equestrians
Canine compatibility: Dogs permitted
Land status: National Forest
Nearest town: Breckenridge
Fees and permits: No fees or permits required
Schedule: Open all year, but often obstructed by snow from fall to early summer
Maps: USGS Breckenridge, CO; Trails Illustrated 109 Breckenridge, Tennessee Pass; Latitude 40 Summit County Colorado Trails
Trail contacts: White River National Forest, Dillon Ranger District, 680 Blue River Pkwy., Silverthorne, 80498; (970) 468-5400; www.fs.usda.gov/whiteriver

Finding the trailhead: From the last traffic light in Breckenridge (Boreas Road), drive south on Hwy. CO 9 for 7.6 miles. Turn west (right) onto Blue Lakes Road (FR 850). Go straight at the fork and follow the road for 2.2 miles to the parking area just below the dam. **GPS: N39 23.208'/ W106 05.993'**

The Hike

From the parking area, walk toward the dam to pass a sign announcing the Quandary Crest Ridge Trail, used to access Quandary Peak's (14,265 feet) South Gully route. Pick up the well-defined, rocky trail skirting the northern edge of Upper Blue Lake, a reservoir providing water to Aurora and Colorado Springs. Nature greets your arrival with clusters of black-tip senecio, American bistort, Colorado columbine, yellow stonecrop,

▶ TIDBIT—Quandary Peak ranks 13th highest among Colorado's 58 fourteeners.

mountain harebell, silky phacelia, and moss campion. Quandary Peak looms large to the north (right).

Skirt the reservoir and head up a rocky, eroded section of trail that climbs through a verdant grove bursting with black-tip senecio, a vibrant display of rosy, scarlet, and western yellow paintbrush and magenta alpine clover. Within gravelly crevices, round patches of tiny, fleshy basal leaves support the delicate white and pink petals of alpine spring beauty. Shrubby cinquefoil, mountain bluebells, bistort, rosy paintbrush, Parry gentian, and yarrow join forces to create a bright foreground for spectacular views of Wheeler Mountain (13,694 feet) as the trail levels.

Cross the creek lined with Parry primrose, elephant heads, and narcissus anemone. From here, the trail cuts back through an area bursting with American bistort, mountain bluebells, and beautiful cinquefoil. Fringed gentian and rosy and western yellow paintbrush greet you on the other side of the creek where Fletcher Mountain towers in the distance. Follow the main trail past elephant heads, yarrow, mountain harebells, king's crown, and marsh marigold. Pause for a moment to absorb the beauty of this rocky, flower-lined path skirting a huge, deep blue lake journeying toward a spectacular bowl encircled by jagged summits.

Follow the trail, which traverses a steep, rocky gradient teeming with alpine thistle and marmots whistling warnings as they dart back and forth over the tundra. Listen for the waterfall announcing its presence more and more loudly with each step you take. Crane your neck to take in North Star Peak rising from the south and Quandary towering overhead to the north.

Balsamroot overlooking reservoir

Parry gentian

Meander through a lush section where the brook and the trail seem to become one. Heartleaf bittercress, Parry primrose, marsh marigold, queen's crown, fringed gentian, and rosy paintbrush thrive in this lush environment.

Continue climbing next to a glimmering, boisterous creek littered with alpine avens, paintbrush of many types, alpine clover, star gentian, and alpine harebell.

As you gain altitude and the willows lessen, look downhill to discover a striking array of yellow, reds, whites, and purples decorating slopes. Mountain parsley, yarrow, beautiful daisy, alpine thistle, old man of the mountain, alpine avens, and lavender daisies paint a rainbow on the tundra. Moss campion and alpine sandwort form a colorful carpet.

Further on, reach historic mining remnants from the Golden Beaver Mine. Though the cabins are now in disrepair, they serve to remind us that many struck it rich in 1860. Climb gently up the valley in the shadow of giant peaks. Enjoy meandering alongside the water where mountain harebells and alpine bistort blossom. Cross the creek and continue through meadows bursting with narcissus anemone, elephant heads, queen's crown, king's crown, and silky phacelia. House-sized boulders litter the meadow, and the trail peters out as you enter a starker, alpine environment. Alpine sorrel, Parry's lousewort, alpine paintbrush, old man of the mountain, alpine columbine, and others spruce up the tundra.

A multitiered waterfall cascades over a talus slope to reach a tarn nestled in a serene meadow. Rest on a lovely rock and absorb the calm sound of rushing water and sublime vistas. Retrace your steps back to the car.

Monte Cristo Gulch

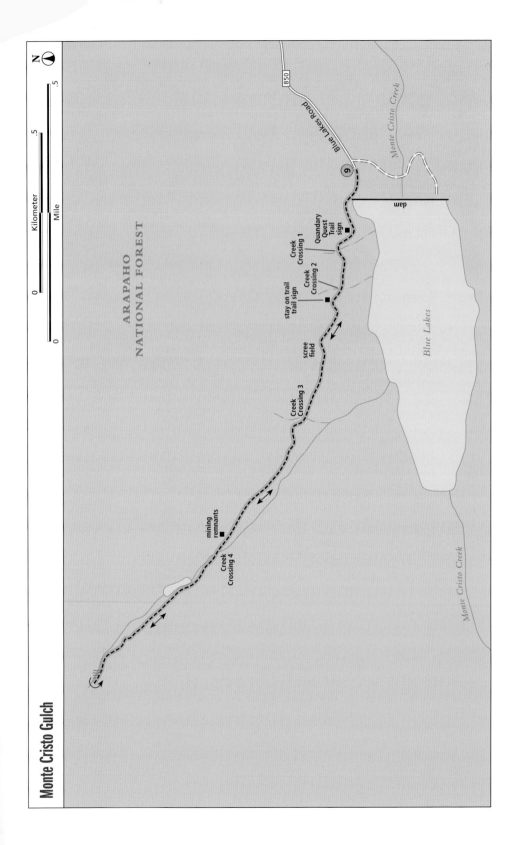

ARAPAHO
NATIONAL FOREST

Blue Lakes Road
850
9

Quandary
Quest
Trail
sign

Creek
Crossing 1

Creek
Crossing 2

stay on trail
trail sign

scree
field

Creek
Crossing 3

Creek
Crossing 4

mining
remnants

dam

Blue Lakes

Monte Cristo Creek

Monte Cristo Creek

N

Kilometer
0   .5

Mile
0   .5

Miles and Directions

0.0 From the parking area, walk uphill to the dam.

0.1 On the northern (right) edge of the dam, walk past the Quandary Crest Ridge Trail sign, cross the walkway and pick up the well-defined rocky trail that heads west and skirts the northern edge of Upper Blue Lake.

0.15 Reach a sign pointing uphill to the north (right). Head right to reach the top, where the trail levels and veers west.

0.2 Cross the creek and follow the trail as it cuts south (left) back toward the lake.

0.3 Turning west, the trail climbs and crosses the creek.

0.32 Veer north and climb a slope to reach a sign urging hikers to stay on the trail. Follow the main trail west.

0.4 Arrive at a scree field where you leave the trees behind and continue climbing steadily.

0.6 Reach the creek, hop over it, and pick up the trail veering uphill to the north (right).

0.8 Continue climbing to reach historic mining remnants from the 1800s.

0.9 Climb gently up the valley to an easy creek crossing that brings you to the west (left) side of the creek. Continue north.

1.2 Reach a tarn nestled in a meadow. Enjoy a picnic or nap before retracing your steps.

2.5 Arrive back at the trailhead.

Hike Information

Local Information

Breckenridge Resort Chamber: Breckenridge; (970) 453-2918 or (888) 251-2417; gobreck.com

Local Events/Attractions

Country Boy Mine: 0542 French Gulch Rd., Breckenridge; (970) 453-4405; countryboymine.com

Town of Frisco: Frisco; (970) 668-5276 or (800) 424-1554; townoffrisco.com

Historic Walking Tour; (970) 453-9767; breckheritage.com/historic-walking-tour

Hike Tours

Guided Hiking Tours: Breckenridge; (970) 453-5000; breckenridge.com/summer-breck-treks.aspx; townofbreckenridge.com/index

Organizations

Friends of the Dillon Ranger District: (970) 262-3449; fdrd.org

10 Mayflower Gulch

On this relaxed but spectacular jaunt through a constricted, forested valley littered with mining remnants, you reach an expansive bowl brimming with wildflowers of all sorts. Discover bits of Colorado's mining past while absorbing impressive views of the toothed summits of the Ten Mile Range on a quick, mellow 4.3-mile hike into the high country. A brief off-trail meander offers the chance for an intimate exploration of hillsides bursting with wildflowers.

Start: From the Mayflower Gulch Trailhead (10,995 feet)
Distance: 4.3 miles out and back
Hiking time: 2–4 hours
Difficulty: Easy due to gradual, smooth terrain and moderate elevation gain
Trail surface: Dirt road and trail
Best season: July to September
Peak bloom: late July to mid-August
Flowers commonly found: elephant heads, globeflower, heartleaf bittercress, glacial daisy, blueleaf cinquefoil, brook saxifrage, Parry clover, heartleaf arnica, yarrow, pygmy bitterroot, rosy, scarlet, and western yellow paintbrush, mountain bluebells, Whipple's penstemon, tall larkspur, Colorado columbine, Parry primrose, bracted lousewort, American bistort, alpine thistle, subalpine arnica, showy ragwort, glacial daisy, marsh marigold, queen's crown, Parry gentian, wild rose, alpine clover, beautiful daisy, narcissus anemone, alpine lousewort

Other trail users: Equestrians, mountain bikers, four-wheel-drive vehicles until the gate
Canine compatibility: Dogs permitted
Land status: National Forest
Nearest town: Frisco
Fees and permits: No fees or permits required
Schedule: Open all year, but often covered in snow from fall to early summer
Maps: USGS Copper Mountain, CO; Trails Illustrated 109 Breckenridge, Tennessee Pass; Latitude 40 Summit County Colorado Trails
Trail contacts: White River National Forest, Dillon Ranger District, 680 Blue River Pkwy., Silverthorne, 80498; (970) 468-5400; www.fs.usda.gov/whiteriver
Special Considerations: Motor vehicles not permitted beyond the gate before the mine

Finding the trailhead: From Frisco, drive west on I-70 for 5 miles. Take exit 195 for Copper Mountain/Leadville and merge onto Hwy. 91. Head south for 6 miles until you reach the trailhead and large parking lot on the left. **GPS: N39 25.810'/W106 09.917'**

The Hike

Turn your back on the highway and begin following this old mining route through dense evergreen forest paralleling Mayflower Creek. Vast wetlands and a beautiful riparian corridor shelter elephant heads, globeflower, and heartleaf bittercress buds. Meandering along the creek's border, find abundant blooms, including lavender glacial daisy, shiny yellow blueleaf cinquefoil, brilliant pink elephant heads, and the minute but artful white blossom of brook saxifrage.

Rosy paintbrush in Mayflower Gulch

Continue along the road as it travels south up the valley revealing Parry clover, heartleaf arnica, yarrow, and the tiny pink and white flowers of the ground-hugging pygmy bitterroot. Less than a mile into this historical adventure, signs of the area's rich mining history appear. Rosy and western yellow paintbrush, mountain bluebells, Whipple's penstemon, and tall larkspur adorn these historic remnants and the surrounding meadows. Tailing piles dapple the hillsides in this area, reminding us that the first people to flock here came in search of their fortune. The forest thins affording exquisite vistas of peaks and ridges. As you hopscotch between meadows and stands of forest, wildflower-viewing opportunities abound. Pale western yellow paintbrush, deep purple Colorado columbine, scarlet paintbrush, mountain bluebells, and tall larkspur burst forth from lush meadows. Vibrant magenta Parry primrose occupies tiny seeps while creamy yellow bracted lousewort and heartleaf arnica add bursts of color to the forest floor.

The trail gently ascends into the Mayflower amphitheater, a spectacular basin enveloped by Fletcher Mountain's (13,995 feet) craggy ridge and the rugged monoliths of Pacific, Crystal, and Atlantic Peaks standing like sentinels to the east (left). Verdant fields bursting with colorful flower clusters set against the backdrop of snow-capped summits create an unforgettable scene.

Finally, the trail fully breaks free from the forest and reaches a fork in the road. The left fork goes southeast toward Boston Mine and parallels the brook as it delves further into Mayflower Gulch.

If flower finding is your priority, follow the road curving south (right) and climbing uphill gradually toward Gold Hill. As the trees thin out, great views of this classic high mountain cirque unfold before you.

▶ **TIDBIT—A mining tipple is an ore chute that employs gravity to move heavy ore.**

Queen's crown

Explore the grassy hillsides around you as they explode in a rainbow made up of rosy, scarlet, and western yellow paintbrush, American bistort, alpine thistle, subalpine arnica, showy ragwort, glacial daisy, and Whipple's penstemon.

Follow this twisty road, which wanders southwest and traverses the grassy slope on the west side of Mayflower Gulch, for as long as you feel like exploring. Be sure to look back for vistas of the Boston Mine across the valley and the rugged peaks encircling this marvelous basin. When the road turns sharply north (right) and begins climbing more directly for Gold Hill, you encounter faint trails continuing southward onto the lush hillsides. One option is to turn around here (unless you are topping out on Gold Hill—see Options) and retrace your steps back to the main road.

For a more intimate exploration of the many colorful blooms at your feet, wander off trail and descend gradually through the lush hillside teeming with rosy paintbrush, elephant heads, marsh marigold, queen's crown, and Parry gentian. Keep an eye on the road as you plunge through the bouncy highlands brimming with wild rose, queen's crown, alpine clover, mountain bluebells, Whipple's penstemon, beautiful daisy, narcissus anemone, and alpine lousewort, a stunning and rare find that grows almost solely in the Colorado Rockies. Explore for as long as you'd like and enjoy the solitude amid this pleasing scenery. When you decide to pry yourself away from this idyllic setting, make your way back to the road and then follow your steps back to the trailhead.

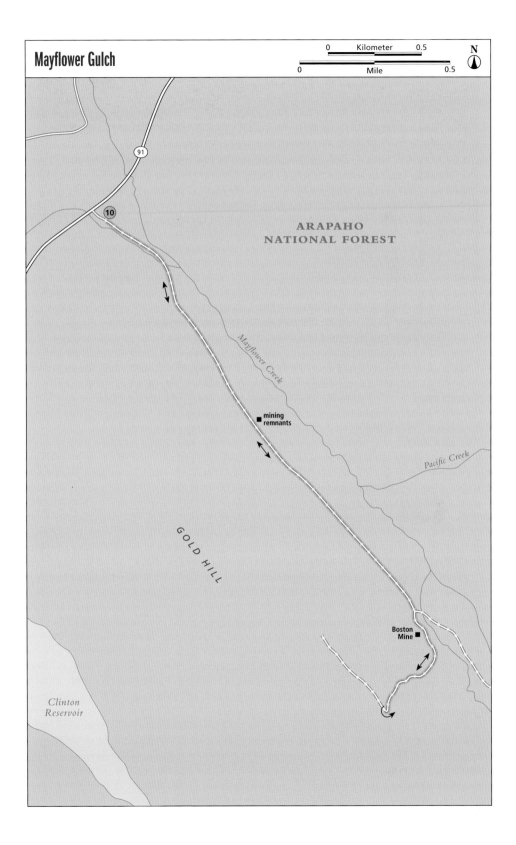

Mayflower Gulch

0   Kilometer   0.5

0   Mile   0.5

N

91

10

ARAPAHO NATIONAL FOREST

Mayflower Creek

■ mining remnants

Pacific Creek

GOLD HILL

Boston Mine ■

Clinton Reservoir

Miles and Directions

0.0 Start from the Mayflower Gulch Trailhead. Walk southeast along the dirt access road paralleling Mayflower Creek.

0.9 Arrive at signs of the area's rich mining history, including a dilapidated ore-loading chute, rusty bits of equipment, and the ruins of a ramshackle cabin.

1.6 At a fork in the road, veer right to follow the road as it curves south (right) and climbs gradually toward Gold Hill.

2.1 The road turns sharply north (right) and begins climbing more directly for Gold Hill. Faint trails continue south onto the lush hillsides. Follow these vague paths across the slopes ahead until you've explored enough. Meander back to the road. Retrace your steps to the trailhead.

4.3 Arrive back at the trailhead.

Options: Instead of turning around, continue upward when the road turns sharply north (right) to reach the tundra-covered top of Gold Hill (11,936 feet), where you can see the countless other peaks and the Clinton Creek Watershed to the west. On the return trip, explore the Boston Mine Camp. Visiting the ghost town left by miners long ago is definitely a worthy goal, but because flowers are our focus, we did not choose to feature the route to the mining cabins. For a worthy side trip after you explore the upper, flower-filled meadows, follow the left fork of the trail to the camp. Explore the remnants of this early mining camp, which include a boarding house and cabins evocative of another era, but please help keep this fragile town site intact.

Hike Information

Local Information

Copper Mountain Resort Chamber: Copper Mountain; (970) 968-2318 or (970) 968-6477; visitcoppermountain.com

Frisco/Copper Visitor Information Center: Frisco; (800) 424-1554; townoffrisco.com—with knowledgeable staff who provide a variety of information including maps and advice on activities and dining options.

Summit County Chamber of Commerce: Frisco; (970) 668-2051; summitchamber.org

Local Events/Attractions

Town of Frisco: Frisco; (970) 668-5276 or (800) 424-1554; townoffrisco.com

Organizations

Friends of the Dillon Ranger District: (970) 262-3449; fdrd.org

11 Linkins Lake

Just below Independence Pass (12,095 feet), this moderately challenging, but short, easily accessible trail travels through an alpine wonderland replete with dazzling wildflower displays and never-ending vistas to reach a high alpine lake (12,008 feet) with decent fishing. Though the brief, steep climb will raise your heart rate, the Linkins Lake Trail (#1979) begins high enough that you can skip the long, leg-busting climb usually needed to reach this sort of exceptional terrain.

Start: From the Linkins Lake Trailhead (11,506 feet)
Distance: 1.4 miles out and back
Hiking time: 1–3 hours
Difficulty: Short, but moderate due to altitude and steep sections
Trail surface: Dirt trail
Best season: July to September
Peak bloom: late July to mid-August
Flowers commonly found: glacial daisy, subalpine arnica, monkshood, fringed gentian, king's crown, death camas, Coulter's daisy, scarlet, northern, western yellow and rosy paintbrush, Parry primrose, yellow monkeyflower, fireweed, golden aster, mountain parsley, dotted saxifrage, Richardson's geranium, Colorado columbine, American bistort, rosy pussytoes, bracted lousewort, tall ragwort, narcissus anemone, elephant heads, marsh marigold, alpine avens, star gentian, black-headed daisy, alpine lousewort, mountain bluebells

Other trail users: Equestrians
Canine compatibility: Leashed dogs permitted
Land status: National Forest, Wilderness
Nearest town: Aspen
Fees and permits: No fees or permits required
Schedule: Open all year, but often covered in snow from fall to summer
Maps: USGS Mount Champion, Independence Pass, CO; Trails Illustrated 127 Aspen, Independence Pass; Latitude 40 Crested Butte, Aspen, Gunnison Trails
Trail contacts: White River National Forest, Aspen Ranger District, 806 W. Hallam Aspen, 81611; (970) 925-3445; www.fs.usda.gov/whiteriver
Special considerations: Managers don't recommend camping at the lake because of concerns about damage to the fragile alpine tundra and exposure to the elements.

Finding the trailhead: From Aspen, drive 18.5 miles east on Hwy. 82. Just past mile marker 59, reach the last switchback before Independence Pass. The trailhead, which is the jumping-off point for Linkins Lake and the Lost Man Trail, is on the left (north) side of the highway at this hairpin turn. **GPS: N39 07.480'/W106 34.908'**

The Hike

Begin your journey just below tree line on the well-marked trail that begins to the left of the river. Follow the trail and climb gradually upward along the west (left) side of the Roaring Fork. Lush willows line this verdant trail already brimming with

Alpine garden near Linkin Lake

glacial daisy, subalpine arnica, monkshood, fringed gentian, king's crown, death camas, Coulter's daisy, and scarlet and rosy paintbrush.

The trail continues north and soon intersects with the river where you find magenta Parry primrose and yellow monkeyflower hiding amid green vegetation. Cross to the north (right) side of the Roaring Fork via a small manufactured bridge. Almost immediately after this crossing, reach a signed Y-junction with the Lost Man Trail, which heads north (right) to Independence Lake and Lost Man Pass. Take the northwest (left) fork to continue onward into the Hunter-Fryingpan Wilderness toward Linkins Lake and past fireweed, golden aster, and mountain parsley.

From here, previously moderate grades give way to steeper terrain. The trail becomes rockier and ascends past a few remaining spruce tree clusters where dotted saxifrage, Richardson's geranium, Colorado columbine, American bistort, and rosy pussytoes make their home. With each foot of elevation gained, new views reveal themselves. Look to the east, toward the Lost Man Trail, and Twining Peak (13,711 feet) appears in the distance. To the west, Geissler Mountain (13,380 feet) towers above.

The trail levels out and traverses the slope where you find bracted lousewort and tall ragwort. Views continue to improve as you climb steadily to reach a switchback where a social trail heads off to your right. Stay on the main trail and take the switchack to the left. As you cut back toward the lake, a gorgeous display of narcissus anemone, tall ragwort, elephant heads, fireweed, American bistort, and rosy, northern, and western yellow paintbrush explode in a rainbow of light. Switchbacks cut

Elephant heads

through splendid slabs of granite that add even more color. The trail climbs steeply, but be sure to take your time and look back toward Independence Pass for a fabulous view of the creek below and stately, never-ending mountains in the distance. From here, you can see dozens of the state's most impressive peaks including La Plata Peak (14,361 feet) looming large to the southeast and Independence Mountain (12,703 feet) towering to the south. As you walk, note the powerful role erosion has played on shaping this slope.

Leaving the switchbacks, the route heads west and climbs through an alpine meadow full of narcissus anemone, marsh marigold, alpine avens, rosy and northern paintbrush, and fringed and star gentian. Curious marmots peer over rocks watching your every step.

Continuing west/southwest, the trail passes a tranquil trickle to reach the glacial cirque sheltering Linkins Lake. Parry primrose, elephant heads, marsh marigold, alpine avens, black-headed daisy, alpine lousewort, and mountain bluebells proliferate along the creek and lake banks. Explore the serene wildflower-filled shores of this pristine glacial lake, but take care not to damage this fragile alpine environment. Magnificent vistas of the Continental Divide and summits abound. From this magical spot, there is no doubt that the effort was worth every moment.

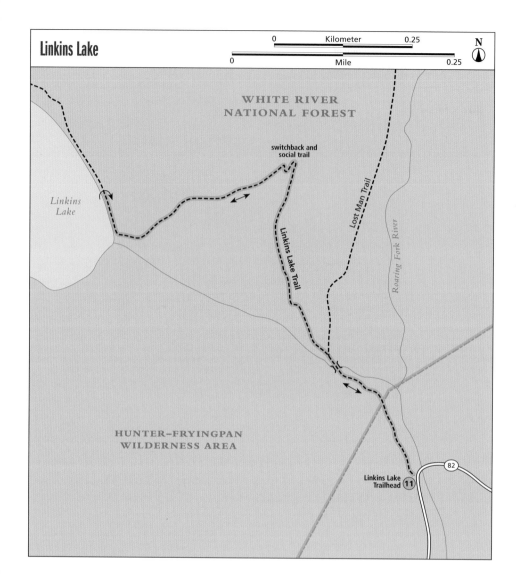

Miles and Directions

0.0 Start from the Linkins Lake/Upper Lost Man Trailhead on the well-marked trail climbing gradually along the west (left) side of the Roaring Fork River.

0.1 Reach the river. Cross to the north (right) side of the Roaring Fork via a small manufactured bridge.

0.2 Arrive at a signed Y-junction with the Lost Man Trail. Take the northwest (left) fork to continue onward into the Hunter-Fryingpan Wilderness toward Linkins Lake.

0.4 Reach a severe switchback where a social trail heads off to the east (right). Follow the switchback to the west (left) to stay on the main trail.

0.7 Pass a stream to reach Linkins Lake. Explore its shores, taking care not to damage this fragile alpine environment.

1.4 Arrive back at the trailhead.

Hike Information

Local Information

Aspen Chamber of Commerce: Aspen; (970) 925-1940; aspenchamber.org

Local Events/Attractions

Aspen Music Festival: Aspen; (970) 925-9042; aspenmusicfestival.com
Basalt River Days: Basalt; (970) 927-4031; basaltchamber.org
Strawberry Days: Glenwood Springs; (970) 945-6589; glenwoodchamber.com/strawberry-days-festival.html

Organizations

Colorado Mountain Club—Aspen Group: Aspen; cmc.org
Roaring Fork Outdoor Volunteers: Basalt; (970) 927-8241; rfov.org
Wilderness Workshop: Aspen; (970) 963-3977; wildernessworkshop.org

Hike Tours

Aspen Alpine Guides: Aspen; (970) 925-6618; aspenalpine.com

Other Resources

Pitkin Outside—A map of hiking trails and more in Pitkin County available online and via a free mobile app. Download it and you can export a GPS file or print a PDF map before setting out. pitkinoutside.org

WHAT ARE THOSE CRAZY-LOOKING SMALL TREES?

As you walk through the zone between subalpine and alpine tundra, especially in rugged environments like cliffs and mountaintops, you will notice islands of stunted and gnarled trees, growing in a pattern called *krummholz*, which aptly means "crooked wood" in German. Typically found between 11,000 and 11,400 feet, these dwarf, matted trees usually stand less than eight feet high and often reach only knee or ankle height. These hardy specimens only have two frost-free months, so they grow exceeding slowly, adding only millimeters in a growing season. For this reason, trees hundreds of years old may only measure a few feet tall and a few inches in diameter; scientists found a tree in Rocky Mountain National Park that measured 37 inches in diameter and was well over 390 years old. A three-inch tree at 11,500 feet cored out at 328 years old!

Notice that one side of most trees has little or no growth. Wind-blown ice and sand prune the limbs off the windward side, which protects the rest of the tree by taking the brunt of the elements. This weather blasting often permits growth of green branches only on the leeward side of the trunk, creating malformed evergreens called flag, or banner, trees. Now that you know how hard these trees work to survive, please don't mess with the 3-foot trees you see out there—they may be up to 200 years old.

Krummholz

12 Cathedral Lake

Challenging, stunning, and not to be missed. This describes the stiff climb through Pine Creek Canyon to reach Cathedral Lake (11,880 feet), a sparkling gem nestled in a breathtaking amphitheater surrounded by craggy granite ridges and toothed summits, including the dramatic serrated Cathedral Peak (13,943 feet). Arguably one of the most magical hikes in the area, this trail rises 2,000 feet along a raging waterway through aspen groves, conifer forest, and flower-filled meadows. Waterfalls, wildlife, and mountain views abound as you work your way to one of the most picturesque picnic spots this side of the Continental Divide.

Start: From the Cathedral Lake Trailhead (9,915 feet)
Distance: 6.0 miles out and back
Hiking time: 3–5 hours
Difficulty: Strenuous due to steep climbs, altitude, and elevation gain
Trail surface: Forested and dirt trail
Best season: June to September
Peak bloom: mid-July to mid-August
Flowers commonly found: lambstongue groundsel, black-tip senecio, yarrow, Gray's angelica, golden aster, twinberry, yarrow, wax currant, star gentian, fireweed, blueberry, squashberry, wild strawberry, lanceleaf chiming bells, wild rose, monument plant, northern goldenrod, tall larkspur, yellow monkeyflower, mountain harebell, shrubby cinquefoil, valerian, mountain dandelion, bracted lousewort, Parry's lousewort, scarlet and western yellow paintbrush, western wallflower, alpine thistle, Whipple's penstemon, pygmy bitterroot, golden draba, yellow stonecrop, mountain bluebells, Colorado columbine, black-headed daisy, Rocky Mountain pussytoes, rosy pussytoes, silky phacelia, common alumroot, death camas, king's crown, heartleaf bittercress, Parry clover, American bistort, Parry gentian,

alpine avens, alpine bistort, subalpine arnica, alpine fleabane, queen's crown, alpine clover, moss campion, alpine sandwort
Other trail users: Equestrians
Canine compatibility: Leashed dogs permitted
Land status: National Forest, Wilderness
Nearest town: Aspen
Fees and permits: No permits or fees required. If you are spending the night in the Maroon Bells-Snowmass Wilderness, you must self-register at the trailhead and carry a copy of your registration. Registration is free, and there is no limit to the number of permits issued. You will need a valid fishing license for Cathedral Lake and along Pine Creek.
Schedule: Open all year, but often obstructed by snow from fall to summer
Maps: USGS Hayden Peak, CO; Trails Illustrated 127 Aspen, Independence Pass
Trail contacts: White River National Forest, Aspen Ranger District, 806 W. Hallam Aspen, CO 81611; (970) 925-3445; www.fs.usda.gov/whiteriver
Special considerations: This is one of the most popular trails in Aspen, so expect heavy traffic on summer and fall weekends.

Finding the trailhead: From Aspen, take Rte. 82 west out of town. After 0.5 mile, go around the roundabout and turn right onto Castle Creek Road toward the hospital and Ashcroft. After 12.2 miles turn right onto a gravel road marked for Cathedral Lake. Continue 0.7 mile up the rough gravel road, passable by passenger cars, to the trailhead. Parking is limited so arrive early.
GPS: N39 02.574'/W106 48.497'

The Hike

Begin by diving into a forest filled with towering aspen trees. Lambstongue groundsel, black-tip senecio, scarlet paintbrush, yarrow, and Gray's angelica thrive in this shady grove. Climbing steadily from the start, the rocky trail quickly intersects with a short trail that brings you to an overlook with gorgeous views. As you climb, the aspens thin giving way to pines and firs as the trail enters the Maroon Bells-Snowmass Wilderness. Curving toward Pine Creek, the rushing waterway born from Cathedral Lake, the forest gives way to steep, open hillsides offering glimpses of rugged peaks ahead. Here golden aster, twinberry, yarrow, wax currant, star gentian, and fireweed bloom.

Swerve back into the woods to find blueberry, squashberry, wild strawberry, and lanceleaf chiming bells hiding amid the trees. Out in the open again, look ahead to see where a narrow chute chokes Pine Creek into a raging torrent. Here the peaks, including Malamute (13,348 feet) and Cathedral, become much more prominent. Wild rose, wild strawberry, monument plant, northern goldenrod, fireweed, tall larkspur, yellow monkeyflower, and star gentian add bursts of color.

▶ **TIDBIT—Electric Pass tops out at 13,500 feet, making it the highest pass accessible by trail in Colorado.**

On the steep ascent, breathe deep and take breaks to become intimate with the many complicated flowers blooming along the trail like mountain harebell, shrubby cinquefoil, squashberry, scarlet paintbrush, valerian, mountain dandelion, bracted lousewort, and Parry's lousewort.

After challenging switchbacks, head away from water to traverse a steep, rocky slope where you find a rainbow made up of scarlet and western yellow paintbrush, western wallflower, alpine thistle, and Whipple's penstemon. Enjoy the variety as you oscillate between being enveloped in thick forest and skipping through open meadows. Showy blooms thrive, but look closely to discover smaller buds like pygmy bitterroot, golden draba, and yellow stonecrop. The route gets rockier until you are crossing

Elephant heads in front of Cathedral Lake

Moss campion

a scree slope punctuated with vegetation. Revel in the amazing mountain vistas available in every direction. Mountain bluebells, Colorado columbine, black-headed daisy, Rocky Mountain pussytoes, and a rainbow of paintbrush decorate the hillside. Here the trail trades aspens for a pine forest full of gnarled, twisted trees, growing sideways. At the upper limits of the subalpine ecosystem, high winds blow over the mountaintops forming stands of stunted and twisted trees known as *krummholz*, a German term meaning crooked wood (see sidebar for the Linkins Lake hike for more information). Continue onward through this funky "forest" over an increasingly rocky trail that climbs up a little ravine where rosy pussytoes, silky phacelia, and common alumroot bloom.

> **GREEN TIP—Countless social trails cut switchbacks. Though it's tempting to shorten a difficult hike, please stay on the trail; it's better for you and the environment.**

The trail levels out, crosses a giant boulder field, and then ascends another very steep slope via switchbacks. At the top, reach a signed junction with the Electric Pass Trail, which heads west (right). Take the left fork and enjoy a respite from climbing as the trail levels. At the next unmarked fork, stay left again and cross Pine Creek on a small log bridge where an observant eye will find death camas, king's crown, and heartleaf bittercress thriving. Continue up through willow patches and small glades dappled with Parry clover, American bistort, and Parry gentian to reach Cathedral Lake. Wander around the lake to find alpine avens, alpine bistort, alpine thistle, subalpine arnica, alpine fleabane, queen's crown, tall larkspur, and alpine clover buds creating a bright yellow, magenta, purple, red, and white kaleidoscope of color reflecting in the lake. Hug the left lakeshore to arrive at the perfect lunch spot. For better perspective and views of Electric Pass, Malamute, Cathedral, and Leahy (13,322 feet) Peaks, climb the gentle hillsides adorned with mats of moss campion and alpine sandwort flanking the lake. Reach the trailhead via the same route.

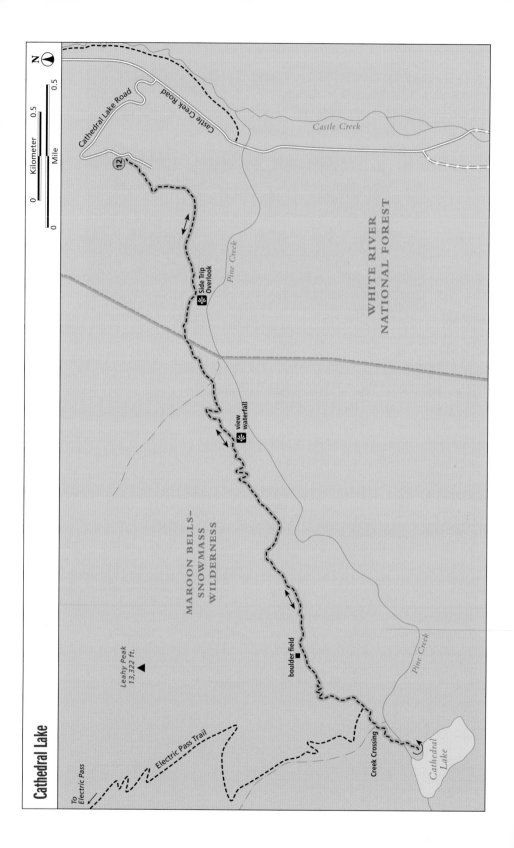

Cathedral Lake

N

0 0.5 Kilometer
0 0.5 Mile

Cathedral Lake Road

Castle Creek Road

Castle Creek

12

Side Trip
Overlook

Pine Creek

WHITE RIVER
NATIONAL FOREST

view
waterfall

MAROON BELLS–
SNOWMASS
WILDERNESS

Leahy Peak
13,322 ft.

boulder field

Pine Creek

Electric Pass Trail

To
Electric Pass

Creek Crossing

Cathedral
Lake

Miles and Directions

0.0 Start at the Cathedral Lake Trailhead.

0.7 Reach a junction with a spur trail traveling to an overlook.

0. 8 Enter the Maroon Bells-Snowmass Wilderness.

1.4 Break out into the open and glimpse the waterfall cutting through the narrow gorge ahead.

2.4 Leveling out, the trail reaches a giant boulder field and then a series of steep switchbacks.

2.6 Reach a signed junction with the Electric Pass Trail. Take the left fork to stay on the main trail to the lake.

2.9 At the next unmarked fork, stay left again and cross Pine Creek on a small log bridge.

3.0 Reach Cathedral Lake.

6.0 Arrive back at the trailhead.

Options: Extend the hike by climbing 1,700 feet in 2.3 miles to reach Electric Pass, a spectacular viewpoint between Cathedral and Leahy Peaks.

Hike Information

Local Information

Aspen Chamber of Commerce: Aspen; (970) 925-1940; aspenchamber.org

Local Events/Attractions

Aspen Music Festival: Aspen; (970) 925-9042; aspenmusicfestival.com

Basalt River Days: Basalt; (970) 927-4031; basaltchamber.org

Strawberry Days: Glenwood Springs; (970) 945-6589; glenwoodchamber.com/strawberry-days-festival.html

Pine Creek Cookhouse: Aspen; (970) 925-1044; pinecreekcookhouse.com—the Pine Creek Cookhouse, just minutes from the trailhead, serves exquisite gourmet lunches and dinners in a stunning setting at the base of the Elk Range. A wonderful post-hike treat!

Organizations

Colorado Mountain Club—Aspen Group: Aspen; cmc.org

Roaring Fork Outdoor Volunteers: Basalt; (970) 927-8241; rfov.org

Wilderness Workshop: Aspen; (970) 963-3977; wildernessworkshop.org

Hike Tours

Aspen Alpine Guides: Aspen; (970) 925-6618; aspenalpine.com

Other Resources

Pitkin Outside—A map of hiking trails and more in Pitkin County (Aspen, Snowmass, and surrounding areas) available online and via a free mobile app. Download it and you can export a GPS file or print a PDF map before setting out. pitkinoutside.org

13 Aspen to Crested Butte via West Maroon Pass

Meander through head-high wildflowers on this lung-busting, must-do hike that brings you from the posh town of Aspen to the historic mining town of Crested Butte via West Maroon Pass. Enjoy breathtaking alpine scenery, splendid panoramas of jagged summits, high alpine lakes, gorgeous pine-covered valleys, and profuse blooms as you explore a challenging trail that climbs ~3,000 feet through the Maroon Bells-Snowmass Wilderness.

Start: From the Maroon Lake-Maroon Snowmass Trailhead (9,580 feet)

Distance: 11.6 miles point-to-point; shuttle or car swap required. Shorter hiking options abound.

Hiking time: 6-10 hours

Difficulty: Strenuous due to distance, altitude, and elevation gain

Trail surface: Forested, dirt trail

Best season: July to September

Peak bloom: mid-July to early August

Flowers commonly found: orange sneezeweed, monkshood, cow parsnip, beautiful daisy, scarlet paintbrush, mountain bluebells, tall ragwort, tall larkspur, showy daisy, wild rose, fireweed, thimbleberry, Wyoming paintbrush, Colorado columbine, dotted saxifrage, golden draba, Rocky Mountain penstemon, beautiful cinquefoil, cutleaf daisy, red columbine, heartleaf arnica, lanceleaf chiming bells, western wallflower, sky pilot, peavine, American bistort, American vetch, Whipple's penstemon, Richardson's geranium, blacktip senecio, shrubby cinquefoil, alpine fireweed, silvery lupine, fringed gentian, elephant heads, brook saxifrage, death camas, monkshood, loveroot, mountain parsley, Coulter's daisy, corn lily, valerian, monument plant, aspen sunflower, bracted lousewort, king's crown, Parry primrose, yellow monkeyflower, blue flax, parrot's beak, northern, rosy, and western yellow paintbrush.

Other trail users: Equestrians

Canine compatibility: Leashed dogs permitted

Land status: National Forest, Wilderness

Nearest town: Aspen

Fees and permits: Maroon Creek Road is open to motorized vehicles before 8 a.m. and after 5 p.m. for a $10.00 fee. Parties spending the night in the Maroon Bells-Snowmass Wilderness must self-register at the trailhead. There is no fee and no limit to the number of permits issued, but you must carry a copy of your registration for the duration of your trip.

Schedule: From mid-June through September, day-use traffic is restricted on Maroon Creek Road between 8 a.m. and 5 p.m. beyond the T-Lazy 7 Ranch. After 8 a.m., take the shuttle from Aspen Highlands Ski Area, which leaves every 20 minutes. Maroon Creek Road is closed to vehicles in winter. Schofield Pass (endpoint) is obstructed by snow from fall to summer.

Maps: USGS Maroon Bells, Snowmass Mountain; Trails Illustrated Maroon Bells, Redstone, Marble; Latitude 40 Crested Butte, Aspen, Gunnison Trails

Trail contacts: White River National Forest, Aspen Ranger District, 806 W. Hallam Aspen, 81611; (970) 925-3445; www.fs.usda.gov/whiteriver

Special considerations: The trail ends at Schofield Park, 14 miles from Crested Butte. You will need to drop a car or arrange for a taxi or shuttle. (See Local Information.)

The Hike

This hike begins at Maroon Lake, an idyllic setting where photographers flock to catch the iconic Maroon Bells reflected in the lake at sunrise. Breathe it all in and hop on the trail north of the lake. Walking in the shadow of the towering Bells, traverse a meadow dappled with orange sneezeweed, monkshood, cow parsnip, beautiful daisy, and scarlet paintbrush. At the Scenic Loop split, head into thick aspens. Notice cow parsnip, mountain bluebells, tall ragwort, tall larkspur, and showy daisy hiding in the lush vegetation. Keep an eye out for moose, elk, deer, and black bears.

Amid quaking aspens, wild rose, fireweed, thimbleberry, and Wyoming paintbrush thrive. For a brief moment, break out of the forest and pick your way upward over some talus. The bright colors of Colorado columbine, dotted saxifrage, golden draba, Rocky Mountain penstemon, beautiful cinquefoil, and cutleaf daisy shine in contrast to the gray rock.

At a junction with the Willow Creek Trail, go left toward Crater Lake. Red and Colorado columbine, heartleaf arnica, lanceleaf chiming bells, alpine wallflower, scarlet paintbrush, sky pilot, and peavine join to form tiny flower gardens.

Flowers heading down toward Crested Butte from Maroon Pass

▶ TIDBIT—What makes Crested Butte the Wildflower Capital of Colorado, and why are they so awesome here? Consistent winter snowfall, perfect soil, and optimal summer climate conditions produce profuse blooms in the West Maroon Valley and the basin drained by the East Fork of the Crystal River.

The Bells tower above a dream-like field teeming with hundreds of monument plants and overflowing with lacy cow parsnip. Wyoming, rosy, and western yellow paintbrush, tall larkspur, and American bistort add bursts of color. American vetch, Whipple's penstemon, Richardson's geranium, northern paintbrush, black-tip senecio, and shrubby cinquefoil adorn the route.

The trail swiftly ascends the valley and nears the rushing creek where there is a subtle sign with an arrow pointing left to cross east over West Maroon Creek. At tree line, nature rewards you with your first full view of the pass and meanders through tundra and flower-filled glades bursting with rosy paintbrush, tall larkspur, alpine fireweed (aka river beauty), silvery lupine, and fringed gentian.

Climb steeply along a rocky trail teeming with dozens of different flowers and majestic vistas of the Bells, Pyramid Peak, and countless other rugged summits. Scan the rocky alpine slopes above for marmots, pika, mountain goats, and bighorn sheep as you huff and puff 945 feet upward along a narrow trail.

Enjoy a well-earned break and snack in the small notch of the headwall known as West Maroon Pass (12,500 feet). No matter which way you turn, a splendid view awaits. Switchbacks guide you into the narrow valley below, which is bursting with meadows of magnificent wildflowers. If you thought the flowers on the Aspen side were incredible, prepare to be "wowed" even further here. An utterly spectacular array of blossoms explodes in every direction while Purple, Treasury, and Treasure Mountains light up the western skyline.

One mile below the junction with Frigid Air Pass, cross a small stream decorated with elephant heads, brook saxifrage, mountain bluebells, mountain death camas, and monkshood. Just before the intersection with the Hasley Basin Trail, loveroot (aka Porter's lovage or Osha) and

Wyoming paintbrush

Aspen to Crested Butte via West Maroon Pass

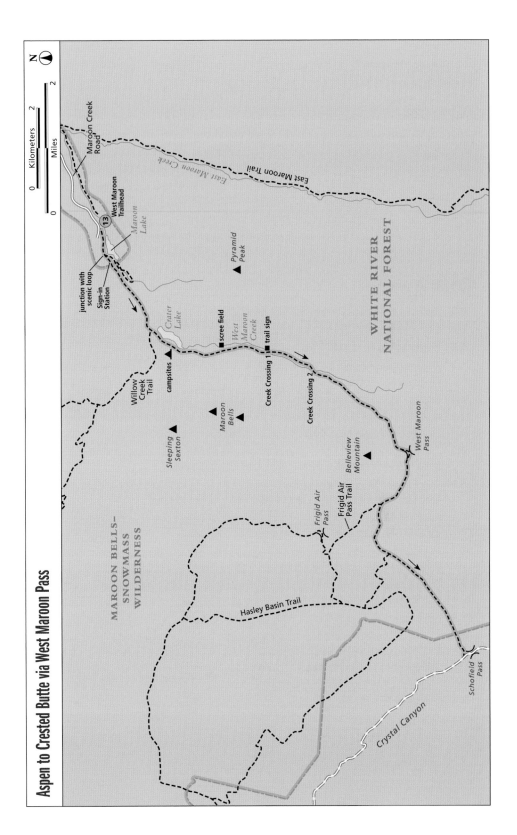

Maroon Creek Road

West Maroon Trailhead

Maroon Lake

junction with scenic loop

Sign-in Station

Crater Lake

Willow Creek Trail

campsites

scree field

Sleeping Sexton

Maroon Bells

West Maroon Creek

trail sign

Creek Crossing 1

Creek Crossing 2

Pyramid Peak

East Maroon Creek

East Maroon Trail

MAROON BELLS–SNOWMASS WILDERNESS

WHITE RIVER NATIONAL FOREST

Frigid Air Pass

Frigid Air Pass Trail

Belleview Mountain

West Maroon Pass

Hasley Basin Trail

Schofield Pass

Crystal Canyon

N

Kilometers

Miles

0   2

13

cow parsnip flourish. Stay left at the junction and pass alpine fireweed, Whipple's penstemon, mountain parsley, and Coulter's daisy.

Flowers grow in size creating lanes lined with a cornucopia of head-high blossoms including corn lily, tall valerian, monument plant, tall larkspur, silvery lupine, Colorado columbine, scarlet paintbrush, and aspen sunflower. Bracted lousewort, elephant heads, king's crown, brook saxifrage, Parry primrose, and yellow monkeyflower hide in seeps. Blooms of orange sneezeweed, northern paintbrush, rosy and scarlet paintbrush, tall larkspur, Colorado columbine, blue flax, loveroot, fireweed, cutleaf daisy, and a host of other vibrant buds continue exploding as you work your way down the valley. Pass an old cabin and follow the trail into stands of spruce where heartleaf arnica, Richardson's geranium, parrot's beak, and mountain bluebells revel in the shade. Schofield Park, this adventure's endpoint, sits just minutes ahead.

Miles and Directions

- **0.0** Start from the Maroon Snowmass Trailhead.
- **0.4** Stay right at the junction with the Scenic Loop Trail.
- **0.5** Reach the sign-in station.
- **1.9** Arrive at a junction with the Willow Creek Trail. Stay left at the fork to follow the sign toward Crater Lake.
- **2.4** Skirt the right side of Crater Lake.
- **3.3** After you pass the lake, the trail follows the stream, cuts through the forest, and emerges on a scree field you must cross.
- **4.0** Find an inconspicuous sign with an arrow pointing left indicating that you should cross the brook. Take care; at high water this can be a wide, swift crossing.
- **5.0** Reach another stream crossing in an open area. Cross carefully and follow the trail as it heads south/southeast (right) and climbs steadily toward the pass.
- **7.2** Reach West Maroon Pass (12,490 feet). Descend via steep, scree-filled switchbacks to the East Fork Creek Trail.
- **8.3** At a junction with the Frigid Air Pass Trail, continue straight following the trail as it curves through the valley and then bears left.
- **9.3** Cross a small stream to intersect with the Hasley Basin Trail. Go left to stay on the main trail heading southwest.
- **11.6** Arrive back at the Schofield Pass parking area where your shuttle or taxi awaits.

Options: Hiking from Aspen to Crested Butte is the less crowded, quieter option. For an easier hike, with 1,000 feet less elevation gain, do it in reverse. You can also do an out-and-back hike to West Maroon Pass from either side. For a shorter option with amazing flowers, begin at Schofield Pass on the Crested Butte side and walk to the Hasley Basin Trail junction (2.3 miles) or the Frigid Air Pass Trail junction (3.2 miles).

Hike Information

Local Information

Aspen Chamber of Commerce: Aspen; (970) 925-1940; aspenchamber.org

Aspen Visitor Center at Aspen Highlands (open May to October: Aspen); (970) 925-3445; www.fs.usda.gov/whiteriver

Dolly's Mountain Shuttle: Crested Butte; (970) 349-2620; crestedbutteshuttle .com—picks hikers up and drives the 30 minutes into Crested Butte.

Roaring Fork Transit Authority: Aspen; (970) 925-8484; rfta.com—offers shuttle to Maroon Lakes.

Local Events/Attractions

Aspen Music Festival: Aspen; (970) 925-9042; aspenmusicfestival.com

Basalt River Days: Basalt; (970) 927-4031; basaltchamber.org

Strawberry Days: Glenwood Springs; (970) 945-6589; glenwoodchamber.com/ strawberry-days-festival.html

Organizations

Colorado Mountain Club—Aspen Group: Aspen; cmc.org

Roaring Fork Outdoor Volunteers: Basalt; (970) 927-8241; rfov.org

Wilderness Workshop: Aspen; (970) 963-3977; wildernessworkshop.org

Hike Tours

Aspen Alpine Guides: Aspen; (970) 925-6618; aspenalpine.com

Crested Butte Hiking Guides: Crested Butte; (970) 349-5430; crestedbutteguides.com

Other Resources

Pitkin Outside—A map of hiking trails and more in Pitkin County (Aspen, Snowmass, and surrounding areas) available online and via a free mobile app. Download it and you can export a GPS file or print a PDF map before setting out. pitkinoutside.org

14 Monument Canyon

After a steep 600-foot drop from the plateau to the canyon floor, this 6.3-mile point-to-point descent through Monument Canyon levels out as it snakes around the base of sandstone cliffs and winds through this tortuous chasm at the heart of the Colorado National Monument. Plentiful blooms offer bits of color that stand out amid the high-desert earthen tones at your feet, while some of the more famous and imposing rock features of the park—including the Kissing Couple and Independence Monument—tower overhead to decorate the sky with pillars of pink, white, tan, and brown.

Start: From the Upper Monument Canyon Trailhead (6,140 feet)
Distance: 6.3-mile through-hike
Hiking time: 3–5 hours
Difficulty: Moderate due to length and terrain
Trail surface: Rocky, dirt trail
Best season: March to June
Peak bloom: mid-April to mid-May
Flowers commonly found: yellow, yellow-eye and slender cryptantha, northern sweetvetch, mountain pepper plant, double bladderpod, prickly pear cactus, mountain mahogany, bitterbrush, chokecherry, Mormon tea, serviceberry, puccoon, woolly locoweed, baccata and narrowleaf yucca, stinking milkvetch, Townsend's daisy, perky Sue, carpet phlox, desert parsley, blanketflower, creamtips, heartleaf twistflower, claret-cup and mountain ball cactus, western wallflower
Other trail users: Hikers only
Canine compatibility: Dogs prohibited
Land status: National Monument
Nearest town: Fruita
Fees and permits: No permits required. Entrance fee (for private, non-commercial vehicles) required for the Colorado National Monument.
Schedule: Open all year
Maps: USGS Colorado National Monument CO; Trails Illustrated 208 Colorado National Monument [McInnis Canyons National Conservation Area]; Latitude 40 Fruita/Grand Junction Trails
Trail contacts: Colorado National Monument, 1750 Rim Rock Dr., Fruita, 81521; (970) 858-3617, ext. 360; www.nps.gov/colm
Special considerations: To make this a 6-mile point-to-point hike, shuttle a car or get picked up at the Lower Monument Trailhead along CO 340, 2.1 miles to the southeast of the west entrance to the Colorado National Monument. From Fruita, head south on Broadway (Hwy. 340) for 3 miles. Pass the Colorado National Monument entrance, continue 2.1 miles, and turn right on a dirt road for the Lower Monument Canyon Trailhead. Drive through a neighborhood to reach the trailhead parking area.

Finding the trailhead: From Fruita, go south for 4 miles on Hwy. 340 to the west entrance of the Colorado National Monument. Pay the fee, pass through the entrance gate, and follow Rim Rock Road for 8 miles until you reach the Upper Monument Canyon Trailhead on the left side of the road, just past the Coke Ovens Overlook. There is a pullout and parking for a few cars on the left. **GPS: N39 04.663'/W108 43.688'**

The Hike

Begin descending on a well-maintained dirt path. Traverse a series of switchbacks that pass yellow-eye cryptantha, northern sweetvetch, and slender cryptantha. At Coke Ovens Trail intersection, stay straight to delve deeper into a wild, remote portion of rugged Monument Canyon.

Sandy switchbacks lined with pinyons, junipers, desert paintbrush, mountain pepper plant, and double bladderpod offer sweeping vistas of red rock cliff walls and dramatic gorges ahead. When the trail crosses a slickrock shelf with a steep drop off to the left, enjoy walking through this narrow gauntlet, hugging the sandstone cliffs on your right, and passing impressive displays of northern sweetvetch, prickly pear cactus, mountain mahogany, bitterbrush, and chokecherry. Descend this rough path past Mormon tea, serviceberry, and blooms of yellow-eye cryptantha. Continuing your downward spiral, pause to look up at the impressive pink, orange, white, and brown sandstone walls. At your feet, the trumpet-shaped flowers of puccoon shine through in splashes of brilliant yellow while woolly locoweed and northern sweetvetch add bits of purple and pink to this thriving desert.

Take your time to peer over the edges of this canyon rife with juniper, prickly pear cactus, and Mormon tea, a tall shrub with straight, bright green stems. The canyon buzzes with life as turkey vultures, ravens, lizards, chipmunks, and jays flitter about. The soil turns rockier and red as you near the canyon bottom. Here a small wash harbors a cottonwood tree, narrowleaf yucca, double bladderpod, prickly pear cactus, serviceberry,

View from rim of canyon

stinking milkvetch, and northern sweetvetch. Once you have explored this tiny oasis, cross the wash and follow the easy trail past more cactus, Townsend's daisy, sagebrush, desert paintbrush, and chokecherry. Soon, you cross another wash and climb some rock steps passing perky Sue, desert paintbrush, larger bunches of northern sweetvetch, and western pepper plant. Continue along the flat, smooth dirt trail as it winds through the canyon dappled with carpet phlox, desert parsley, blanketflower, and creamtips, a tall slender stalk with several small flower heads colored by dozens of yellow disk flowers.

Enjoy cruising over the rolling terrain on this very obvious route surrounded by sandstone walls and spires sheltering baccada yucca. Many people think the desert is barren, but you know different after walking through this canyon burgeoning with blooms. As you near the Kissing Couple, heartleaf twistflower, woolly loco-weed, prickly pear cactus, claret-cup, and mountain ball cactus appear. Wind past the romantic duo to find that little gardens of yellow cryptantha, yellow-eye cryptantha, mountain pepper plant, Townsend's daisy, desert phlox, and puccoon pop up.

Wind further past sandstone monoliths and giant boulders to find desert parsley, blanketflower, western wallflower, and more brilliant red paintbrush. The trail climbs gradually and turns sharply east (right) to reach and then pass the Independence Monument, a 450-foot-high monolith, the largest freestanding rock formation in the park. Descend gradually through pinyon-juniper to reach the signed junction with the Wedding Canyon Trail. Turn east (right) to continue exploring lower Monument Canyon as it narrows and turns even rockier. The trail snakes back and forth, skirting the canyon edge and passing huge rock chunks that have fallen at the hands of wind, water,

Creamtips

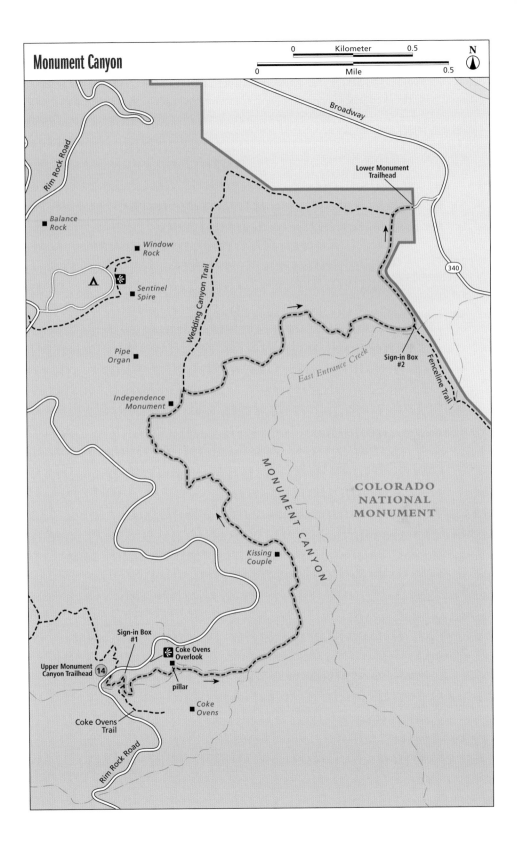

and time. Continue descending to reach a sandier, wider trail. Swing sharply north (left), climb a few steps, and follow the fence line bordering a neighborhood. Pass the intersection with the Wedding Canyon Trail and continue downhill to find the trailhead.

Miles and Directions

0.0 Start at the Upper Monument Canyon Trailhead.

0.2 Reach a signed intersection with the Coke Ovens Trail. Continue north (left) to stay on the main trail.

0.3 Pass a sign-in box and continue as the trail narrows to cross a rock shelf.

1.0 Pass a pillar to the right of the trail with tiny stones on top of it.

1.1 Reach the canyon bottom, cross a small wash, and find a sign pointing east (left).

3.2 Pass the Kissing Couple, cross a drainage, and follow the trail away from the rock monolith toward Independence Monument.

3.8 Curve sharply east (right) to reach and then pass the Independence Monument.

4.0 Turn east (right) at a junction with the Wedding Canyon Trail.

5.5 Descending, reach a wider trail that passes a sign-in box. Swing sharply north (left), climb steps, and follow the fence line.

6.2 At a junction with Wedding Canyon Trail continue downhill and turn east (right).

6.3 Arrive back at the Lower Monument Trailhead.

Options: Without a shuttle, you can still experience the canyon by hiking from the upper trailhead to Independence Monument and back. This 6-mile hike requires climbing 1,100 feet to get out of the canyon. For a side trip, turn right at the first intersection to reach an overlook offering views of the Coke Ovens, a series of massive sandstone domes formed by the natural sculpting forces of wind, water, and ice.

Hike Information

Local Information

Grand Junction Visitor and Convention Bureau: 740 Horizon Dr., Grand Junction; (970) 244-1480 or (800) 962-2547; visitgrandjunction.com

Local Events/Attractions

Colorado Mountain Winefest: Palisade; (970) 464-0111; winecolorado.org

Colorado National Monument: Fruita; (970) 858-3617; www.nps.gov/colm

Dinosaur Journey Museum: 550 Jurassic Court, Fruita; (970) 858-7282; museumofwesternco.com/visit/dinosaur-journey

Fort Uncompahgre History Museum: open April to October; Confluence Park, Delta; (970) 874-8349; forttours.com/pages/fortuncompahgre.asp

Organizations

Colorado Mountain Club—Western Slope Group: 970-640-4160; cmc.org

LOOKING AT LOWER ELEVATIONS: SEMIDESERT LIFE ZONE

In the arid valleys west of the Continental Divide, we find the semidesert shrub ecosystem, dominated by low-growing, drought-tolerant, deciduous shrubs like salt bush, greasewood, or sagebrush. In Colorado, we find that this life zone extends to 7,000 feet in the Colorado Plateau region (which includes the Colorado National Monument) and the San Luis Valley. Receiving less than 10 inches of precipitation on average, diversity here tends to be lower in comparison to grasslands due to less moisture and colder winters. But, just like the prairie, plants here have adapted to drought and high salt concentrations. Many semidesert species have also developed a series of defenses—think spines, thorns, chemical interactions, and hairs—to thwart herbivore attacks. Visitors will find beautiful flowers here including prickly pear cactus, scarlet globe-mallow, northern sweetvetch, double bladderpod, and yellow cryptantha. The desert cottontail, black-tailed jackrabbit, coyote, short-horned lizard, and Swainson's hawk also manage to thrive in this harsh environment. The Colorado, Gunnison, White, Yampa, and Dolores Rivers cross this life zone at various spots across the state, providing important riparian corridors that aid the survival of various plant and animal species.

Monument Canyon, Colorado National Monument

15 CCC Trail

A short steep ascent along a rugged and historic trail lined with sandstone slabs, giant boulders, and juniper trees rewards hikers with never-ending vistas. Along the way, showy blooms add splashes of color to the desert while delicate blossoms hide in rocky crevices. Views of rainbow cliffs and unique rock formations that define the Colorado National Monument, a hidden, often-overlooked gem of the state, abound as you climb to reach a grassy open meadow where sage, cactus, and a range of vibrant flowers bloom.

Start: From the Upper Monument Canyon Trailhead (6,140 feet)
Distance: 1.6-mile round-trip
Hiking time: 1.5-2 hours
Difficulty: Easy due to distance, moderate elevation gain, and terrain
Trail surface: Rocky, dirt trail
Best season: March to June
Peak bloom: mid-April to mid-May
Flowers commonly found: northern sweet-vetch, beautiful rockcress, double bladder-pod, yellow, yellow-eye cryptantha, heartleaf twistflower, Townsend's daisy, rimrock milkvetch, golden aster, mountain pepper plant, thrifty goldenweed, desert paintbrush, stinking milkvetch perky Sue, narrowleaf yucca, crescent milkvetch, desert parsley, carpet and long-leaved phlox, Westwater tumble mustard, cushion buckwheat, desert dandelion, prickly pear cactus
Other trail users: Hikers only
Canine compatibility: Dogs prohibited
Land status: National monument
Nearest towns: Grand Junction/Fruita
Fees and permits: No permits required. Entrance fee (for private, non-commercial vehicles) required for the Colorado National Monument.
Schedule: Open all year
Maps: USGS Colorado National Monument CO; Trails Illustrated 208 Colorado National Monument [McInnis Canyons National Conservation Area]; Latitude 40 Fruita/Grand Junction Trails
Trail contacts: Colorado National Monument, 1750 Rim Rock Dr., Fruita, 81521; (970) 858-3617, ext. 360; www.nps.gov/colm

Finding the trailhead: From Fruita, go south for 4 miles on Hwy. 340 to the west entrance of the Colorado National Monument. Pay the fee, pass through the entrance gate, and follow Rim Rock Road for 8 miles until you reach the Upper Monument Canyon Trailhead on the left side of the road, just past the Coke Ovens Overlook. There is a pullout and parking for a few cars on the left. **GPS: N39 04.684'/W108 43.656'**

The Hike

From the Monument Canyon Trailhead, begin climbing gradually along a wide dirt path that immediately passes a series of boulders hiding a brilliant display of northern sweetvetch, whose creeping magenta blooms stand out against the tan sandstone. Look closely within the rock crevices to find the more subtle, but equally wonderful, beautiful rockcress flourishing. The Civilian Conservation Corps, which was active between 1930 and 1942, put a great deal of work into creating this trail—a fact that becomes obvious as you scale the rock steps in several sections. Gradual switchbacks traverse past double bladderpod, yellow-eye cryptantha, and heartleaf twistflower, a perennial with a smooth, light-colored stem, bluish-green spatula-shaped basal leaves, and unique flowers with four dark purple and yellow sepals that pinch inward at the top, almost obscuring four purple petals.

Climbing through pinyon-juniper forest and a rocky area with big slabs of sandstone, double bladderpod adds splashes of yellow sunshine, while purple, pink, and white cross-shaped flowers of long-leaved phlox adorn the otherwise brownish soil. Juniper trees offer periodic but sparse shade while prickly pear cactus lines the trail in a spiny show. Notice less showy plants including narrowleaf yucca, mountain mahogany, and Mormon tea proliferating.

Rimrock milkvetch against view from CCC trail

As you continue climbing, sweet Townsend's daisies push though the soil to bring forth blooms that barely leave the ground and are characterized by whitish-purple rays surrounding a pale yellow center. Rimrock milkvetch, a low-growing perennial with pink-purple or two-toned flower petals also makes an appearance. A flat area offers stunning vistas in all directions.

The trail narrows, turns rocky, and climbs past golden aster, yellow cryptantha, phlox, mountain pepper plant, thrifty goldenweed, yellow-eyed cryptantha, and rimrock milkvetch to reach a subtle drainage coming in from the left. At this drainage, brilliant specimens of desert paintbrush join forces with dense pockets of stinking milkvetch to create a colorful red and white display.

Perky Sue, yucca, crescent milkvetch, desert paintbrush, phlox, and various cryptantha adorn the trail. Expansive views of canyon country, the Kissing Couple, and various other stone figures greet you at the top of a rise. The hillsides above and below the trail are littered with giant boulders as well as yellow cryptantha, daisy, desert parsley, and both carpet and long-leaved phlox. Patches of yellow, red, white, and magenta stand out amid the earthy tones of the soil, rocks, and trees to create a palette of contrasts.

Heartleaf twistflower

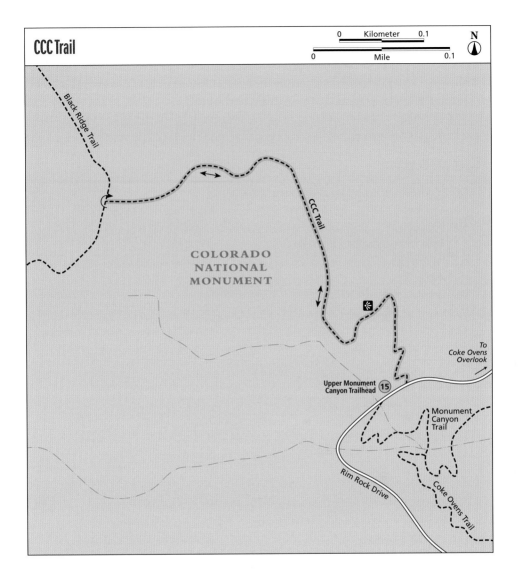

The route shifts character, becoming rockier with each step upward. Keep an eye out for expansive clusters of phlox, double bladderpod, and crescent milkvetch scattered about.

Climbing more steeply, paintbrush, phlox, and cryptantha appear until the trail levels and turns into a skinny rut. It would be easy to just walk cross-country here, but stay on the designated trail to avoid damaging the fragile biological soil crusts (formerly known as cryptobiotic soils), which provide soil stability and serve as a nitrogen source utilized by other plants and organisms. Look closely for tiny lavender, pinkish, or white puffs of cushion buckwheat and delicate light purple blooms of Westwater tumble mustard.

Impressive amounts of phlox flourish in a range of lavender, pink, and cream as do double bladderpod, desert paintbrush, and heartleaf twistflower. The trail, which turns to a two-track, cuts through an open field and heads toward a hillside fully covered with trees. Desert dandelion, prickly pear cactus, phlox, and desert parsley add bits of color to this landscape dominated by dark green sage.

At the edge of the open area, a signed intersection with the Black Ridge Trail marks our turnaround point. Retrace your steps back to the trailhead.

Miles and Directions

0.0 Start from the Upper Monument Canyon Trailhead.

0.2 Climbing moderately, the trail turns sharply southwest (left) to reach a flat area.

0.4 Narrowing, the trail climbs north to reach a subtle drainage, coming in from the left. Continue following the main trail north.

0.8 At the edge of a grassy field, reach our turnaround point—a signed intersection with the Black Ridge Trail.

1.6 Arrive back at the trailhead.

Options: From the CCC intersection with the Black Ridge Trail, the Monument's highest trail, continue left for 2 miles to reach the Upper Liberty Cap Trailhead or continue right for 3 miles to reach the Visitor Center.

Hike Information

Local Information

Grand Junction Visitor and Convention Bureau: 740 Horizon Dr., Grand Junction; (970) 244-1480 or (800) 962-2547; visitgrandjunction.com

Local Events/Attractions

Colorado Mountain Winefest: Palisade; (970) 464-0111; winecolorado.org

Colorado National Monument: Fruita; (970) 858-3617; www.nps.gov/colm

Dinosaur Journey Museum: 550 Jurassic Court, Fruita; (970) 858-7282; museumofwesternco.com/visit/dinosaur-journey

Fort Uncompahgre History Museum: open April to October; Confluence Park, Delta; (970) 874-8349; forttours.com/pages/fortuncompahgre.asp

Organizations

Colorado Mountain Club—Western Slope Group: (970) 640-4160; cmc.org

16 Pollock Bench Trail

With each step of this pleasant and varied 7-mile lollipop loop hike through the Black Ridge Wilderness, the subtle brilliance of the desert reveals itself. Meander along the rim of a canyon dappled with deep green pinyon pines and junipers past wind-sculpted sandstone formations, deep ravines, and heaps of shattered boulders. Hearty, wildly adapted flowers add welcome bursts of yellow, red, purple, white, and magenta to the drab soil and red rock slabs while long-distance views draw your eyes skyward across canyon country.

Start: From the Pollock Bench Trailhead (4,490 feet)
Distance: 6.9-mile lollipop loop
Hiking time: 3–5 hours
Difficulty: Moderate due to length, climbing, and terrain
Trail surface: Rocky, dirt trail
Best season: March to May
Peak bloom: mid-April to mid-May
Flowers commonly found: double bladderpod, claret-cup cactus, cranesbill, dwarf evening primrose, desert paintbrush, yellow and yellow-eye cryptantha, mountain pepper plant, Mormon tea, Indian breadroot, perky Sue, heartleaf twistflower, aromatic sumac, scarlet globemallow, antelope-horn milkweed, northern sweetvetch, desert trumpets, carpet phlox, freckled milkvetch, narrowleaf yucca, cushion buckwheat, prickly pear cactus, Easter daisy
Other trail users: Equestrians
Canine compatibility: Dogs permitted
Land status: Bureau of Land Management land
Nearest town: Fruita
Fees and permits: No fees or permits required
Schedule: Open all year
Maps: USGS Mack CO; Trails Illustrated 208 Colorado National Monument [McInnis Canyons National Conservation Area]; Latitude 40 Fruita/Grand Junction Trails
Trail contacts: Bureau of Land Management, Grand Junction Field Office, 2815 H Road Grand Junction, 81506; (970) 244-3000; www.blm.gov/co/st/en/fo/gjfo.html

Finding the trailhead: From Fruita, go south for 2 miles on Hwy. 340 to the Kingsview Estates subdivision. Turn west (right) onto Kingsview Road into the subdivision. Stay on the main road (which changes to Horsethief Canyon Road) all the way through the subdivision. After 0.5 mile, pass a sign for the Devils Canyon Trailhead. Continue another 2.5 miles to reach the signed Pollock Bench Trailhead, which is directly off the main road on your left. **GPS: N39 09.344'/W108 46.714'**

The Hike

Head south away from the parking lot on a dirt two-track. At the first junction, turn west (right) onto Pollock Bench Trail (P1), a well-defined trail meandering through canyon country. The commanding walls of Devils Canyon rise to the south. Yellow bursts of double bladderpod and brilliant red claret-cup cactus flank the trail. Cranesbill or filaree, a noxious weed, covers large areas with a carpet of tiny pink flowers. Reach a knoll offering views of the Colorado River effortlessly meandering

Milvetch and view from canyon rim

westward. The delicate flowers of dwarf evening primrose, with four lobed petals and yellow stamens, stand out in a grassy field dappled with sagebrush. The trail levels to reveal a dazzling display of desert paintbrush right before you reach a gate. Pass through and travel over slickrock to find yellow-eye and yellow cryptantha and mountain pepper plant. Enter Black Ridge Wilderness, a 75,000-acre area designated in 2000, that straddles the Utah-Colorado border and includes a wild array of red rock canyons, cliffs, waterfalls, and mesas. At the top of another knoll, follow the contours of a sandstone bench dappled with pinyon pine and juniper.

The walking is easy so you can enjoy quintessential canyon country vistas dominated by red and white spires, jumbles of broken boulders, cliffs, and deep ravines. The rolling trail oscillates between sand and slickrock to pass Townsend's daisy, Mormon tea, and Indian breadroot, a small but alluring plant that hugs the ground. After a short climb over a narrow sandstone ramp, a sheer slope overlooks a deep canyon to the left while interesting rock structures occupy the right side of the trail, which follows the bench and passes impressive displays of dense desert paintbrush. Perky Sue, yellow cryptantha, and double bladderpod combine to color the earth gold. Heartleaf twistflower and western pepper plant proliferate on this mesa where pinyon, juniper, aromatic sumac, and prickly pear cactus thrive. Scarlet globemallow and antelope-horn milkweed periodically occupy openings.

At a trail junction that begins the loop portion of the hike, continue straight through a heavily treed section where prolific rows of yellow, red, and white reveal the subtle brilliance of the desert. Spiny cactus plants intermingle with bright red desert paintbrush growing in dense clusters. The trees give way to reveal views of intricate canyons carving their way through expansive areas of red rock. Clusters of magenta northern sweetvetch burst forth from rocky outcrops. After another junction with the Flume Canyon Trail, curve around a hairpin turn to head north along the edge of the East Fork of Pollock Canyon, a vegetated, deeply carved chasm. Heartleaf twistflower, double bladderpod, perky Sue, Indian breadroot, and yellow-eye cryptantha line the canyon rim. Mormon tea, desert trumpets, carpet phlox, and freckled milkvetch greet you as your view-filled journey continues.

The trail turns east (right), narrows, and a big drop off to the left provides a glimpse deep into the canyon below. Signs of wildlife—jackrabbits, deer, lizards, bighorn sheep, mountain lions, and

Yellow-eye cryptantha

eagles abound. Stick to the rim as the trail turns north again passing yucca and more eye-catching paintbrush to reach a signed junction with the Rattlesnake Canyon Trail (R1). Go southeast (right) up a short but steep hill away from the canyon rim. Continue in this direction as the trail undulates across a few washes to reach an open plateau where cushion buckwheat awaits. Continue east (right) at the junction to pick up the two-track trail that passes through a grassy open area with dwarf evening primrose, prickly pear cactus, northern sweetvetch, and Townsend's daisy. At a familiar signed junction where the loop started, turn north (left) and retrace your steps back to the trailhead.

Miles and Directions

0.0   Start from the Pollock Bench Trailhead.

0.03 Reach the Flume Canyon Trail junction. Turn west (right) to stay on the Pollock Bench (P1).

0.4   Go straight through the gate and then south (straight) at an intersection with the Flume Canyon Trail (F1).

0.6   Pass the Black Ridge Wilderness boundary and follow the trail west (right).

1.6   Reach a trail junction that begins the loop portion of the hike. Continue southwest (straight) to stay on the Pollock Bench Trail.

2.9   Reach another junction with the Flume Canyon Trail. Curve right around the hairpin turn to head north.

4.7   At the Rattlesnake Canyon Trail (R1) junction, turn southeast (right) up a steep hill away from the rim.

5.0   Arrive at another junction with R1. Continue east (right) at junction.

5.2   Reach the start/end of the loop. Turn north (left) and head downhill toward the trailhead.

6.9   Arrive back at the trailhead.

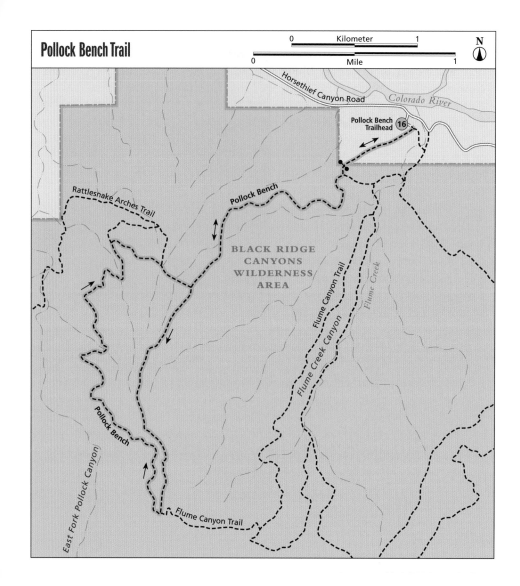

Hike Information

Local Information

Delta Country Tourism: Delta; (970) 874-9532; deltacountycolorado.com
   Grand Junction Visitor and Convention Bureau: 740 Horizon Dr., Grand Junction; (970) 244-1480 or (800) 962-2547; visitgrandjunction.com

Local Events/Attractions

Colorado Mountain Winefest: Palisade; (970) 464-0111; winecolorado.org
   Colorado National Monument: Fruita; (970) 858-3617; www.nps.gov/colm

Dinosaur Journey Museum: 550 Jurassic Court, Fruita; (970) 858-7282; museumofwesternco.com/visit/dinosaur-journey

Fort Uncompahgre History Museum: open April to October; Confluence Park, Delta; (970) 874-8349; forttours.com/pages/fortuncompahgre.asp

Organizations

Colorado Mountain Club—Western Slope Group: (970) 640-4160; cmc.org

HONORABLE MENTIONS

Northwest

Here are a couple great hikes in the Northwest region that didn't make the A-list this time around but deserve recognition.

A. Shrine Mountain Trail (#2016)

This popular 4.2-mile out-and-back ascends gradually through open meadows teeming with wild-flowers. It then climbs through pine forest dappled with unique rock formations to reach Shrine Mountain where spectacular 360-degree views await. Travel east from Vail on I-70 to exit 190 for Vail Pass. Exit here and turn right, heading west, onto the Shrine Pass dirt road (FR 709). Follow this road for 2.3 miles to reach the trailhead on the left near the gravel driveway for the Shrine Mountain Inn. Information: Contact White River National Forest at (970) 827-5715 or visit the website at www.fs.usda.gov/whiteriver.

B. Three Island Lake

Just an hour north of Steamboat sits the Mount Zirkel Wilderness where you will find the moderately challenging, popular 7-mile round-trip hike, which climbs over 1,500 feet to reach Three Island Lake. This delightful adventure follows the rushing south fork of the Elk River, climbs through tranquil aspen groves, cruises through meadows dotted with a range of colorful blooms, and provides stunning vistas along the way. The lake, surrounded by pines and craggy peaks, offers a prime picnic locale. Go west of Steamboat on US 40 for 2 miles to the Elk River Road (CR 129). Turn right and go north about 18 miles. Just past the Glen Eden Ranch, turn east on Seedhouse Road #400. Travel about 10 miles to FR 443. Turn right and the Three Island Trailhead is about 3 miles down this road. Information: Contact the Medicine Bow–Routt National Forest at (970) 870-2299 or visit the website at www.fs.usda.gov/mbr.

Southwest

The spine of the snow-capped San Juan Mountains, the longest mountain chain in the Rockies and the highest mountain range (average elevation) in North America, forms the region's impressive backbone. Birthed from explosive volcanoes and later carved into sharp pinnacles and cirques by several glacial periods, these rugged peaks and passes offer endless exploration opportunities as do towns like Ouray, Telluride, and Silverton that rest in their shadows. With more shimmering lakes and raging rivers than any other part of the state and countless giant peaks, the Southwest's wildness is unmatched. The Durango-Silverton Narrow Gauge Railroad provides access to the remote Weimnuche Wilderness, Colorado's largest Wilderness area boasting jagged peaks, alpine lakes, and miles of trails, including the terminus of the 485-mile Colorado Trail.

Heading south, mountains and forested slopes give way to the arid bluffs and plateaus of the Four Corners area where you can discover what life was like for Ancestral Puebloans at Mesa Verde National Park, Ute Mountain Tribal Park, and Canyons of the Ancients National Monument.

Moving north and east, find the Gunnison River carving its way through the rugged, 2,600-foot-deep gorge of the Black Canyon, which was preserved as a National Park in 1999. North of Gunnison, Crested Butte, a quaint mining town nestled amid towering peaks, has earned its place as the "official wildflower capital of Colorado." This mountain biking, hiking, and skiing mecca near the Raggeds and Maroon Bells-Snowmass Wilderness areas hosts a wildflower festival each July to celebrate the truly dazzling displays of head-high blooms. Due to the area's diversity in wildlife, plants, and ecosystems, the town of Gothic, just miles from Crested Butte, has been converted to a scientific research center drawing scientists and students from across the world to study at the Rocky Mountain Biological Institute.

17 Rustler Gulch

From the start, vibrant, striking colors define this route through a basin flanked by impressive, remote, and rugged peaks. Mind-blowing views and a plethora of fragrant, head-high blooms overwhelm the senses while exploring one of Crested Butte's most scenic valleys. This gradual but longer trail through verdant forest and lush meadows bursting with a rainbow of over a hundred different species crosses the creek multiple times to reach a striking cirque with mining ruins and a cascading waterfall.

Start: From the Rustler Gulch lower parking/intersection with Gothic Road (9,700 feet)
Distance: 9.4 miles out and back
Hiking time: 4-6 hours
Difficulty: Moderate due to length, gradual, smooth terrain, and moderate elevation gain
Trail surface: Two-track road and dirt trail
Best season: June to October
Peak bloom: mid-July to mid-August
Flowers commonly found: scarlet gilia, mountain bluebells, mule's ears, tall larkspur, corn lily, aspen sunflower, cow parsnip, triangularleaf senecio, yarrow, blue flax, loveroot, beautiful daisy, showy daisy, Richardson's geranium, scarlet, northern and rosy paintbrush, beautiful cinquefoil, mountain harebell, heartleaf bittercress, heartleaf arnica, monkshood, silvery lupine, orange sneezeweed, bracted lousewort, yellow monkeyflower, blue violets monkshood, alpine fireweed, shrubby cinquefoil, western chainpod, Colorado columbine, elephant heads, fringed and star gentian, ball-head waterleaf, monument plant, glacier lily, king's crown, horsemint, silky phacelia, mountain harebells, Parry primrose, marsh marigold, queen's crown
Other trail users: Equestrians
Canine compatibility: Leashed dogs permitted
Land status: National Forest, Wilderness
Nearest town: Crested Butte
Fees and permits: No fees or permits required
Schedule: Open all year, but often covered in snow from fall to summer
Maps: USGS Snowmass Mountain, Oh-Be-Joyful, Maroon Bells, Gothic, CO; Trails Illustrated 131 Crested Butte, Pearl Pass; Latitude 40 Crested Butte, Aspen, Gunnison Trails
Trail contacts: Grand Mesa, Uncompahgre and Gunnison National Forests, Gunnison District Office, 216 N. Colorado, Gunnison, 81230; (970) 641-0471; www.fs.usda.gov/gmug
Special considerations: Due to muddy spots and frequent creek crossings, we recommend wearing gators and using hiking poles for extra stability.

Finding the trailhead: From Crested Butte, drive north out of town on Hwy. 135 (also Sixth Street). Pass through Mount Crested Butte and bear right past the Snodgrass Trailhead. After 7.7 miles, the road now named Gothic Road (also CR 317 and Schofield Pass Road) turns to dirt and drops into the East River Valley. Continue for 3.8 miles until you reach the town of Gothic. Drive 2.7 miles past Gothic and watch for a turn on the right signed for Rustler Gulch. Park at the intersection with Gothic Road or turn right and park along this narrow road. Cross the East River by foot to begin your hike. **GPS: N38 59.344'/W107 00.655'**

Note: If you have a four-wheel-drive or high-clearance vehicle, you can drive across the river (check its depth) and park on the other side, or you can even continue driving for one mile up the steep, rocky road to the trailhead. If you choose to walk across, we recommend removing your hiking boots (bring river shoes) since it is often too deep to cross without getting wet.

The Hike

From your car, head toward the East River keeping an eye out for scarlet gilia, which is hard to miss thanks to the showy, long clusters of red to pink, trumpet-shaped flowers. Cross the water and climb up a steep road cutting through spruce, fir, and aspen to reach a field full of chest-high mountain bluebells, mule's ears, tall larkspur, corn lily, aspen sunflower, cow parsnip, triangularleaf senecio, and yarrow. Steps from the car, astounding flower displays and remarkable views of jagged peaks make it feel as if you are deep in the wild.

Looking up Rustler Gulch toward waterfall

Tackling the steepest part of the day, go slowly and enjoy wildflowers galore, including blue flax, loveroot, beautiful daisy, showy daisy, and Richardson's geranium.

Reach the Rustler Gulch Trail (#599). Leave the road to find mountain bluebells, scarlet paintbrush, tall larkspur, beautiful cinquefoil, and mountain harebell. Enter the Maroon Bells-Snowmass Wilderness, one of five areas in Colorado designated in the original 1964 Wilderness Act. Turning to rocky singletrack, cruise through conifer forest going wild with flowers, including heartleaf bittercress, heartleaf arnica, monkshood, cow parsnip, Richardson's geranium, and silvery lupine. Leveling, the trail meanders alongside a creek providing a delightful soundtrack for your journey. Brilliant yellow cinquefoils, vibrant orange sneezeweed, and creamy yellow bracted lousewort flowers create a thrilling contrast against plentiful deep purple blooms of lupine, larkspur, and monkshood. The intimidating, broad red rock face of Avery Peak (12,653 feet) rises high above the valley floor.

Look for delicate yellow monkeyflower and blue violets hiding in tiny trickles. The deep green of spruce and pine, the dark purple of monkshood, the brilliant pink of rosy paintbrush, the blood red of scarlet paintbrush and the crimson, gold, and green peaks towering overhead combine to create an exquisite scene. With each step, a new hue reveals itself in the sky, a blossom, or a precipice.

Continue north to reach the water. Cross twice in a row; the second crossing is a little deeper, but depending on water level, hop rocks or take off shoes and walk across. The landscape cracks open and Mount Bellview (12,526 feet) towers overhead. Sweeping views of rugged, crimson peaks punctuated by statuesque spires draw your eyes to the skyline while one of the most dazzling and overwhelming wildflower displays in the state fights to keep your attention on the meadow floor. Alpine fireweed,

Whipple's penstemon

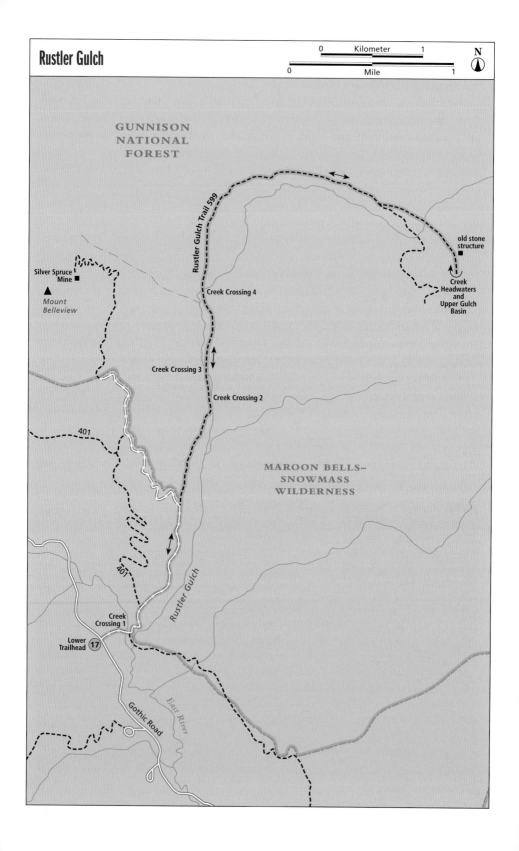

shrubby cinquefoil, and dense clusters of silvery lupine, orange sneezeweed, and western chainpod explode in a medley of captivating color.

Reach the water for one final time. The swiftest crossing of the day can rage with force; choose a fording option based on water level and comfort level. Dense clusters of Colorado columbine and elephant heads add intense color, while dainty purple blooms of fringed and star gentian reveal themselves to those paying attention. Ballhead waterleaf appears while monkshood, cow parsnip, tall larkspur, and paintbrush grow even larger.

Cliff walls encroach from the west forcing the trail to veer sharply east (right). Impressive specimens of monument plant stand out amid hordes of columbines, bluebells, larkspur, and paintbrush. Traversing a rocky slope toward the double summit of Precarious Peak (13,380 feet), find exquisite yellow glacier lilies dangling from slender stems near lingering patches of snow. Fields brimming with northern and rosy paintbrush, king's crown, queen's crown, horsemint, silky phacelia, and mountain harebells greet your arrival.

At a trail split, stay on the upper route and climb eastward toward a waterfall pouring over distant cliffs. Pass overgrown mining, reminders of those who came seeking riches. Climb briefly before descending to the creek headwaters where Parry primrose and marsh marigold add bits of brightness. Brilliant blooms, views, and rushing water conspire to create an idyllic spot for a picnic. Retrace your steps back to the car.

Miles and Directions

0.0 From the lower parking area, follow the road east to the East River.

0.2 Cross the river, continue past the campground on the east (right) side of the road, and climb along the moderately steep road.

0.4 At a junction with Trail 401, continue straight on the road.

1.0 Reach the gate marking the start of the Rustler Gulch Trail (#599). Follow a two-track north (right) around the gate.

1.1 Arrive at the Wilderness boundary sign.

1.8 Cross to the east (left) side of the creek.

2.0 Continuing north, cross the water again.

2.4 Reach a more formidable creek crossing; choose a way across based on your skill and water level. For the most direct approach, but perhaps the toughest in terms of waterpower, remove your shoes and walk straight across following the main trail. For a potentially drier crossing, walk upstream (right) on a less defined trail to a narrower spot where you can jump across.

4.0 At a trail split, continue on the upper trail.

4.6 The trail dives south, bringing abandoned mine tailings into view and passing on the left (east) the overgrown ruins of a stone structure and rusting machinery.

4.7 Descend to the creek and the Upper Rustler Gulch Basin (11,400 feet), our turnaround point.

9.4 Arrive back at the trailhead.

Options: Though the trail becomes fainter, it does continue past the falls for a short distance. Ambitious hikers can meander further up the basin for even better vistas of the valley.

Hike Information

Local Information

Gunnison–Crested Butte Tourism Association: Gunnison; (970) 641-7992; gunnisoncrestedbutte.com

Local Events/Attractions

Wildflower Festival: Crested Butte; (970) 349-2571; www.crestedbuttewildflowerfestival.com

Crested Butte Historic District Walking Tour: 331 Elk Ave., Crested Butte; (970) 349-1880

Crested Butte Mountain Heritage Museum: 331 Elk Ave., Crested Butte; (970) 349-1880; crestedbuttemuseum.com

Hike Tours

Crested Butte Mountain Guides: Crested Butte; (970) 349-5430; crestedbutteguides.com

Organizations

High Country Conservation Advocates: Crested Butte; (970) 349-7104; hccacb.org

18 Judd Falls

If you're looking for a short, mellow, but colorful hike with a great payoff, Judd Falls is the one for you. Boasting great views of Gothic Mountain (12,631 feet), plentiful midsummer wildflowers, and a sweet picnic spot overlooking a huge cascade, this hike is perfect for nature lovers of all abilities. The fact that it's close to town, gains only a few hundred feet, and wanders through a shady forest makes it the perfect pick for a half-day jaunt with the entire family. But, don't expect solitude since easy access and spectacular scenery draw many.

Start: From the signed Copper Creek parking lot (9,560 feet)

Distance: 2.5 miles out and back

Hiking time: 1–2 hours

Difficulty: Easy due to gradual, smooth terrain and minimal elevation gain

Trail surface: Dirt two-track, forested and dirt trail

Best season: June to October

Peak bloom: July

Flowers commonly Found: cow parsnip, loveroot, Richardson's geranium, scarlet gilia, orange sneezeweed, beautiful cinquefoil, showy daisy, yellow monkeyflower, northern green bog orchid, wild rose, Colorado columbine, monkshood, tall larkspur, valerian, aspen sunflower, dotted saxifrage, mule's ears, Whipple's penstemon, mountain bluebells, beautiful daisy, triangularleaf senecio, American vetch, giant lousewort, mariposa lily, blue flax, corn lily, mountain harebell, curly-cup gumweed, ball-head sandwort, death camas, yellow stonecrop, northern bedstraw, sulphur flower, sagebrush buttercup, shrubby cinquefoil, whiplash daisy, northern and scarlet paintbrush, scarlet gilia.

Other trail users: Equestrians

Canine compatibility: Dogs permitted

Land status: National Forest

Nearest town: Crested Butte

Fees and permits: No fees or permits required

Schedule: Open all year, but often obstructed by snow from fall to summer

Maps: USGS Gothic, CO; Trails Illustrated 131 Crested Butte, Pearl Pass; Latitude 40 Crested Butte, Aspen, Gunnison Trails

Trail contacts: Grand Mesa, Uncompahgre and Gunnison National Forests, Gunnison District Office, 216 N. Colorado, Gunnison, 81230; (970) 641-0471; www.fs.usda.gov/gmug

Special considerations: Enjoy your time at the overlook, but do not wander near the edge. There is no barrier to protect against falls and rocky, loose terrain proliferates. Respect all Rocky Mountain Biological Lab (RMBL) signs regarding research sites.

Finding the trailhead: From Crested Butte, travel north on Gothic Road (FR 317). Pass through Mount Crested Butte, bear right past the Snodgrass Trailhead, and follow the road, which is now dirt, for approximately 7 miles as it drops into the East River Valley. Only 0.5 mile past the town of Gothic, you reach a signed intersection with FR 317.3A on the right. Park here to begin the hike to Judd Falls described below. High-clearance or four-wheel-drive vehicles can continue on FR 317.3A for 0.5 mile to reach the upper Copper Creek Trailhead, but then you would miss a flower-filled part of the route. **GPS: N38 57.968'/W106 59.621'**

The Hike

From the lower parking lot, follow the road as it climbs gently through an aspen-dominated forest where flowers including cow parsnip, loveroot, Richardson's geranium, scarlet gilia, orange sneezeweed, beautiful cinquefoil, and showy daisy line both sides. Blooms make this extra half-mile worth every step, but beware of mountain bikers who may be hauling downhill since this road intersects with the renowned 401 Trail. Observant hikers will find yellow monkeyflower and northern green bog orchid hiding in trailside seeps. Ascend to find wild rose, Colorado columbine, monkshood, tall larkspur, valerian, aspen sunflower, red clover (a widespread, nonnative plant), dotted saxifrage, and mule's ears blooming against a backdrop of stunning mountain views.

Judd Falls

The forest thickens, and the trail turns east and reaches the upper trailhead. Pass through the metal gate to continue along the wide, tranquil route lined with huge pines. Dark purple Whipple's penstemon, vibrant pink roses, huge cow parsnip, delicate mountain bluebells, beautiful daisy, brilliant yellow triangularleaf senecio, and magenta American vetch burst from the ground and greet each step. Giant lousewort and scarlet paintbrush stand out amid the lush green vegetation.

Soon, you notice some odd equipment resting in the grass on the right. This is the Judd Falls weather station, which is operated by RMBL in Gothic, a highly esteemed research station that hosts field biologists from institutions across the world. Continue traveling south to reach a sign asking you to remain on the path, which now turns into a slender singletrack. The rocky trail gently rolls through mellow contours along the steep hillside and heads deeper into the forest where cow parsnip, tall larkspur, northern paintbrush, blue flax, mountain bluebells, and monkshood, many of which tower head-high, line the trail. Periodically the trail breaks into a clearing full of corn lily, monkshood, tall larkspur, and cow parsnip to offer excellent views in all directions. To the right, Gothic Mountain (12,625 feet) casts a shadow over the valley, while straight ahead, you get unfettered vistas of Snodgrass Mountain (11,145 feet), Mount Crested Butte, and the ski resort. Keep an eye out for flowers you haven't seen yet like the mariposa lily, mountain harebell, curly-cup gumweed, ball-head sandwort, death camas, yellow stonecrop, northern bedstraw, and sulphur flower.

The trail flattens and curves southwest (right) rewarding you with fantastic views of Gothic and more flowers including sagebrush buttercup, shrubby cinquefoil, whiplash daisy, scarlet paintbrush, and scarlet gilia. Though many hikes near Crested Butte have fields overflowing with flowers, the route to Judd Falls requires a more observant, discerning eye in spots. Scan above and below the trail so you don't miss a small, less showy flower like northern bedstraw or yellow monkeyflower.

As you descend, the forceful sound of raging water announces the presence of a mighty falls well before it appears. Reach a wide T junction, walk a few steps forward, and pause to peer over a ridge offering a spectacular glimpse of Judd Falls crashing into Copper Creek. Go right and downhill a few yards to a safer, more comfortable overlook with unfettered views of the cascade. Relax on the bench dedicated to Garwood Hall Judd, a silver miner drawn to Gothic in 1880 by the promise of riches; he stayed until his death in 1930. Enjoy the fury of the waterfall and the majesty of the mountains towering in the distance. Retrace your steps back to the trailhead keeping an eye out for deer that frequent the area.

Mariposa lily

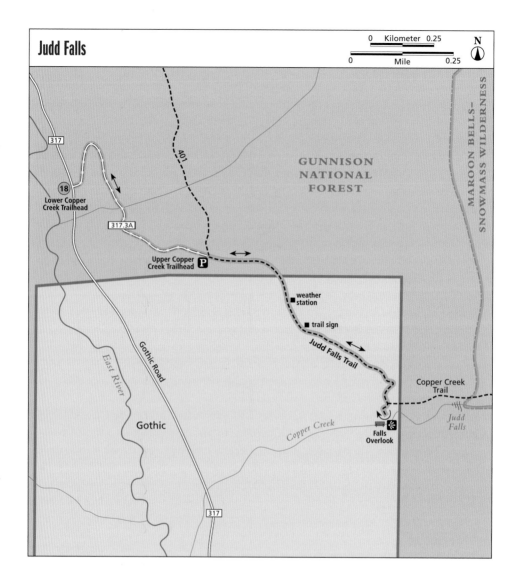

Miles and Directions

0.0 Start at the Judd Falls Lower Trailhead and parking area.

0.5 Reach the Judd Falls Upper Trailhead.

0.8 Arrive at the Judd Falls weather station operated by the RMBL. Continue south on the trail.

0.9 Pass a trail sign pointing you straight toward Judd Falls and Copper Creek.

1.2 Reach a T junction and the first overlook for Judd Falls. Turn right.

1.25 Arrive at a more comfortable overlook where you can relax on a bench and watch the falls. Retrace your steps back to the trailhead.

2.5 Arrive back at the trailhead.

Options: From the T junction, continue up the wide dirt road toward Copper Creek and Copper Lake. Explore the trail for a short amount of time or continue to Copper Lake for a total 10-mile round-trip excursion.

Hike Information

Local Information

Gunnison-Crested Butte Tourism Association: Gunnison; (970) 641-7992; gunnisoncrestedbutte.com

Local Events/Attractions

Wildflower Festival: Crested Butte; (970) 349-2571; www.crestedbuttewildflowerfestival .com

Crested Butte Historic District Walking Tour: 331 Elk Ave., Crested Butte; (970) 349-1880

Crested Butte Mountain Heritage Museum: 331 Elk Ave., Crested Butte; (970) 349-1880; crestedbuttemuseum.com

Hike Tours

Crested Butte Mountain Guides: Crested Butte; (970) 349-5430; crestedbutteguides .com

Organizations

High Country Conservation Advocates: Crested Butte; (970) 349-7104; hccacb.org

MYSTERIES OF THE MONTANE (8,000–9,500 FEET)

Spring comes later to these elevations than the lowlands. This region of aspen, ponderosa pine, Douglas fir, and Colorado columbine epitomizes the splendor of the mountains for most people. Various shrubs like wax currant and red elderberry often grow in the shadows. Mosses and lichens carpet the earth and share the forest floor with flowers like single delight, twinflower, and heartleaf arnica. Under proper conditions, wildflowers carpet meadows. Penstemon and silvery lupine paint the hillsides blue while Colorado loco forms a sea of magenta. Arrowleaf balsamroot flowers fill valleys with yellow. Watchful hikers may spot mountain chickadees, elk, and American beaver. From central Colorado northward, great forests of lodgepole pine are common. These trees colonize areas burned by fire and produce dense stands.

The montane zone contains a host of different habitats, ranging from wet to dry, open to wooded, and sunny to shady. For this reason, the montane ecosystem can support the largest variety of trees, plants, wildflowers, and wildlife and boasts the greatest amount of biodiversity across life zones.

Montane

19 Long Lake (aka Meridian Lake)

Cool, swimmable waters, stunning vistas, a plethora of blooms, and a short easy hike draw visitors to the narrow, natural Meridian Lake (called Long Lake by most). Resting in a tranquil bowl, this slender glacial body surrounded by a colorful display of wildflowers rewards hikers with a wild experience very close to town. The perfect introduction to Crested Butte's amazing flowers and divine scenery without a long drive or much effort!

Start: From the small signed parking area across from the dam on Washington Gulch Road (9,550 feet)
Distance: 2.0 miles out and back to lake; add a 0.5- to 1.5-mile round-trip for lake exploration
Hiking time: 1–3 hours
Difficulty: Easy due to distance, minimal elevation gain, and smooth terrain
Trail surface: Dirt two-track, dirt trail
Best season: April to October
Peak bloom: July
Flowers commonly found: cow parsnip, Richardson's geranium, golden aster, butter 'n' eggs, tall larkspur, silvery lupine, yarrow, aspen sunflower, scarlet and western yellow paintbrush, beautiful cinquefoil, American vetch, orange sneezeweed, Parry clover, thick-bract senecio, mountain dandelion, showy goldeneye, showy daisy, fireweed, northern goldenrod, mule's ears, scarlet gilia, mariposa lily, rosy pussytoes, dogbane, sulphur flower, wild rose, blue flax, Rocky Mountain penstemon, northern bedstraw, nettle-leaf giant-hyssop

Other trail users: Hikers only
Canine compatibility: Dogs permitted
Land status: National Forest
Nearest town: Crested Butte
Fees and permits: No fees or permits required
Schedule: Open all year
Maps: USGS Oh-be-joyful, CO; Trails Illustrated 133 Kebler Pass, Paonia Reservoir; 1 Latitude 40 Crested Butte, Aspen, Gunnison Trails
Trail contacts: Grand Mesa, Uncompahgre and Gunnison National Forests, Gunnison District Office, 216 N. Colorado, Gunnison, 81230; (970) 641-0471; www.fs.usda.gov/gmug
Special considerations: Please stay on the trail and obey all signs. The trail crosses onto private ranching property and the Allen Family Ranches provide access, but ask that all visitors abide by the closure signs.

Finding the trailhead: From Crested Butte, take Gothic Road (FR 317) north 1.7 miles. Turn left onto Washington Gulch Road (811) and drive 1.5 miles. Park in a small parking area in front of tennis courts on the right side across from a dam. **GPS: N38 54.476'/W106 59.525'**

The Hike

Leave the trailhead and walk southwest across the dam toward a forested area. Pass through a gate and follow the wide two-track climbing gradually into a tranquil forest lined with aspens and pines. The forest floor comes alive with cow parsnip, Richardson's geranium, golden aster, butter 'n' eggs, and tall larkspur. At a sharp bend in the trail, the route turns northwest (right) to pass silvery lupine, yarrow, aspen sunflower, and western yellow paintbrush.

Beautiful cinquefoil, American vetch, orange sneezeweed, Parry clover, thick-bract senecio, mountain dandelion, showy goldeneye, and showy daisy adorn the trail as it climbs steadily but gradually through mixed conifer forest.

Just as the trail levels, a sign marks the beginning of private property and the turn-off to Long Lake, which, despite the fact that most maps call it Meridian Lake, is more commonly referred to as Long Lake by locals and visitors alike. Turn southwest (left) to follow a trail lined with fireweed, northern goldenrod, lupine, and orange sneezeweed. After just a few hundred yards, reach a plateau overlooking the lake. Here, the trail splits: one fork heads northwest (right) and one goes southeast (left). You can head in either direction and explore. Heading northwest (right) you find scarlet paintbrush, mule's ears, and scarlet gilia amid a field of sweet-smelling sagebrush. Meander around the northeast side of the lake (stay on the trail) through an area lined with tiny aspens, mariposa lily, rosy pussytoes, dogbane, aspen sunflower, sulphur flower, and wild rose. As you near the lake, its cool, crystalline waters may entice you. Feel free to cool off with a dip in one of Crested Butte's sweetest swimming spots.

▶ **GREEN TIP—Avoid sensitive ecological areas. Hike, rest, and camp at least 200 feet from streams, lakes, and rivers.**

When you reach the sign for the dam, turn around and head back to the split in the trail. Go straight through the junction to skirt above the lake's southwest shore.

Paintbrush and Long Lake

Blue flax, tall larkspur, Rocky Mountain penstemon, northern bedstraw, aspen sunflower, and nettle-leaf giant-hyssop await your arrival in this tranquil spot. The rocky and colorful summit of Mount Emmons, aka Red Lady, (12,392 feet) dominates the southwest horizon.

Wander around the lake until you run out of energy. Turn around and enjoy views of Gothic, Mount Crested Butte and other far-flung snow-capped peaks as you return to the spot where the trail divides. Breathe in panoramic vistas before retracing your path to the trailhead.

Blue flax

Miles and Directions

0.0 Start at the parking area across from the dam. Cross the street and walk southwest across the dam.

0.2 Pass through a gate signed for pedestrian access only. Continue south up a gravel road.

0.9 At a sign announcing private property, turn west (left). After 0.02 mile, reach a lake overlook and a split in the trail. Turn northwest (right) to explore this direction first.

1.3 Reach the Lake Brennard Dam sign. Retrace your steps to the split in the trail. Head southeast (straight) to explore the other side of the lake.

2.2 When the trail starts to descend, turn around and retrace your steps to the trailhead.

3.4 Arrive back at the trailhead.

Options: Continue to skirt the southern edge of the lake. Please respect any signs signaling private property or closed trails as the status of trails on private property may change without notice.

Hike Information

Local Information

Gunnison-Crested Butte Tourism Association: Gunnison; (970) 641-7992; gunnisoncrestedbutte.com

Local Events/Attractions

Wildflower Festival: Crested Butte; (970) 349-2571; www.crestedbuttewildflowerfestival.com

Crested Butte Historic District Walking Tour: 331 Elk Ave., Crested Butte; (970) 349-1880

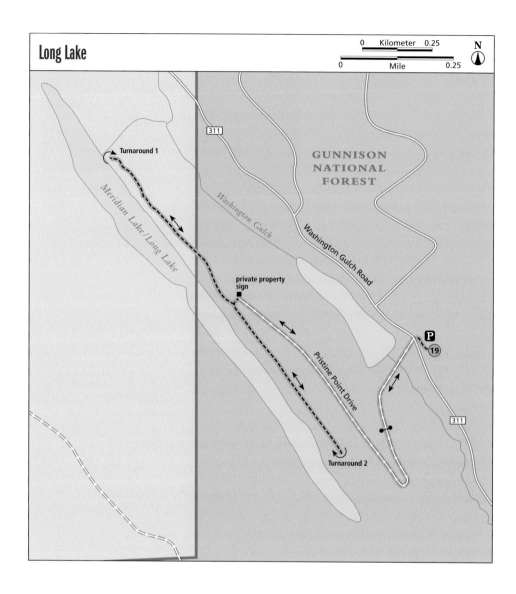

Crested Butte Mountain Heritage Museum: 331 Elk Ave., Crested Butte; (970) 349-1880; crestedbuttemuseum.com

Hike Tours

Crested Butte Mountain Guides: Crested Butte; (970) 349-5430; crestedbutteguides. com

Organizations

High Country Conservation Advocates: Crested Butte; (970) 349-7104; hccacb.org

20 Copley Lake

Enjoy a moderately steep climb through verdant forest to reach a stunning lake surrounded by lush flower-filled meadows and towering pines. Located close to town, this relatively short, easily accessible trail delivers big; amazing arrays of rainbow blossoms line the route while phenomenal mountain views await your arrival at the lake.

Start: From the Copley Lake Trailhead (9,580 feet)
Distance: 3.9 miles out and back
Hiking time: 2–3 hours
Difficulty: Moderate due to rocky terrain and elevation gain
Trail surface: Rocky, dirt two-track, dirt trail
Best season: June to October
Peak bloom: July
Flowers commonly found: northern bedstraw, mountain harebell, scarlet gilia, aspen sunflower, cow parsnip, beautiful cinquefoil, western yellow, rosy, scarlet, northern paintbrush, wild rose, yarrow, northern goldenrod, twinberry, parrot's beak, American vetch, wild strawberry, heartleaf and subalpine arnica, orange sneezeweed, mule's ears, Whipple's penstemon, bracted lousewort, towering and subalpine Jacob's ladder, Canada violet, cowbane, mountain parsley, Fendler's meadow rue, Case's fitweed, pearly everlasting, golden

aster, blue flax, rosy pussytoes, red and Colorado columbine, heartleaf bittercress, king's crown, tall larkspur, marsh marigold, white bog orchid, globeflower, elephant heads, yellow monkeyflower, American speedwell, corn lily
Other trail users: Equestrians, mountain bikers
Canine compatibility: Dogs permitted
Land status: National Forest
Nearest town: Crested Butte
Fees and permits: No fees or permits required
Schedule: Kebler Pass is closed in winter. For more information call (970) 641-0044
Maps: USGS Mount Axtell, CO; Trails Illustrated 133 Kebler Pass, Paonia Reservoir; Latitude 40 Crested Butte, Aspen, Gunnison Trails
Trail contacts: Grand Mesa, Uncompahgre and Gunnison National Forests, Gunnison District Office, 216 N. Colorado, Gunnison, 81230; (970) 641-0471; www.fs.usda.gov/gmug

Finding the trailhead: Heading west out of Crested Butte, take Whiterock Avenue, which turns to Kebler Pass Road (CR 12) at the edge of town. Drive 3.5 miles past town limits to an unsigned parking area on the south (left) side of the road. The trailhead is directly across the road on the north side. If you pass signs for Splains Gulch (a left turn), you have gone about 0.7 mile too far.
GPS: N38 51.416'/W107 03.598'

The Hike

Begin climbing steeply next to the water along Elk Creek Trail, a well-defined but unsigned old road. The Wagon Trail (also unmarked) follows Kebler Pass Road and heads due west (left) from the trailhead, so be sure to choose the route heading uphill and northwest (straight) over rocky rugged terrain.

Take your time climbing the first section—the steepest of the whole day—pausing to enjoy northern bedstraw, mountain harebell, scarlet gilia, and aspen sunflower brightening the rocky soil below your feet. Cow parsnip, beautiful cinquefoil, northern paintbrush, and wild rose blossom near the creek. Leveling briefly, the trail enters a thicker stand of forest to pass yarrow, northern goldenrod, twinberry, and Richardson's geranium.

Climbing gradually, the trail oscillates between stands of shaded conifer forest and open meadows where parrot's beak, western yellow paintbrush, goldenrod, American vetch, and geranium thrive. Climbing this thin creekside ravine surrounded by towering ridges on both sides, notice wild strawberries sprawling alongside you. Yarrow, heartleaf arnica, cow parsnip, orange sneezeweed, mule's ears, cinquefoil, paintbrush, and aspen sunflowers turn green meadows into a feast for the eyes. At a private property sign, stay on the road and continue northwest to find Whipple's penstemon and bracted lousewort adding colorful trailside adornments.

Further on, impressive clumps of Colorado columbine and towering Jacob's ladder turn the hillside varying shades of purple while Canada violet, cowbane, mountain parsley, and Fendler's meadow rue add smaller but equally stunning bits of color to the forest floor.

Continuing upward it becomes apparent that this is an unrelenting wildflower lover's paradise; new flowers like Case's fitweed, scarlet paintbrush, pearly everlasting, and

Meadow filled with elephant heads at Copley Lake

golden aster appear while the density of familiar purples, yellows, reds, oranges, and whites continues to astound with each step. Climbing higher along a soothing creek, blue flax, subalpine Jacob's ladder, rosy pussytoes, red columbine, and subalpine arnica light up the hillsides flanking this rugged road.

Nearing a seep, we find heartleaf bittercress, rosy paintbrush, cowbane, bluebells, king's crown, tall larkspur, and cow parsnip. The left side of the trail turns into a tiny creek where we find moisture-loving species like elephant heads, king's crown, marsh marigold, white bog orchid, globeflower, and a plethora of paintbrush, geranium, and bluebells.

Leveling, cross the brook and break out into a flower-filled open meadow where a huge cairn marks a

Case's fitweed

path leading west (left). Turn left to follow this small, forested path that reaches a wet area teeming with elephant heads, western yellow paintbrush, geranium, mountain dandelion, and yellow monkeyflower. Following the creek, climb a bit further past arnica, Whipple's penstemon, American speedwell, corn lily, orange sneezeweed, geranium, rosy pussytoes, cinquefoil, and subalpine Jacob's ladder to reach Copley Lake resting in an untouched, tree-lined bowl with peaks towering on the horizon. Meander around the lakeshore to discover king's crown, rosy paintbrush, globeflower, marsh marigold, arnica, and shiny yellow buttercups hiding amid a sea of magenta elephant heads.

Enjoy a break and rejoice in the faraway feeling of this tranquil setting before returning the way you came.

Miles and Directions

0.0   Start from the Copley Lake Trailhead.

0.4   Reach a private property sign. Stay on the road and continue northwest (left) past it.

1.4   Find a seep crossing the road. Continue north along the route, which now passes through a more lush area.

1.6   Cross a small creek, break out into open meadow and reach a cairn. Turn west (left) on a faint path that heads into the forest.

1.9   Reach Copley Lake.

3.8   Arrive back at the trailhead.

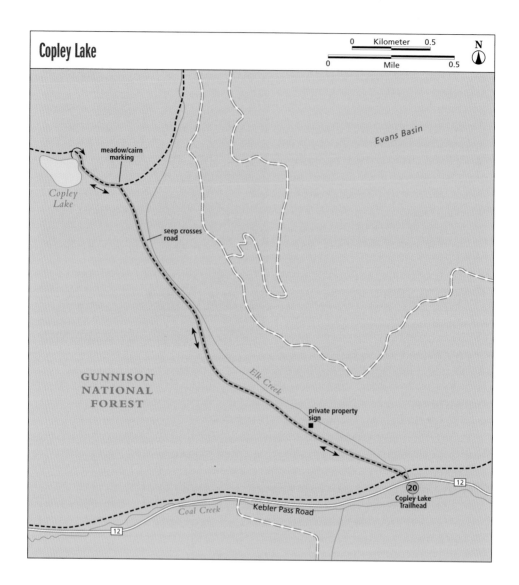

Hike Information

Local Information

Gunnison–Crested Butte Tourism Association: Gunnison; (970) 641-7992; gunnisoncrestedbutte.com

Local Events/Attractions

Wildflower Festival: Crested Butte; (970) 349-2571; www.crestedbuttewildflowerfestival.com

Crested Butte Historic District Walking Tour: 331 Elk Ave., Crested Butte; (970) 349-1880

Crested Butte Mountain Heritage Museum: 331 Elk Ave., Crested Butte; (970) 349-1880; crestedbuttemuseum.com

Hike Tours

Crested Butte Mountain Guides: Crested Butte; (970) 349-5430; crestedbutteguides.com

Organizations

High Country Conservation Advocates: Crested Butte; (970) 349-7104; hccacb.org

21 East River (aka Brush Creek)

A favorite among locals and visitors alike, the East River Trail (commonly called Brush Creek) parallels a soothing river as it curves around Crested Butte Mountain and works its way through a verdant valley with expansive vistas and overwhelming fields of wildflowers. Fairly short, relatively flat, and close to town, this easy hike along a road through the East River valley delivers great rewards with minimal effort.

Start: From the East River Trailhead (8,950 feet)
Distance: 4.4 miles out and back
Hiking time: 2-3 hours
Difficulty: Easy due to distance, minimal elevation gain, and smooth terrain
Trail surface: Dirt two-track
Best season: April to October
Peak bloom: late June to mid-July
Flowers commonly found: scarlet gilia, false dandelion, silvery lupine, sulphur flower, mountain harebells, blue flax, tall larkspur, yarrow, beautiful and shrubby cinquefoil, northern and Wyoming paintbrush, mule's ears, orange sneezeweed, wild rose, nettle-leaf giant-hyssop, Fremont and Richardson's geranium, twinberry, cow parsnip, monkshood, yellow monkeyflower, monument plant, mariposa lily, giant lousewort,

northern goldenrod, American vetch, elephant head, white bog orchid
Other trail users: Equestrians and mountain bikers
Canine compatibility: Dogs permitted
Land status: National Forest
Nearest town: Crested Butte
Fees and permits: No fees or permits required
Schedule: Open year-round
Maps: USGS Crested Butte, CO; Trails Illustrated 131 Crested Butte, Pearl Pass; Latitude 40 Crested Butte, Aspen, Gunnison Trails
Trail contacts: Grand Mesa, Uncompahgre and Gunnison National Forests, Gunnison District Office, 216 N. Colorado, Gunnison, 81230; (970) 641-0471; www.fs.usda.gov/gmug

Finding the trailhead: From Crested Butte, follow Hwy. 135 south for 2 miles. At the East River Country Club sign, turn left onto Brush Creek Road (CR 738). Follow the road (which turns from pavement to dirt) for 2.7 miles to reach the East River Trailhead on your left. **GPS: N38 51.903'/ W106 54.771'**

The Hike

Leave your car, and immediately a rainbow of giant blooms greets your arrival. Amid your first steps along the dirt two-track traveling north, find scarlet gilia, false dandelion, silvery lupine, sulphur flower, mountain harebells, blue flax, tall larkspur, yarrow, and shrubby cinquefoil. Not only are these blossoms extremely colorful, but they are also supersized. Giant specimens—shoulder-height or higher—of brilliant red, yellow, purple, blue, orange, and white unfold across the lush valley ahead.

Moving onward, stands of aspen tower on the hillside above giving rise to slopes full of Wyoming paintbrush, mule's ears, orange sneezeweed, and larkspur. Wild rose, nettle-leaf giant-hyssop and Richardson's geranium add bits of pink and white to the vibrant scene.

Curving slightly right to pass cow parsnip, yarrow, and fireweed, Teocali Mountain (13,208 feet), a recognizable and rough pyramid-shaped peak, appears on the horizon before the trail drops down to a clump of aspens where twinberry, geranium, cow parsnip, and beautiful cinquefoil proliferate. Hop across a tiny creek crossing, but only after looking closely to find velvety purple monkshood and sunshine-colored yellow monkeyflower flourishing in the damp creekside. Continue north to reach another open spot teeming with huge, healthy examples of gilia, lupine, penstemon, blue flax, cinquefoil, and hyssop. Enjoy cruising along the next section as it oscillates between shady groves and open meadows with expansive views of the river and summits ahead. Stay alert since this combo—water, lush vegetation, and a range of habitats in a small area—makes the area a favorite with bears, deer, moose, foxes, and other critters.

At a junction with an unnamed two-track coming in from the right, continue straight along the trail to enter a rainbow-filled meadow punctuated by enormous monument plants, which make their debut here. A sublime aspen grove forms the upper perimeter of meadow, which offers the most impressive mountain vistas yet.

View from East River Trail

Continue wading through head-high mule's ears, aspen sunflowers, hyssop, and lupine, being sure to keep your eyes peeled for the periodic mariposa lily peeking out its delicate white, yellow, and purple head. Below, the river gracefully weaves its way through the verdant valley while mountains tower overhead to create an idyllic and classically Colorado scene. Cross another small rivulet and listen carefully as a louder waterway announces its presence with a boisterous song well before you can see it.

Begin a slight descent through an explosion of purples, reds, yellows, whites, and greens to reach a lush forested grove sheltering a rushing cascade lined with impressively large specimens of giant lousewort, cow parsnip, and northern goldenrod. Just beyond the falls, find rose, Fremont geranium, yellow monkeyflower, and American vetch lining the trail. An especially delightful display of yellow, magenta, and white—in the form of elephant head, northern paintbrush, and white bog orchid—adorn the moist left side of the trail.

Giant lousewort

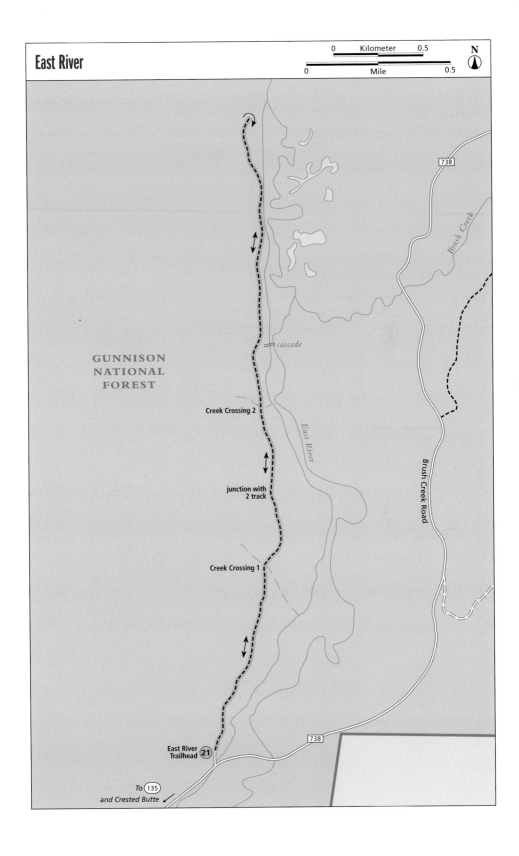

East River

0   Kilometer   0.5

0   Mile   0.5

N

738

Brush Creek

GUNNISON
NATIONAL
FOREST

cascade

East River

Creek Crossing 2

Brush Creek Road

junction with
2 track

Creek Crossing 1

East River
Trailhead 21

738

To 135
and Crested Butte

After reveling in this wildflower paradise, move down the trail as it narrows and continues dropping toward the river passing through wet meadows full of clover, elephant heads, northern paintbrush, sunflowers, and corn lily. As you get closer and closer to the water, the reds, purples, and yellows of gilia, larkspur, lupine, and sunflower obscure parts of the trail with their enormity and density. Nearing the river, a gate signals private property and your turnaround point. Take a break to absorb the breathtaking views and soothing sounds before leaving. The hike back offers a different perspective of the river and the incredible fields of flowers that characterize the area, so enjoy every step while working your way back to the trailhead.

Miles and Directions

0.0 Start from the East River Trailhead.

0.7 Arrive at a tiny creek crossing.

1.0 Reach a junction with an unnamed two-track coming in from the east (right). Continue north (straight) along the trail that heads into an open meadow.

1.2 Hop across another small trickle and follow the trail as it descends toward the sound of raging water.

1.4 Reach a small cascade hiding in a stand of aspens.

2.2 Nearing the river, reach a fence that is your turnaround point.

4.4 Arrive back at the trailhead.

Hike Information

Local Information

Gunnison-Crested Butte Tourism Association: Gunnison; (970) 641-7992; gunnisoncrestedbutte.com

Local Events / Attractions

Wildflower Festival: Crested Butte; (970) 349-2571; www.crestedbuttewildflowerfestival .com

Crested Butte Historic District Walking Tour: 331 Elk Ave., Crested Butte; (970) 349-1880

Crested Butte Mountain Heritage Museum: 331 Elk Ave., Crested Butte; (970) 349-1880; crestedbuttemuseum.com

Hike Tours

Crested Butte Mountain Guides: Crested Butte; (970) 349-5430; crestedbutteguides.com

Organizations

High Country Conservation Advocates: Crested Butte; (970) 349-7104; hccacb.org

22 American Basin

Don't expect to make good time on this breathtaking short hike through an alpine wonderland. The sea of dazzling flowers set against the stunning backdrop of craggy, vertical cliffs will surely compel you to stop often so you can snap photos of the impressive scene and enjoy every new blossom close-up. A meander up this glacially carved valley rewards hikers with a rushing creek, an intense waterfall, breathtaking views, and one of the most brilliant wildflower displays in the state.

Start: From the interpretive signs in the first parking area you encounter on your left after turning onto the American Basin Road (11,300 feet)

Distance: 2.1 mile out and back

Hiking time: 1–3 hours

Difficulty: Easy due to smooth terrain and moderate elevation gain

Trail surface: Dirt road, dirt, and rocky trail

Best season: July to October

Peak bloom: mid-July to early August

Flowers commonly found: rosy, western yellow and northern paintbrush, tall larkspur, mountain bluebells, yarrow, annual sunflower, elephant heads, Whipple's penstemon, cowbane, beautiful daisy, Gray's Angelica, beautiful and shrubby cinquefoil, Colorado columbine, Coulter's daisy, alpine avens, American bistort, Parry clover, Colorado thistle, subalpine arnica, alpine sorrel, heartleaf bittercress, king's crown, monkshood, queen's crown, yellow monkeyflower, marsh marigold, Parry primrose, Arctic gentian, snow lover, alpine bistort, old man of the mountain, moss campion

Other trail users: Moderate jeep traffic along the road to the official trailhead

Canine compatibility: Dogs permitted

Land status: Bureau of Land Management (BLM) land/National Forest

Nearest town: Lake City

Fees and permits: No fees or permits required

Schedule: Open all year, but often obstructed by snow from fall to summer. Parts of American Basin are avalanche-prone.

Maps: USGS Handies Peak, Redcloud Peak; Trails Illustrated 141 Telluride, Silverton, Ouray, Lake City

Trail contacts: BLM Gunnison Field Office, 210 W. Spencer St., Gunnison, 81230; (970) 642-4940; www.blm.gov/co/st/en/fo/gfo .html. Grand Mesa, Uncompahgre and Gunnison National Forests, Gunnison District Office, 216 N. Colorado, Gunnison, 81230; (970) 641-0471; www.fs.usda.gov/gmug

Special considerations: In summer, thunderstorms happen nearly every afternoon in Colorado's high country. Because American Basin is perched above tree line, it's important to get an early start and stay alert for sudden changes in weather.

Finding the trailhead: From Lake City, drive south on Hwy. 149 for 2.5 miles. Turn south (right) onto CR 30 at the Lake San Cristobal sign. Follow this paved road as it curves around the lake for another 4 miles where it turns to dirt. Follow the dirt road for another 16.3 miles. Bear left at a fork in the road marked by a sign that reads "Cinnamon Pass/American Basin." Once you are on the American Basin road, there are multiple parking options. For the best flower viewing, we advise you to bear left at the fork to enter the basin, drive 0.10 miles and park in the first lot on the left where you will see two interpretive signs. There are two parking areas further up the road, but getting to them requires high clearance and four-wheel drive. Plus, if you drive the road, you'll miss some of the most splendid flowers, since huge concentrations of blossoms grow in meadows and along the creek below the trailhead. **GPS: N37 55.755'/W107 30.844'**

Note: Half the adventure of this hike is getting there, so take care as you drive. As you climb up the valley, the Cinnamon Pass Road gets rougher, bumpier, and narrower especially after you pass the Grizzly Gulch/Silver Creek Trailheads, which are approximately 4 miles from the signed turnoff to American Basin. Driving the Cinnamon Pass Road is not for the faint of heart or the low of clearance. Though you will see passenger cars braving this route, we recommend high clearance and four-wheel drive.

The Hike

Though getting to this point on the rocky, rough road is a bit of a chore, from the moment you leave your car, nature makes it apparent that the drive was more than worth it. Up ahead you can see meadows dotted with color set against the backdrop of towering cliffs.

Follow the road north toward this idyllic scene. Enjoy the sound of the rushing creek beside you and the lush green vegetation, wildflowers, and the host of songbirds this waterway supports. Along the roadside, you begin seeing rosy paintbrush, tall larkspur, mountain bluebells, yarrow, and annual sunflowers in huge numbers. Because it is so gorgeous, this part can be busy with dirt bikers and four-wheelers, but there is plenty of room to walk next to the road.

Columbines dominate meadow in American Basin

Flower-filled meadow en route to American Basin

Shortly after you begin, the road crosses the creek. Depending on the river level, you may be able to stay dry by hopping rocks, or you may want to remove shoes and socks. From here, the wildflowers and scenery improve with each step. Orange sneezeweed and triangularleaf senecio peek out from the thick willows lining the creek while elephant heads, Whipple's penstemon, cowbane, rosy and western yellow paintbrush, beautiful daisy, Gray's Angelica, and beautiful cinquefoil burst forth from the wild open meadows flanking the road.

The road climbs gently toward the rocky cliffs towering ahead. Soon, you reach a split in the trail. Though both options end at the same place, stay north (straight) on the two-track to avoid vehicle traffic. Continue to enjoy nature's bounty as you ascend gradually up the basin. Vibrant blossoms of bright pink, red, yellow, purple, orange, and white form a dazzling rainbow that continues to grow. Varying shades of Colorado columbine, Coulter's daisy, alpine avens, American bistort, mountain blue-bells, Whipple's penstemon, rosy paintbrush, elephant heads, tall larkspur, Parry clover, Colorado thistle, subalpine arnica, sunflowers, beautiful and shrubby cinquefoil, and alpine sorrel join together to create a melodic symphony of color.

The ever-captivating Handies Peak (14,048 feet) looms large and alone on your left. A waterfall thunders nearby and the forest of flowers thickens with each step upward. Here you enter an area brimming with heartleaf bittercress, king's crown, monkshood, and huge fields of tall larkspur. Nearing the water, you find queen's crown, yellow monkeyflower, marsh marigold, and Parry primrose in plentiful supply.

When the two-track rejoins the road, it's likely that you'll see a few, if not many, marmots busily scurrying back and forth. Don't fret if they stand on their hind legs and whistle loudly at you. These harmless "whistle pigs" are merely alerting the rest of their clan to your presence.

Clusters of Colorado columbines, northern paintbrush, and larkspur wave in the wind making it hard to get anywhere because the never-ending fields of beauty force you to stop often and take it all in.

After climbing a little more, you reach the actual American Basin Trailhead. This is where many people begin their adventure up Handies Peak, the 40th tallest of Colorado's 54 fourteeners. Continue straight along the rocky path that ascends more steeply amid vibrant fields of shoulder-high yellows, reds, whites, pinks, and purples. Soon you reach a spot where you can see the beautiful cascade you have been hearing all along. Arctic gentian, snow lover, alpine bistort, old man of the mountain, and moss campion create an alpine wonderland.

Continue climbing through a sea of wildflowers until you reach the trail register. Turn around here or continue wandering upward for as long as you like. On the way back, enjoy vistas of Whitecross Mountain (13,542 feet), which towers high in the north.

Flower-filled meadow in American Basin

Rosy paintbrush

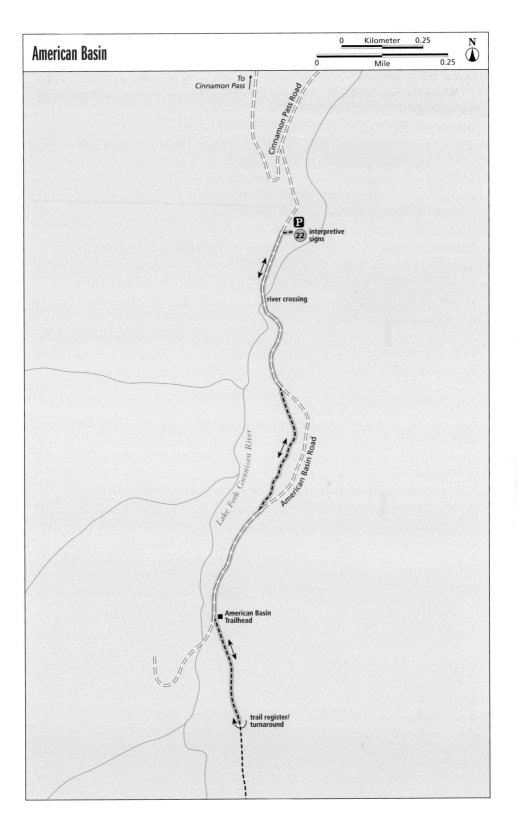

American Basin

0 Kilometer 0.25

0 Mile 0.25

N

To Cinnamon Pass

Cinnamon Pass Road

P 22 interpretive signs

river crossing

Lake Fork Gunnison River

American Basin Road

American Basin Trailhead

trail register/ turnaround

Miles and Directions

0.0 Start from the interpretive signs located in the first parking area on your left, 0.1 mile after you turn onto the American Basin Road.

0.1 Follow the road as it crosses the Lake Fork Gunnison River.

0.3 The main road intersects with a two-track, which you can take to avoid vehicle traffic.

0.6 The trail reconnects with the main road. Continue straight on the road.

0.8 The road ends at the signed American Basin Trailhead (11,600 feet). Continue straight and ascend further into the basin along the rocky path.

1.0 Reach the trail register box. Turn around here.

2.0 Arrive back at the parking area.

Options: From the trail register, you can continue to Sloan Lake, home of the threatened Colorado cutthroat trout. More ambitious climbers can continue up to Handies Peak, one of five 14,000-foot peaks in the area. The view from the top of Handies Peak is one of the best in the San Juan Mountains.

Hike Information

Local Information
Lake City Chamber of Commerce: Lake City; (970) 944-2527; lakecity.com

Local Events/Attractions
Alferd Packer Cannibal Massacre Site: Hwy. 149, Lake City, CO; 2.5 miles south of the Lake City miniature golf course. Turn left off Hwy. 149 at the sign directing you to the site. Hinsdale County Museum: Lake City; (970) 944-2050; museumtrail .org/hinsdale-county-museum.html

Silver Thread Scenic Byway: Creede; (719) 658-2374; http://www.codot.gov/travel/scenic-byways/south-central/silver-thread

Slumgullion Slide: Lake City; (800) 569-1874 or (970) 641-0471; http://www.lakecity .com/mountain-town-activities/scenic-drives-byways/29-slumgullion-earthflow

Hike Tours
The Sportsman Outdoors & Fly Shop: Lake City; (970) 944-2526; lakecitysportsman.com

23 Bear Creek Falls

Enjoy an easy but steady climb of a thousand feet through a serene forested canyon surrounded by rugged rock walls to reach a raging cataract. A favorite among locals and visitors alike, this flower-filled hike is the perfect start to any summer day especially if you are short on time or just want a casual but superb meander. Great for youngsters or as an acclimatization hike if you have just arrived at the mountains.

Start: From the Bear Creek Trailhead on the end of South Pine Street (8,780 feet)

Distance: 5.4 miles out and back

Hiking time: 2–3 hours

Difficulty: Easy due to gradual, smooth terrain and moderate elevation gain

Trail surface: Forested and dirt trail

Best season: June to September

Peak bloom: late June to mid-July

Flowers commonly found: cow parsnip, monument plant, twinberry, Richardson's geranium, scarlet paintbrush, mountain harebell, shrubby cinquefoil, fireweed, red elderberry, wolf's currant, wild rose, monkshood, mountain parsley, beautiful daisy, Fremont geranium, northern bedstraw, baneberry, yarrow, giant lousewort, orange sneezeweed, Coulter's daisy, heartleaf arnica, cowbane, towering Jacob's ladder, triangularleaf senecio, red columbine, wild raspberry, aspen sunflower, yellow avens, stinging nettles, One-sided wintergreen, twinflower, yellow monkeyflower, bog pyrola, brook saxifrage, northern green bog orchid and fringed grass of Parnassus, Whipple's penstemon, mountain bluebells, alpine fireweed, Colorado columbine, Drummond's rockcress

Other trail users: Equestrians, mountain bikers

Canine compatibility: Dogs permitted

Land status: Public open space

Nearest town: Telluride

Fees and permits: No fees or permits required

Schedule: Open all year, but often covered in snow from fall to summer

Maps: USGS Telluride; San Juan National Forest map

Trail contacts: Telluride Parks & Recreation Department, 500 E. Colorado Ave., PO Box 397, Telluride, 81435; (970) 728-2173; http://www.telluride-co.gov/

Special considerations: Get an early start to avoid crowds. Parking in Telluride can be challenging. Permits are required on many residential streets in town and Colorado Avenue is limited to two-hour parking. Free parking is available at the Carhenge Lot (off West Pacific Avenue) near the base of lift 7 or at the south end of Mahoney Drive, near the west entrance to town.

Finding the trailhead: From Telluride's main street (Colorado Avenue), turn south onto Pine Street. Proceed two blocks and cross the bridge over the San Miguel River. The street turns into a dirt road that becomes the Bear Creek Trail. **GPS: N37 56.055'/W107 48.714'**

The Hike

This serene jaunt along Bear Creek, a quiet sanctuary so close to town, makes an excellent morning option. Follow the gradual and wide tree-lined road, built by miners, but now closed to motorized vehicles. At the intersection with the Camel's

Garden Trail, continue straight. Enter the Bear Creek Preserve, a 320-acre parcel preserved in 1995 as public open space thanks to a partnership between the San Miguel Conservation Foundation and the town of Telluride. Climbing through a forest medley of aspens, pine, oak, and spruce, you follow in the footsteps of Utes who used to hunt and perform sacred ceremonies here.

Busy beaver's work—cut tree branches, chewed logs, and gnawed stumps—on the left provides evidence of this industrious but elusive forest-shaper's presence. Monument plant, twinberry, cow parsnip, Drummond's rockcress, and Richardson's geranium line the route. The bright red elegant blooms of scarlet paintbrush merge with the purple of mountain harebell, the yellow buds of shrubby cinquefoil, and the bright pink flowers of fireweed to form a rainbow that brightens the forest depths.

Breaks in the trees offer superb views of peaks towering over town and cliffs to the north.

Views from trail

Note red elderberry bushes and low crawling shrubs of wolf's currant as you ascend along the west side of Bear Creek, whose sound soothes. Prolific rosebushes bud with fragrant pink blooms. Hillsides come alive with thickets of deep purple monkshood and lacy cow parsnip. Both stand taller than many people do. Big clusters of mountain parsley, beautiful daisy, Fremont geranium, baneberry, and northern bedstraw pop with vibrancy.

Reach a tiny overlook showcasing the powerful creek below. The trees thin, the trail opens up, and stunning vistas of the rocky pinnacles defining the canyon's eastern wall dominate the scene. Look up canyon to see Ballard Mountain and La Junta Peak or down canyon for equally impressive views of Telluride. Lush meadows support fields of flowers including yarrow, giant lousewort, cow parsnip, orange sneezeweed, Coulter's daisy, heartleaf arnica, cowbane, towering Jacob's ladder, and triangularleaf senecio.

Meandering back near the creek, the trail opens, making the dramatic canyon walls appear even more impressive and offering a glimpse of a distant giant falls. A trickle of water crosses the trail as you climb over rocky slabs past giant boulders.

Narrowing as you near the torrent, the trail is easy to follow and at times muddy, so be ready to hop some rocks across a stream or two.

Fireweed

Near the creek, a giant boulder marks where you head right and uphill to follow the increasingly narrow and lush route. Vegetation thickens and the call of the falls grows louder. Delicate harebells, red columbine, wild raspberry, aspen sunflower, yellow avens, monkshood, and stinging nettles bloom here.

Just below the falls, walk over a giant rocky slab to find a huge flat boulder offering views. The final bit of trail before the falls bursts with buds, but some like the slender One-sided wintergreen and dainty twinflower require a keen eye. Yellow monkeyflower, bog pyrola, brook saxifrage, northern green bog orchid, and fringed grass of Parnassus revel in the moisture. Others like the showy scarlet paintbrush, aspen sunflower, Whipple's penstemon, and tall beautiful daisy form eye-catching colonies.

Flanked by 13,000-foot peaks that tower dramatically on either side of this narrow canyon, the 100-foot Bear Creek Falls, full of power and splash, cascades down the mountain at the top of the trail. Mountain bluebells droop delicately, alpine fireweed bursts forth in a spray of magenta, brook saxifrage blooms from rock, and clumps of Colorado columbine triumphantly wave in the wind. Take care exploring the slippery terrain near the falls. As you retrace your steps back down the canyon, breathe in the spectacular vistas.

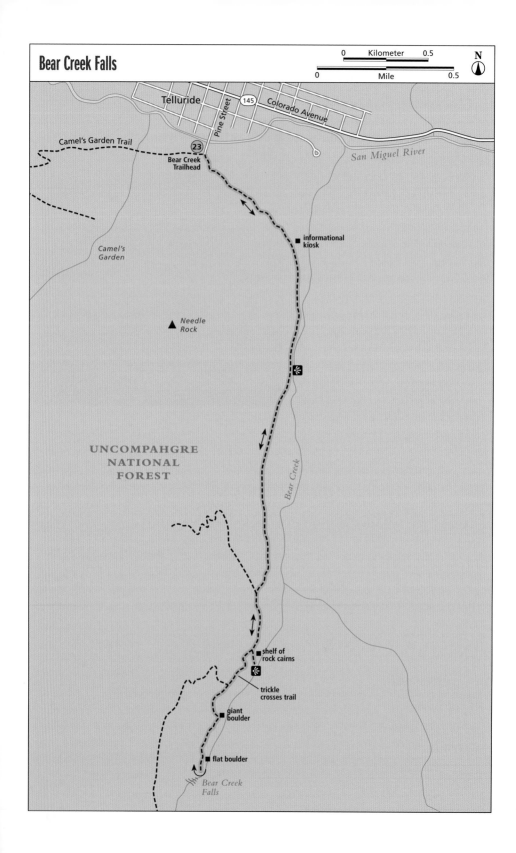

Miles and Directions

0.0 Start at the Bear Creek Trailhead.

0.1 Reach a junction with the Camel's Garden Trail. Continue straight.

0.6 An informational kiosk provides details about the Bear Creek Preserve.

1.0 Reach an overlook where you can see the creek rushing by.

2.0 A shelf of rock cairns on the left marks a popular swimming and rock-skipping spot.

2.3 A trickle crosses the trail as you climb over rocky slabs past giant boulders, and you get a view of the falls from a distance.

2.4 Near the water, a giant boulder marks the spot to head right and uphill.

2.6 A huge flat boulder on the left of the trail makes a great spot for photos, a picnic, and a view of the falls.

2.7 The Bear Creek Falls cascade down the mountain at the top of the trail.

5.4 Arrive back at the trailhead.

Options: Adventurous hikers with time and energy can head further up the canyon on the Wasatch Trail, which provides options for longer loop hikes to Telluride's ski area and Bridal Veil Basin.

Hike Information

Local Information

Telluride Tourism Board: Telluride; (970) 728-3041 or (888) 605-2578; visittelluride.com

Local Events / Attractions

Jazz Celebration: Telluride; (970) 728-7009; telluridejazz.org
    Telluride Bluegrass Festival: Telluride; (800) 624-2422; bluegrass.com/telluride
    Telluride Blues & Brews Festival: Telluride; (866) 515-6166; tellurideblues.com

Hike Tours

San Juan Outdoor School: Telluride; (970) 728-4101; tellurideadventures.com
    Bootdoctors: Telluride; (970) 728-4525; bootdoctors.com

Organizations

Telluride Mountain Club: Telluride; telluridemountainclub.org

Other Resources

Greer, Diane. 2013. *Best Hiking in Southwest Colorado around Ouray, Telluride, and Silverton*. New York: Boot Jockey Press, Inc.
    Scarmuzzi, Don J. 2013. *Telluride Trails*. Portland, OR: Westwinds Press.

24 Blue Lake

Climb high above the town of Telluride through magnificent Bridal Veil Basin to reach a turquoise lake nestled at 12,200 feet in a glacial cirque. Dazzling wildflower displays, gushing waterfalls, and historic mining relics including cabins, a bunkhouse, and the remnants of an old tram make this lung buster worth the effort.

Start: From the top of Bridal Veil Falls (10,400 feet)
Distance: 6.8 miles out and back
Hiking time: 3–6 hours
Difficulty: Strenuous due to length, altitude, and elevation gain
Trail surface: Rocky road and dirt trail
Best season: July to September
Peak bloom: mid-July to early August
Flowers commonly found: cow parsnip, hairy arnica, twinberry, monkshood, tall larkspur, Geyer's onion, shrubby cinquefoil, corn lily, scarlet and western yellow paintbrush, snowball saxifrage, yellow stonecrop, elephant heads, king's crown, death camas, queen's crown, marsh marigold, Colorado columbine, beautiful cinquefoil, subalpine arnica, Gray's angelica, bracted lousewort, moss campion, alpine sandwort, alpine avens, old man of the mountain
Other trail users: Equestrians, mountain bikers

Canine compatibility: Dogs permitted
Land status: National Forest
Nearest town: Telluride
Fees and permits: No fees or permits required
Schedule: Open all year, but often obstructed by snow from fall to summer
Maps: USGS Telluride, CO; Trails Illustrated 141 Telluride, Silverton, Ouray, Lake City; Latitude 40 Telluride–Silverton–Ouray Trails
Trail contacts: Grand Mesa, Uncompahgre and Gunnison National Forest, 2250 Hwy. 50, Delta, 81416; (970) 874-6600; www.fs.usda.gov/gmug
Special considerations: Don't confuse this with the Blue Lake hike that travels through Yankee Boy Basin in the Mount Sneffels Wilderness, which begins from a trailhead along the Dallas Creek Road (CR 7/FR 851) off CO 62 between Ridgway and Telluride.

Finding the trailhead: From Telluride, drive east on Colorado Avenue past the Pandora Mill. After just over 2 miles from the center of town, the road turns to dirt. Shortly after this, you will reach a large unmarked parking area on your right. Park here if you have a two-wheel-drive vehicle, and walk the road the rest of the way (which adds 4 miles to your round-trip total). The road features brilliant views of Bridal Veil Falls, Telluride, and the restored historic power plant at the top of the falls. With four-wheel drive continue straight on the rough dirt road (shown as FR 636 on maps) for another 2.5 miles up a series of switchbacks to reach the top of Bridal Veil Falls. Park right before the gate, but don't block it. Roadside parking is extremely limited and fills up quickly. If parking at the top is full, drive back down the road until you find a safe spot off the road or continue 0.8 mile down to base of the waterfall. **GPS: N37 55.137'/W107 46.065'**

The Hike

As you saw on the drive up, Bridal Veil Falls, the tallest free-falling falls in Colorado, plunges 365 feet to a stream feeding the San Miguel River. Starting above this mighty force, follow the old mining road above the power plant, built in 1907 to power the Smuggler's Union Mine and now listed on the National Register of Historic places even though it still provides power to Telluride.

The rocky road climbs moderately along the east (left) side of Bridal Veil Creek through a stunning, dense forest of Engelmann spruce and subalpine fir. Gifts from the forest floor include giant lacy blooms of cow parsnip, yellow bursts of hairy arnica, and colorful buds of the shrubby twinberry. Picturesque waterfalls, the stream raging beside you, and vistas of Ballard Mountain (12,818 feet) and nearby jagged peaks make the ascent worthwhile.

▶ **TIDBIT—Saxifrage means "rock breaker," which could refer to the fact that this species often grows in rock crevices. The name could also come from the belief that saxifrage—because it grows in stony areas—has medicinal properties that could dissolve kidney stones.**

Hillsides awash with brilliant wildflowers flank the road. Sunny, open areas give rise to a kaleidoscope of color in the form of monkshood, tall larkspur, cow parsnip, Geyer's onion, shrubby cinquefoil, corn lily, and tantalizing variations of scarlet and western yellow paintbrush.

The trees thin even more, offering views of the iconic and distant Mount Sneffels (14,150 feet), the town of Telluride, and the steep canyon walls that contain it. Tiny flowers like the artistic blooms of dotted saxifrage and alpine sorrel break forth from nooks and crannies in the stone, while snowball saxifrage, with a showy but small white cluster resting atop a leafless stalk, calls your attention downward amid giant boulders.

Sprouting from seeps and trickle crossing the trail are the oddly shaped magenta sprays of elephant heads, the brick-red blooms of king's crown, the elegant star-shaped flowers of the deadly death camas, the

Cluster of columbine against views en route to Blue Lake

Snowball saxifrage

singular white blossom of marsh marigold and the pinkish-white flowers of succulent queen's crown. Continue climbing to find impressive colonies of brilliant purple Colorado columbine merging with beautiful cinquefoil, subalpine arnica, cow parsnip, Gray's angelica, tall larkspur, and scarlet and western yellow paintbrush. Bracted lousewort stands tall.

Reaching the true alpine, mining ruins litter the landscape and a series of steep switchbacks lead you further away from the creek. After the upper Bridal Veil Basin junction, the trail climbs a few rough steep sections and passes a gate prohibiting access to an old mining road. Keep your eyes peeled for remnants of the Royal Mine and the Atlanta Tunnel Mine scattered below the road.

A half-mile below Blue Lake, the trail crests a hill and passes an old mining shack holding a tram historically used to bring materials up and down the basin. The grade subsides as you pass several wood mining buildings on a trail flanked by flower-filled meadows. Giant pipes snake their way alongside the road, and you pass buildings that are part of the San Miguel Watershed project, which brings water to Telluride. Please stay on the road since the area around Blue Lake is private property.

Wind through tundra to a rocky overlook above Blue Lake, situated above tree line in a breathtaking glacial cirque surrounded by 13,000-foot peaks. The craggy ridge of East Basin looms large to the south (straight ahead) while La Junta Peak (13,472') and Wasatch Mountain (13,555') fill the skyline to the west (right). Mats of magenta moss campion and creamy alpine sandwort hug the ground. Bright alpine avens form a golden and green carpet. The dazzling yellow sunflower-like blooms of old man of the mountain, which look like giants compared to the other tiny tundra wildflowers, add brilliance to this stark setting.

Explore the lakeshore and rest in this ravishing alpine landscape. Return the way you came.

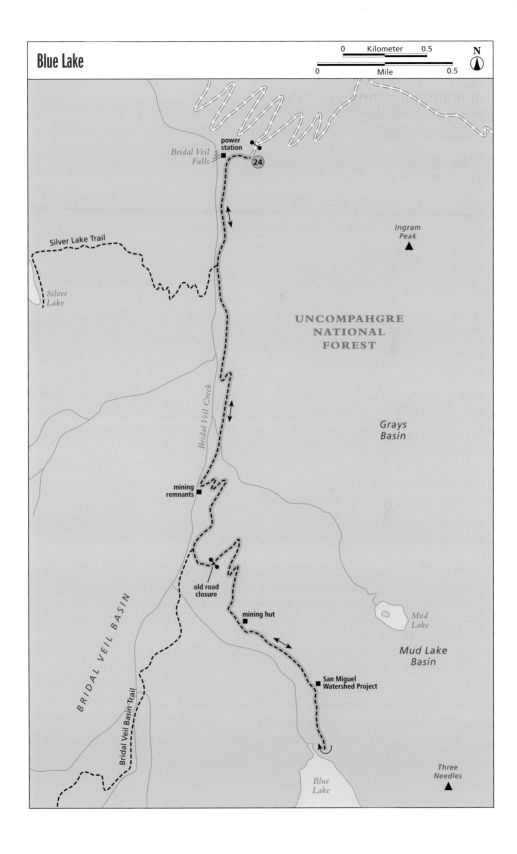

Blue Lake

0　Kilometer　0.5

0　Mile　0.5

N

Bridal Veil Falls

power station

24

Silver Lake Trail

Silver Lake

Bridal Veil Creek

Ingram Peak

UNCOMPAHGRE
NATIONAL
FOREST

Grays Basin

mining remnants

old road closure

mining hut

Mud Lake

Mud Lake Basin

San Miguel
Watershed Project

BRIDAL VEIL BASIN

Bridal Veil Basin Trail

Blue Lake

Three Needles

Miles and Directions

0.0 Start at the road closure gate at the top of Bridal Veil Falls.

0.1 Follow the old mining road south as it travels above the power plant.

0.3 Reach an unsigned junction with the Silver Lake Trail, which comes in from the west (right) and begins across the creek. Stay on the main road heading south.

1.7 Mining ruins litter the landscape, and a series of steep switchbacks leads you even further above the brook offering spectacular views.

2.3 Follow the trail due south until you reach an unsigned junction with a trail coming in from the southwest (right) that goes to upper Bridal Veil Basin and the turnoff to the Lewis Mill and Lake. Take the left fork to stay south toward Blue Lake.

2.4 After the trail climbs a few rough, steep sections, it passes a gate prohibiting access to an old mining road.

2.9 A half-mile below Blue Lake, the trail crests a hill and passes an old mining shack holding a tram historically used to bring materials up and down the basin.

3.3 Pass building and giant pipes that are part of the San Miguel Watershed Project.

3.5 Reach Blue Lake nestled above tree line in a breathtaking glacial cirque surrounded by 13,000-foot peaks.

7.0 Arrive back at the trailhead.

Hike Information

Local Information

Telluride Tourism Board: Telluride; (970) 728-3041 or (888) 605-2578; visittelluride.com

Local Events/Attractions

Jazz Celebration: Telluride; (970) 728-7009; telluridejazz.org
  Telluride Bluegrass Festival: Telluride; (800) 624-2422; bluegrass.com/telluride
  Telluride Blues & Brews Festival: Telluride; (866) 515-6166; tellurideblues.com

Hike Tours

San Juan Outdoor School: Telluride; (970) 728-4101; tellurideadventures.com
  Bootdoctors: Telluride; (970) 728-4525; bootdoctors.com

Organizations

Telluride Mountain Club: Telluride; telluridemountainclub.org

Other Resources

Greer, Diane. 2013. *Best Hiking in Southwest Colorado around Ouray, Telluride and Silverton*. New York: Boot Jockey Press, Inc.
  Scarmuzzi, Don J. 2013. *Telluride Trails*. Portland, OR: Westwinds Press.

25 Lake Hope

From start to finish this hike is bursting with reasons to love being outside: wildflowers galore, breathtaking mountain scenery, and babbling forest brooks, to name just a few. Expect this trail, which climbs gradually through tranquil spruce forest to reach a pristine mountain lake, to buzz with activity in summer. Start early to earn a few moments of solitude at Lake Hope (11,900 feet), a high alpine pond nestled in a marvelous basin surrounded by towering summits including San Miguel Peak (13,752 feet).

Start: From the Lake Hope Trailhead (10,789 feet)

Distance: 6.2 miles out and back

Hiking time: 3–5 hours

Difficulty: Moderate due to altitude and elevation gain

Trail surface: Forested and dirt trail

Best season: June to September

Peak bloom: mid to late July

Flowers commonly found: heartleaf arnica, arrowleaf balsamroot, yarrow, scarlet paintbrush, tall larkspur, Gray's angelica, Whipple's penstemon, loveroot, yellow monkeyflower, valerian, orange sneezeweed, northern goldenrod, mountain dandelion, little gentian, king's crown, monkshood, mountain bluebells, monument plant, beautiful daisy, kinnikinnick, parrot's beak, subalpine Jacob's ladder, glacial daisy, false Solomon's seal, red elderberry, horsemint, queen's crown, king's crown, elephant heads, Richardson's geranium, triangularleaf senecio, cow parsnip, American bistort, bracted lousewort, Colorado columbine, silky phacelia, alpine sorrel, dotted saxifrage, cowbane, corn lily, Parry primrose, Canada violet, red columbine, wild strawberry, fireweed, northern paintbrush, Geyer's onion, hairy arnica, wild candytuft, beautiful cinquefoil, rosy paintbrush, mountain harebell, shrubby cinquefoil, black-headed daisy, graceful buttercup, alpine avens, moss campion, marsh marigold, globeflower, alpine bistort

Other trail users: Equestrians

Canine compatibility: Dogs permitted

Land status: National Forest

Nearest town: Telluride

Fees and permits: No fees or permits required

Schedule: Open all year, but often obstructed by snow from fall to summer

Maps: USGS Ophir, CO; Trails Illustrated 141 Telluride, Silverton, Ouray, Lake City; Latitude 40 Telluride–Silverton–Ouray Trails

Trail contacts: Grand Mesa, Uncompahgre and Gunnison National Forests, Norwood District Office, PO Box 388, Norwood, 81423; (970) 327-4261; www.fs.usda.gov/gmug

Special Considerations: Though some can negotiate FR 627 by driving carefully in a passenger car, we recommend a high-clearance, four-wheel-drive vehicle instead. Check road conditions with the Forest Service.

Finding the trailhead: From downtown Telluride, drive 3 miles west on West Colorado Avenue to the junction with Hwy. 145. Turn south (left) and follow Hwy. 145 for 10 miles. Turn east (left) 0.6 mile past milepost 61 onto FR 626, signed for Trout Lake. Follow the road as it curves around the northwest shore of Trout Lake. After 1.7 miles, turn left onto FR 627. Follow this rough, rocky road for 2.5 miles to reach the Lake Hope Trailhead, which is located on the sharp curve of a switchback and marked with a large sign and map. Parking is limited. **GPS: N37 48.298'/W107 51.095'**

The Hike

Leave the car behind and dive deep into the dense forest via a smooth, eastbound trail that weaves its way through spruce and firs. In this shady wonderland, tiny golden bursts of heartleaf arnica and arrowleaf balsamroot explode alongside stately yarrow blooms. Soon, the trail turns south (left) and crosses Poverty Gulch, a creek lined with patches of colorful scarlet paintbrush, tall larkspur, Gray's angelica, Whipple's penstemon, and loveroot. The brilliant but tiny yellow monkeyflower thrives in seeps.

Weaving in and out of shady conifers and sunny patches, absorb sweeping vistas of Mount Wilson, Wilson Peak, El Diente, and the Lizard Head Wilderness back to the northwest (right). Enjoy these open areas overflowing with shoulder-height vegetation and bedazzling wildflowers including valerian, orange sneezeweed, northern goldenrod, mountain dandelion, little gentian, king's crown, monkshood, mountain bluebells, tall larkspur, monument plant, beautiful daisy, and loveroot. Back in the forest, note the tiny, white, or pink urn-shaped flowers of kinnikinnick dangling from short branches, the curled white flowers of parrot's beak, the light blue blooms of subalpine Jacob's ladder sprawling across the forest floor, and patches of light purple glacial daisy blooming in sunny spots. Cross the brook again and follow the trail as it veers southwest (left) and ducks back into the forest. This trail has multiple small creek crossings to navigate; in big snow years, shallow flowing water actually captures the trail for a portion of the hike. Though your feet may not appreciate it, this moisture makes this one of the best flower hikes in the region. False Solomon's seal, red elderberry, horsemint, queen's crown, king's crown, elephant heads, Richardson's

Lake Hope with flowers

geranium, triangularleaf senecio, cow parsnip, American bistort, and bracted lousewort thrive here. Rocky patches give life to Colorado columbine, silky phacelia, alpine sorrel, and dotted saxifrage.

Marsh marigold

After crossing the water for a third time, the trail nears the main stem of the Lake Fork, a stream flowing from Lake Hope. Pass a waterfall on the right and continue climbing gradually past bushes of mountain currant. When the trail intersects with the fast-flowing Lake Fork, follow the sign pointing you east (left). Notice cowbane, corn lily, Parry primrose, Canada violet, red columbine, wild strawberry, tall larkspur, bracted lousewort, and Richardson's geranium joining forces near the creek to bring the trail to life.

From there, climb switchbacks decorated by fireweed, northern paintbrush, Geyer's onion, hairy arnica, wild candytuft, and beautiful cinquefoil.

Nearing a bench just above tree line, look back for views of the valley and Trout Lake below. Leveling and paralleling a precious tiny stream, the trail opens into a huge alpine meadow thick with willows, littered with large boulders and teeming with colorful cover in the form of rosy paintbrush, mountain harebell, shrubby cinquefoil, black-headed daisy, graceful buttercup, alpine avens, and moss campion. The trail cuts south across grassy tundra to reach Lake Hope, which remains hidden until you are right on it.

Follow the faint trail around the south (left) side of this sparkling lake. Colorful patches of marsh marigold, globeflower, Parry primrose, and alpine bistort line the lakeshore while San Miguel Peak (13,752 feet) and Vermillion Peak (13,894 feet) surround you in a spectacular and jagged mountainous mess. Enjoy a picnic lunch keeping an eye out for native cutthroat trout that make their home in these clear waters.

Retrace your steps back to the trailhead. Reap the rewards of your hard work and absorb the spectacular views toward Trout Lake, Sheep Mountain, and Lizard Head.

Miles and Directions

0.0 Start from the Lake Hope Trailhead. Travel east on a trail weaving its way through the forest.

0.4 The trail turns south (left), crosses Poverty Gulch, and continues, gradually ascending.

1.3 Cross the creek again and follow the trail as it veers southwest (left) and ducks back into the forest.

1.6 After crossing the creek for a third time, the trail nears the main stem of Lake Fork and passes a torrent.

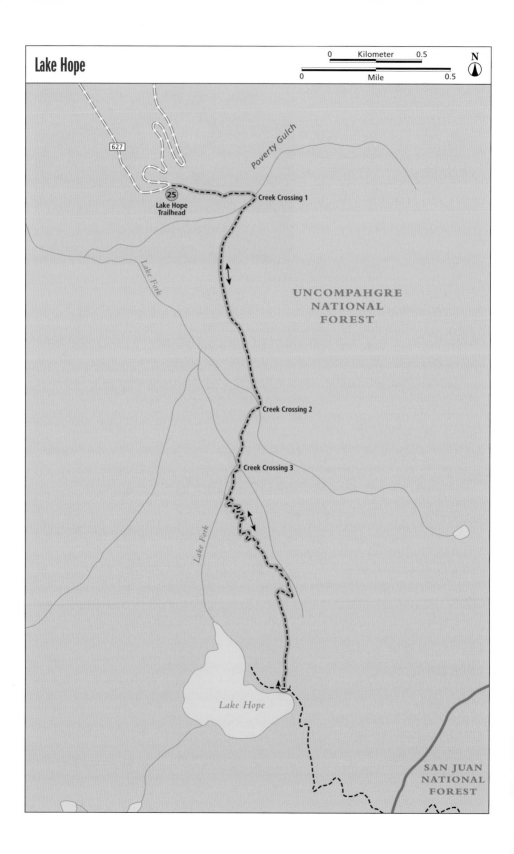

Lake Hope

0   Kilometer   0.5
0   Mile   0.5

N

627

25
Lake Hope
Trailhead

Poverty Gulch

Creek Crossing 1

Lake Fork

UNCOMPAHGRE
NATIONAL
FOREST

Creek Crossing 2

Creek Crossing 3

Lake Fork

Lake Hope

SAN JUAN
NATIONAL
FOREST

1.8 At an intersection with the fast-flowing Lake Fork, follow a sign pointing east (left) to stay on the main trail, which climbs a series of switchbacks.

3.1 Leveling, the trail parallels a small stream and enters a huge alpine meadow. Walk south to reach Lake Hope.

6.2 Arrive back at the trailhead.

Options: Continue to the unnamed pass above Lake Hope via the trail heading south (left) at the lake. Follow the trail left to ascend switchbacks up the rocky hillside below the pass. This side trip will add 0.7 mile and 545 feet one-way and offers vistas of Rolling Mountain (13,693 feet), the Twin Sisters (13,374 feet), and San Miguel Peak (13,432 feet).

Hike Information

Local Information
Telluride Tourism Board: Telluride; (970) 728-3041 or (888) 605-2578; visittelluride.com

Local Events/Attractions
Jazz Celebration: Telluride; (970) 728-7009; telluridejazz.org
 Telluride Bluegrass Festival: Telluride; (800) 624-2422; bluegrass.com/telluride
 Telluride Blues &Brews Festival: Telluride; (866) 515-6166; tellurideblues.com

Hike Tours
San Juan Outdoor School: Telluride; (970) 728-4101; tellurideadventures.com
 Bootdoctors: Telluride; (970) 728-4525; bootdoctors.com

Organizations
Telluride Mountain Club: Telluride; telluridemountainclub.org

Other Resources
Greer, Diane. 2013. *Best Hiking in Southwest Colorado around Ouray, Telluride and Silverton*. New York: Boot Jockey Press, Inc.
 Scarmuzzi, Don J. 2013. *Telluride Trails*. Portland, OR: Westwinds Press.

THE POWER OF WATER

Built in the early 1900s, Lake Hope, which is actually a reservoir, was a main source of water for the Ames Hydroelectric Power Plant near Ophir. In 1891, Ames set the standard for alternating current in the United States by becoming the first power plant to provide industrialized alternating current electricity. Even today, water flows from Lake Hope to Trout Lake, where it is diverted into a big pipe that travels over 2.5 miles to reach the Ames Hydroelectric Plant, which turns it into electricity.

26 Cross Mountain

Experience varied and dazzling wildflower displays while wandering through moist grassy meadows, cool dense evergreen forest, exposed subalpine ridges, and intense alpine tundra to reach the base of Lizard Head Peak, a prominent 13,113-foot craggy rock spire towering overhead. Despite climbing only 3.6 miles into the Lizard Head Wilderness, this well-worn trail rewards adventurers with the feeling of being totally alone and deep in the wild. Enjoy solitude, expansive views, and an array of jaw-dropping wildflowers that will not disappoint.

Start: From the Cross Mountain Trailhead marked by the Lizard Head Wilderness sign (10,200 feet)

Distance: 7.2 miles out and back

Hiking time: 3-5 hours

Difficulty: Strenuous due to distance, altitude, and elevation gain

Trail surface: Dirt two-track, forested and dirt trail

Best season: July to September

Peak bloom: mid-July to mid-August

Flowers commonly found: beautiful cinquefoil, shrubby cinquefoil, Geyer's onion, beautiful daisy, Coulter's daisy, orange sneezeweed, western yellow, rosy, scarlet and northern paintbrush, aspen sunflower, edible valerian, western chainpod, corn lily, black-tip senecio, towering Jacob's ladder, golden aster, Richardson's geranium, heartleaf arnica, Parry's lousewort, northern goldenrod, parrot's beak, mountain bluebells, mountain dandelion, cow parsnip, baneberry, Whipple's penstemon, Gray's angelica, red columbine, death camas, monument plant, white clover, Colorado columbine, giant lousewort, wild strawberry, rattlesnake plantain orchid, One-sided wintergreen,

single delight, bracted lousewort, graceful buttercup, Canada violet, Parry gentian, mountain currant, whiplash daisy, subalpine Jacob's ladder, subalpine arnica, showy daisy, largeleaf avens, wild iris, heartleaf bittercress, Parry primrose, tall larkspur, mountain harebell, marsh marigold, blue violet, alpine sorrel, king's crown, western wallflower, sky pilot, alpine bistort, silky phacelia, old man of the mountain, alpine avens, Rocky Mountain trifolium, American Smelowsky

Other trail users: Equestrians

Canine compatibility: Leashed dogs permitted; dogs under verbal control permitted

Land status: National Forest, Wilderness

Nearest town: Telluride

Fees and permits: No fees or permits required

Schedule: Open all year, but often obstructed by snow from fall to summer

Maps: USGS Mount Wilson, CO; Trails Illustrated 141 Telluride, Silverton, Ouray, Lake City; Latitude 40 Telluride-Silverton-Ouray Trails

Trail contacts: San Juan National Forest, Dolores Ranger District, 29211 Hwy. 184, Dolores, 81323-9308; (970) 882-7296; www.fs.usda.gov/sanjuan

Finding the trailhead: From Telluride drive south for 12.5 miles on CO 145 to reach Lizard Head Pass. Go over the pass and continue south for 2.2 miles. Turn right into a large dirt parking lot signed for Cross Mountain Trailhead. **GPS: N37 47.785'/W107 56.242'**

The Hike

From the trailhead, cross a tiny footbridge to enter a meadow bursting with beautiful and shrubby cinquefoil, scarlet paintbrush, Geyer's onion, beautiful daisy, Coulter's daisy, and orange sneezeweed. Impressive and uniquely shaped peaks including Sheep Mountain, Vermilion Peak, Golden Horn, and Pilot Knob dominate the skyline. The dramatic spiny summit of Lizard Head (13,113 feet) beckons from a distance. Western yellow, rosy, scarlet, and northern paintbrush, aspen sunflower, edible valerian, and western chainpod burst forth from the ground in bright bunches. Ascending through the moist grassy meadow, a different bloom greets each step upward. Fields of corn lily, black-tip senecio, and elephant heads appear en masse.

At the Groundhog Stock Trail junction, stay right. Entering the forest, towering Jacob's ladder, golden aster, Richardson's geranium, heartleaf arnica, Parry's lousewort, northern goldenrod, and both cinquefoil variations herald your arrival. parrot's beak, mountain bluebells, rosy paintbrush, mountain dandelion, and cow parsnip bloom in remarkable fashion.

Cross a tiny rivulet to find baneberry's shiny red and white berries creating a tantalizing, but toxic, display. A dense glade of trees provides the perfect home for Whipple's penstemon, parrot's beak, Gray's angelica, heartleaf arnica, red columbine, and death camas. Delicious meadows occupy breaks in the pines full of monument plant, white clover, northern goldenrod, Colorado columbine, corn lily, and giant lousewort, an impressive stout-stemmed perennial that can grow 2- to 4-feet tall.

Back in the forest, look closely to find wild strawberry plants creeping along the ground amid dense and glowing stands of arnica, Richardson's geranium, parrot's beak, and paintbrush of all colors. Keen observers can find the even tinier blooms of rattlesnake plantain orchid, One-sided

Spectacular flowers and views line the way on this trail

Silky phacelia

wintergreen, and single delight lurking gracefully amid the underbrush.

As you gain elevation along this lush, fertile area, edible valerian, bracted lousewort, graceful buttercup, Canada violet, Parry gentian, mountain currant, and baneberry appear.

After entering the Wilderness, the trail levels and then heads downhill to break out of the forest for a sensational view of Lizard Head. Whiplash daisy, subalpine Jacob's ladder, subalpine arnica, showy daisy, largeleaf avens, and wild iris paint the grassy meadow with color. Amazing displays of paintbrush provide a spectacular foreground for the high peaks of the San Miguel Range including Cross Mountain and Gladstone Peak.

Climbing steeply, reach a small, rocky creek where heartleaf bittercress, corn lily, mountain bluebells, Parry primrose, tall larkspur, mountain harebell, Geyer's onion, marsh marigold, blue violet, and paintbrush bloom wildly.

Trees slowly disappear giving way to a rugged singletrack trail cutting through colorful displays of alpine sorrel, king's crown, western wallflower, American Smelowsky, sky pilot, alpine bistort, rosy paintbrush, silky phacelia, and wallflower.

Marmots' warning whistles sound. The soil turns black, and you traverse a slope filled with old man of the mountain, Colorado columbine, alpine avens, and the brilliant Rocky Mountain trifolium, which grows in eye-catching mats bursting with brilliantly colored clusters of magenta blossoms. Turn a corner and Lizard Head towers above in all its glory.

Walking toward the area's sentinel, views improve in every direction. Pry your eyes from the mountains periodically to enjoy the orange, blue, purple, red, and magenta blooms underfoot.

▶ **GREEN TIP—Consider the packaging of any products you bring with you. It's best to properly dispose of packaging at home before you hike. If you're on the trail, pack it out with you.**

Flanked by endless blossoms of old man of the mountain, avens, silky phacelia, and countless others, the trail contours around Lizard Head to reach a junction with the Lizard Head Trail. Here, in the shadow of this distinctive 400-foot rock spire, which is an old eroded volcanic plug said to look like the gaping jaws of a lizard with its face to the sky, enjoy a well-earned break until deciding to return to the trailhead.

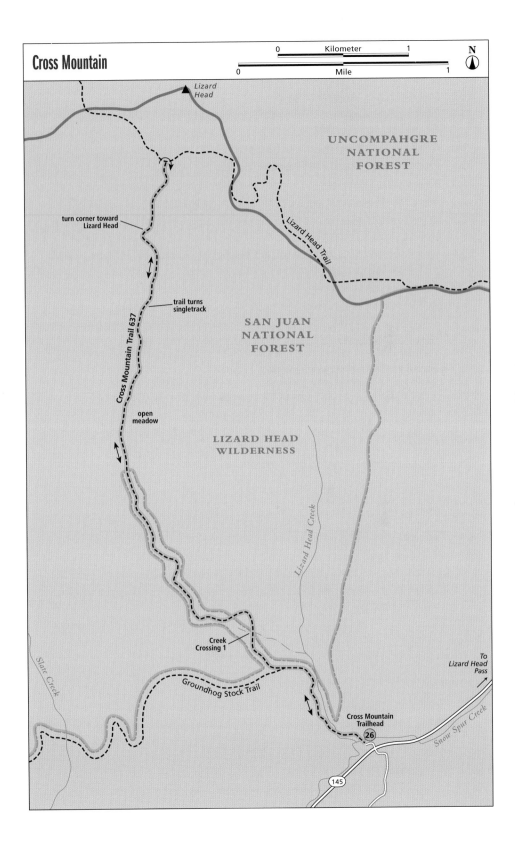

Cross Mountain

0 Kilometer 1
0 Mile 1

N

Lizard Head

UNCOMPAHGRE
NATIONAL
FOREST

turn corner toward
Lizard Head

Lizard Head Trail

trail turns
singletrack

SAN JUAN
NATIONAL
FOREST

Cross Mountain Trail 637

open
meadow

LIZARD HEAD
WILDERNESS

Lizard Head Creek

Creek
Crossing 1

Groundhog Stock Trail

Slate Creek

To
Lizard Head
Pass

Snow Spur Creek

Cross Mountain
Trailhead

26

145

Miles and Directions

0.0 Start at the Cross Mountain Trailhead.

0.6 Reach a junction with the Groundhog Stock Trail. Stay right on the Cross Mountain Trail (#637).

0.8 The trail veers northwest. Hop rocks to cross a creek.

2.1 Reach the signed Lizard Head Wilderness Boundary.

2.3 Break out of the forest into an open meadow with a stunning view of Lizard Head.

2.9 The trail breaks into the alpine and turns to rocky singletrack.

3.2 After traversing a slope covered in volcanic soil, you turn a corner, and Lizard Head towers above you in all of its glory.

3.6 At a junction with the Lizard Head Trail, which is your turnaround point, enjoy a well-earned break in the shadow of this distinctive 400-foot rock spire.

7.2 Arrive back at the trailhead.

Options: For a shorter adventure full of mountain views and a range of flowers, walk through the first meadow and the start of the forest. Choose your turnaround point based on available energy and time. For a longer loop (11.7 miles), use the Lizard Head Trail and Railroad Grade route for the return trip. Another option involves adding the Bilk Basin Overlook Extension. Turn left at the last junction described to follow Lizard Head trail northwest for 0.3 mile to the top of a ridge. Going the extra distance will result in excellent vistas of Cross Mountain, Mount Wilson (14,245 feet), Gladstone Peak (13,913 feet), and Wilson Peak (14,017 feet).

Hike Information

Local Information

Telluride Tourism Board: Telluride; (970) 728-3041 or (888) 605-2578; visittelluride.com

Local Events/Attractions

Jazz Celebration: Telluride; (970) 728-7009; telluridejazz.org
  Telluride Bluegrass Festival: Telluride; (800) 624-2422; bluegrass.com/telluride
  Telluride Blues & Brews Festival: Telluride; (866) 515-6166; tellurideblues.com

Hike Tours

San Juan Outdoor School: Telluride; (970) 728-4101; tellurideadventures.com
  Bootdoctors: Telluride; (970)728-4525; bootdoctors.com

Organizations

Telluride Mountain Club: Telluride; telluridemountainclub.org

Other Resources

Greer, Diane. 2013. *Best Hiking in Southwest Colorado around Ouray, Telluride and Silverton.* New York: Boot Jockey Press, Inc.
  Scarmuzzi, Don J. 2013. *Telluride Trails.* Portland, OR: Westwinds Press.

27 Lower Highland Mary Lakes

This aerobic adventure follows a rushing creek through a lush valley to reach a series of high-altitude, crystalline lakes resting in a serene expanse of verdant tundra. Colorful blooms and expansive views define this classic Colorado experience through the majestic San Juan Mountains. Despite being one of the most scenic, idyllic, flower-filled hikes in the region, relatively few people find their way here, so for those seeking a quieter experience, this hike's for you!

Start: From the Highland Mary Lakes/Cunningham Gulch Trailhead (10,750 feet)

Distance: 5.0 miles out and back

Hiking time: 3-5 hours

Difficulty: Moderate due to altitude, elevation gain, and rocky terrain

Trail surface: Rocky, dirt trail

Best season: July to September

Peak bloom: late July to mid-August

Flowers commonly found: corn lily, Gray's angelica, Colorado columbine, tall larkspur, king's and queen's crown, mountain parsley, beautiful cinquefoil, loveroot, twinberry, monument plant, triangularleaf senecio, mountain dandelion, orange sneezeweed, fireweed, cow parsnip, towering Jacob's ladder, mountain bluebells, wild strawberry, parrot's beak, Fremont geranium, subalpine Jacob's ladder, heartleaf arnica, shrubby cinquefoil, Whipple's penstemon, yarrow, alpine fireweed, brook saxifrage, Coulter's daisy, cowbane, showy ragwort, death camas, glacial daisy, golden aster, aspen sunflower, beautiful daisy, valerian, Geyer's onion, heartleaf bittercress, American bistort, Parry primrose, elephant heads, death camas, bracted lousewort, marsh marigold,

Parry clover, subalpine arnica, cowbane, alpine avens, graceful buttercup, rosy, scarlet and northern paintbrush, American bistort, monkshood, blue violet, northern goldenrod, blueleaf cinquefoil, moss campion, black-headed daisy, cutleaf daisy, Parry's lousewort, marsh marigold, old man of the mountains, brook saxifrage, alpine violet

Other trail users: Equestrians (first 0.3 mile)

Canine compatibility: Leashed dogs permitted; dogs under verbal control permitted

Land status: National Forest, Wilderness

Nearest town: Silverton

Fees and permits: No fees or permits required

Schedule: Open all year, but often obstructed by snow from fall to midsummer

Maps: USGS Howardsville and Storm King Peak, CO; Trails Illustrated 140 Weimnuche Wilderness; Latitude 40 Telluride-Silverton-Ouray Trails

Trail contacts: San Juan National Forest, Columbine Ranger District, 367 South Pearl St., PO Box 439, Bayfield, 81122; (970) 884-2512; www.fs.usda.gov/sanjuan

Special considerations: Due to muddy spots, creek crossings, and the chance for persistent snow, we recommend wearing gators and using hiking poles for extra security on slippery rocks.

Finding the trailhead: From downtown Silverton, drive north on Greene Street (CO 11) through town. After 1 mile, merge east (right) onto CR 2 and continue north. After 2 miles, the road turns to gravel. Continue for another 2.1 miles (total of 4.1 miles on CR 2) until you reach the tiny "town" of Howardsville, where you turn south (right) onto CR 4. After 0.1 mile, reach a fork where a sign points left for the gold mine tour. Take the right, unsigned fork. Continue for another 1.5 miles to another fork where a sign points left for Stony Pass. Take the right, unsigned fork again to parallel the creek. After another 1.9 miles, you reach another fork. Continue right for 0.1 mile to reach the first parking area, where those with two-wheel drive or trailers may want to park. From here, the road gets rockier and steeper as it winds through narrow switchbacks to climb above the valley. After 0.7 mile, those with high clearance should follow the road as it forks east (left) down a short steep ravine that brings you across Cunningham Creek and up another short, steep climb to reach the upper trailhead. For those without high clearance or in early summer when the water may be too high, a pullout before the creek and above the ravine offers plenty of parking. The trail starts just 0.2 mile from this point. **GPS: N37 46.851'/W107 34.787'**

The Hike

Immediately after picking up the gravel path heading south along Cunningham Creek, Gray's angelica, Colorado columbine, tall larkspur, king's crown, mountain parsley, beautiful cinquefoil, and scarlet paintbrush greet you in a flurry of color. A torrent of powerful water flows through a splendid black rock chasm on the right. Loveroot, twinberry, monument plant, triangularleaf senecio, and mountain dandelion thrive creekside. Leaving the water, enter an alluring, open area full of orange sneezeweed, fireweed, cow parsnip, towering Jacob's ladder, monument plant, and mountain bluebells. Continue climbing to enter a treed alleyway where wild strawberry, parrot's beak, Fremont geranium, subalpine Jacob's ladder, and Colorado columbine flourish.

Continue upward, gaining elevation quickly, through a section lined with tall silvery willows, yellow blossoms of heartleaf arnica, shrubby cinquefoil, glittering rosy paintbrush, intense Whipple's penstemon, and the ever-present yarrow. Go right at the signed stock trail junction and cross the brook to find alpine fireweed, brook saxifrage,

Awesome views from above the last lake

and Colorado columbine. As the trail constricts, huge rock cliffs tower above, while at your feet Coulter's daisy, mountain bluebells, cowbane, showy ragwort, heartleaf arnica, death camas, glacial daisy, and golden aster bloom.

Scale rock steps to climb the increasingly steep trail through a narrow rocky band cut into the cliff. Rosy paintbrush, beautiful cinquefoil, aspen sunflower, beautiful daisy, valerian, Geyer's onion, heartleaf bittercress, and American bistort decorate this section.

Traverse a slope strewn with boulders and teeming with flowers to reach the signed Weimnuche Wilderness Boundary. The route turns wet and muddy giving life to king's and queen's crown, Parry primrose, elephant heads, death camas, bracted lousewort, and

Heartleaf bittercress

marsh marigold. Briefly walk through a forested and heavily willowed area to reach another creek crossing where Parry clover, subalpine arnica, cowbane, and yellow monkeyflower present themselves. The trail cuts a path through a dense thicket, and ahead there are willows for as far as you can see. Interwoven amid the thicket are wide-open meadows blooming with alpine avens, graceful buttercup, rosy, scarlet, and northern paintbrush, mountain bluebells, and a rainbow of countless other blossoms.

Leveling, the trail continues south along sparkling Cunningham Creek as it cuts through a huge slope dappled with willows, spruce trees, and wild rocky outcroppings.

Climbing again, move into a lush forest bursting with mountain bluebells, heartleaf bittercress, subalpine Jacob's ladder, American bistort, and king's crown. Cross the creek again and follow a wider, willow-lined trail that passes over fine slabs of granite. Corn lily, loveroot, cinquefoil, Geyer's onion, monkshood, and bluebells line the way as you make your way toward giant peaks.

Leaving most trees behind, the rough trail ascends a small cliff and enters a breathtaking, picturesque basin where wild strawberry and blue violets provide tiny bursts of vivid color. Follow the verdant, often wet route deeper into a lovely stony basin bursting with elephant heads, subalpine arnica, northern goldenrod, tall larkspur, blueleaf cinquefoil, king's crown, and northern and scarlet paintbrush.

High above the water, traverse a slope, pass another waterfall, and continue climbing. With each step, the flowers shrink. Moss campion, black-headed daisy, blue violet, cutleaf daisy, and the oddly shaped yellow Parry's lousewort populate this part of the trail with style.

Halfway up the slope, the dirt trail peters out and disappears into a maze of huge boulders. Cross the boulder field alive with shrubby cinquefoil, thistle, and cutleaf daisy to reach a boggy spot without a defined trail. Move toward the creek and cross to its east side to rejoin a distinct dirt trail. After a short climb, the first lake, which seems to be suspended in mid-air, snaps into view. Explore both shores, which are full of marsh marigold, old man of the mountain, Parry primrose, heartleaf bittercress, brook saxifrage, queen's crown, alpine fireweed, and a rainbow of paintbrush.

The second lake appears soon. Climb gently through the picturesque glacial basin to reach the third and largest lake. Mellowing, the trail opens up to extremely impressive, vast fields teeming with willows, marsh marigold, moss campion, alpine violet, old man of the mountain, Colorado columbine, king's crown, and Parry primrose. High mountain ridges that encircle the lakes combine with fields of bright yellow cinquefoil dappled with colonies of scarlet, rosy, and western yellow paintbrush to create the perfect setting for tundra exploration or a picnic. Distinctly shaped Vestal and Arrow Peaks tower overhead. After you've absorbed all the beauty possible, head back the way you came.

Miles and Directions

- **0.0** Start from the upper trailhead to pick up the Highland Mary Lakes Trail (#606) heading south.
- **0.3** Reach a signed junction with a stock trail. Hikers should take the right fork and continue south.
- **0.4** Cross to the east side of the creek.
- **0.6** Arrive at the signed Weminuche Wilderness Boundary.
- **0.8** Cross the creek again.
- **1.1** Arrive at a braided, formidable creek crossing. Proceed with caution to reach the west (right) side of the creek.

Note: About 0.5 mile up this narrow gulch, there is a faint trail that goes east (left) and climbs closer to the water instead of going across the boulder field (as we describe in the upcoming steps). Though this route is shorter and more direct, it is easy to miss on the way up. Sometimes there is a cairn marking the split in the trail, but we missed it on the way up and only saw it on the way down. If you see it, consider coming down this way.

- **1.8** Halfway up the slope, the trail turns faint and disappears into a maze of huge boulders. Cross the boulder field to your left keeping an eye out for cairns (rock piles) leading the way, but don't rely on them since they may get knocked down or obscured. Pass through a boggy spot without a definite trail, and cross to the east side of the creek to rejoin a distinct trail.
- **2.0** Arrive at the first lake.
- **2.1** Follow the narrow trail around the west (right) side of the lake to reach the second lake.
- **2.5** The trail mellows, meanders south through the basin, and reaches the third and largest lake.
- **5.0** Arrive back at the trailhead.

Options: Continue past the last lake for another 0.6 mile to a viewpoint, which overlooks Verde Lakes and the Grenadier Range to the south. Or, extend this journey into a short backpacking trip by hopping on the Continental Divide Trail (CDT) above the lakes.

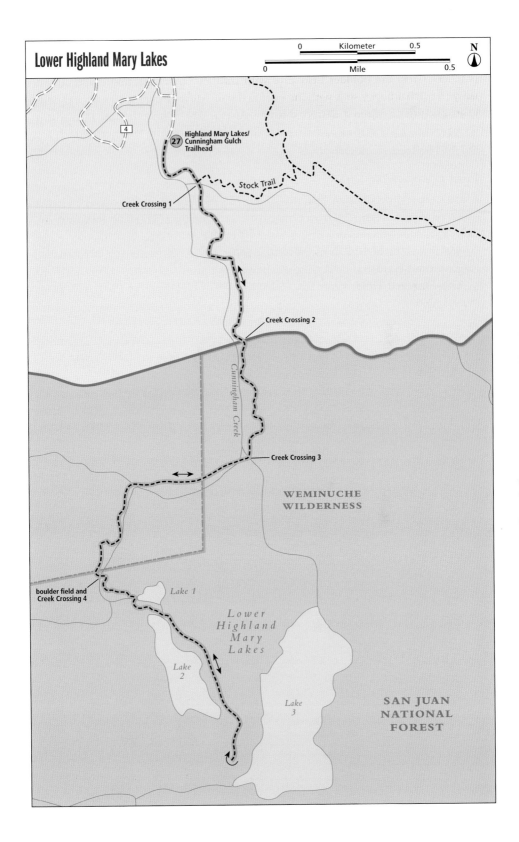

Lower Highland Mary Lakes

0   Kilometer   0.5

0   Mile   0.5

N

Highland Mary Lakes/
Cunningham Gulch
Trailhead

27

Stock Trail

Creek Crossing 1

Creek Crossing 2

Cunningham Creek

Creek Crossing 3

WEMINUCHE
WILDERNESS

boulder field and
Creek Crossing 4

Lake 1

Lower
Highland
Mary
Lakes

Lake
2

Lake
3

SAN JUAN
NATIONAL
FOREST

4

Hike Information

Local Information

Durango Area Tourism Office and Visitor Center: Durango; (970) 247-3500; durango.org

Silverton Area Chamber of Commerce: Silverton; (800) 752-4494 or (970) 387-5654; silvertoncolorado.com

Local Events/Attractions

Christ of the Miners Shrine: Silverton; (800) 752-4494 or (970) 387-5654

Durango & Silverton Narrow Gauge Railroad: Durango; (877) 872-4607 or (970) 247-2733; durangotrain.com

Mayflower Gold Mill Tour: Silverton; (970) 387-0294 (summer); http://www.sanjuancountyhistoricalsociety.org/mayflower-mill.html

Old Hundred Gold Mine Tour: Silverton; (800) 872-3009 or (970) 387-5444; minetour.com

Organizations

San Juan County Historical Society: Silverton; (970) 387-5838; sanjuancountyhistoricalsociety.org

San Juan Mountains Association: Durango; (970) 385-1210; sjma.org

Trails 2000: Durango; (970) 259-4682; trails2000.org—a 501(c)(3) organization that builds and maintains trails; educates trail users; and encourages connectivity on road, path, and trail.

Other Resources

Poe, Anne and Mike. 2013. *Southwest Colorado High Country Day Hikes: Ouray, Silverton, & Lake City.* Las Vegas, NV: Take a Hike Guidebooks.

28 Ice Lakes

This quintessential Colorado hike has it all! Wander through tranquil meadows, walk past rivulets, discover scores of wildflowers, and absorb spectacular vistas on your way to a remarkable turquoise pool perched in a cirque surrounded by rugged cliffs. The trail begins in the trees, breaks above tree line to pass through the lush Lower Ice Lakes Basin, and climbs higher to reach the impressive upper basin. Though this route is relentlessly uphill, its popularity with visitors and locals alike proves the rewards are absolutely worth the effort.

Start: From the northwest corner of the Ice Lakes Trailhead parking lot (9,840 feet)

Distance: 8.6 miles out and back

Hiking time: 4-6 hours

Difficulty: Strenuous due to distance, altitude, elevation gain, and steep sections

Trail surface: Forested and dirt trail

Best season: July to September

Peak bloom: late July to mid-August

Flowers commonly found: white clover, talk larkspur, yarrow, northern goldenrod, silverleaf phacelia, showy daisy, towering Jacob's ladder, beautiful cinquefoil, Richardson's geranium, cow parsnip, black-tip senecio, cowbane, giant lousewort, heartleaf arnica, mountain bluebells, yellow monkeyflower, Canada violet, wild strawberry, bog pyrola, mountain dandelion, orange sneezeweed, beautiful daisy, monkshood, aspen sunflower, Wyoming paintbrush, triangularleaf senecio, Coulter's daisy, Lamb-stongue groundsel, Gray's angelica, scarlet, rosy, western yellow and northern paintbrush, fireweed, twinberry, red elderberry, yellow avens, wild rose, parrot's beak, alpine milkvetch, mountain harebell, monument plant, shrubby cinquefoil, blue flax, mountain parsley, dwarf golden aster, red columbine, graceful buttercup, blueberry, loveroot, valerian, subalpine Jacob's ladder, Colorado columbine, Whipple's penstemon, elephant heads, corn lily, king's crown, fringed gentian, marsh marigold, blue violet, western wallflower, alpine avens, black-headed daisy, old man of the mountains, sky pilot, silky phacelia, moss campion, alpine bistort, alpine spring beauty, Parry's lousewort, Parry primrose, alpine sandwort

Other trail users: Equestrians

Canine compatibility: Leashed dogs permitted; dogs under verbal control permitted

Land status: National Forest, Wilderness

Nearest town: Silverton

Fees and permits: No fees or permits required

Schedule: Open all year, but often obstructed by snow from fall to summer

Maps: USGS Ophir, CO; Trails Illustrated 141 Telluride, Silverton, Ouray, Lake City; Latitude 40 Telluride-Silverton-Ouray Trails

Trail contacts: San Juan National Forest, Columbine Ranger District, 367 South Pearl St., PO Box 439, Bayfield, 81122; (970) 884-2512; www.fs.usda.gov/sanjuan

Special considerations: If you're skilled, bring your fishing rod since brook and cutthroat trout make their home in Ice Lake.

Finding the trailhead: From Silverton, follow US 550 north for 1.9 miles. Turn west (left) onto CR 7 (also called FR 585 and South Mineral Creek Road). Follow this good gravel road for 4.5 miles until you reach the South Mineral Campground on the south side (left) of the road. Park across from the campground in the large lot on the north side (right) of the road.
GPS: N37 48.403'/W107 46.445'

The Hike

Without wasting a moment, the trail thrusts you into a meadow bursting with white clover, tall larkspur, yarrow, northern goldenrod, silverleaf phacelia, showy daisy, towering Jacob's ladder, and beautiful cinquefoil. Minutes later, enter the cool shade of the forest where monkshood appears amid Richardson's geranium, cow parsnip, black-tip senecio, giant lousewort, and cowbane.

Ascend switchbacks past heartleaf arnica, mountain bluebells, and tiny trailside seeps harboring yellow monkeyflower and delicate white Canada violet. Look closely for wild strawberry creeping along the forest floor and bog pyrola, with its nodding, pink to rose-purple waxy flowers growing in a tall raceme, hiding amid the undergrowth.

The trail levels out and opens up into a meadow where mountain dandelion, orange sneezeweed, beautiful daisy, tall larkspur, monkshood, aspen sunflower, Wyoming paintbrush, triangularleaf senecio, yarrow, Coulter's daisy, and lambstongue groundsel await your arrival. When you come to Clear Creek, pick your way across to the west (left) side via a series of smartly placed logs. From here, hoof it up another set of well-graded switchbacks that pop into dense stands of trees and then burst out into open meadows offering periodic vistas of the Twin Sisters rising to the south. Clusters of monkshood, cow parsnip, Gray's angelica, scarlet paintbrush, and fireweed explode in a flurry.

Ice Lake

Near the end of the switchbacks, a tiny trail heads to a view of the waterfall thundering nearby. Back on the main trail, twinberry, red elderberry, northern goldenrod, yellow avens, and wild rose elegantly fill in the gaps between trees. Trailside openings fill with impressive giant louseworts, parrot's beak, and a plethora of paintbrush in red, pink, orange, and yellow. After a dry creek crossing, giant cliffs tower above, a waterfall cascades over rocks below, and alpine milkvetch, mountain harebell, fireweed, monument plant, wild rose, and scarlet and northern paintbrush line the trail.

The trail weaves in and out of the aspen-dominated forest. Pass a mining cabin and climb past giant

Another view of Ice Lake

bushes of shrubby cinquefoil and colorful clusters of rosy and western yellow paintbrush, blue flax, mountain parsley, and dwarf golden aster. After another dry crossing, swim through a giant, never-ending sea of yellow, orange, red, magenta, blue, and purple. Curving south toward the creek, red columbine, graceful buttercup, blueberry, loveroot, valerian, and subalpine Jacob's ladder appear. After glimpsing the waterfall below, break free from the trees to find yourself in another prolific meadow bursting with an astounding display of blooms.

The trail levels to reveal bursts of Whipple's penstemon, beautiful cinquefoil, and loveroot. The trail skirts a wet area where elephant heads, corn lily, monument plant, Colorado columbine, and king's crown thrive. Fuller Peak (13,761 feet), Vermillion Peak (13,894 feet), Golden Horn (13,780 feet), and Pilot

▶ **GREEN TIP—Stay on the trail. Cutting through from one part of a switchback to another can destroy fragile plant life.**

Knob (13,738 feet) rise above the ridge enveloping the lower basin. Following a gentle gradient, pass Lower Ice Lake, which rests nestled among trees.

Dropping down into the lower basin, head-high blooms envelope you. A large cascade flows over towering cliffs. After crossing the sizeable brook, where queen's crown and alpine fireweed thrive, climb steeply through thick willows sheltering fringed gentian, marsh marigold, blue violet, western wallflower, and northern paintbrush.

The willows shrink, making room for alpine avens, black-headed daisy, king's crown, old man of the mountain, sky pilot, silky phacelia, moss campion, blue violet, alpine bistort, alpine spring beauty, and Parry's lousewort. Finally, the trail levels and turns west (left) spitting you out onto open tundra where the aptly named Ice Lake (12,270 feet) rests encircled by jagged, toothy cliffs. Nature has scattered Parry primrose, marsh marigold, western yellow paintbrush, rosy paintbrush, alpine sandwort, and moss campion everywhere. Explore the shoreline and absorb this scene from every angle. Retrace your steps back to the car.

Miles and Directions

0.0 Start at the Ice Lake Trailhead. Pick up the Ice Lake Trail (#505) from the northwest edge of the parking lot.

0.8 Cross to the west (left) side of Clear Creek.

1.4 Follow the tiny trail east for a brief side trip to a waterfall viewpoint. After this brief diversion, return to the main trail, which levels out as it heads west away from Clear Creek.

1.7 The trail widens and you reach a dry creek crossing.

1.8 Pass a cabin on the left as you climb higher and higher.

2.1 Cross another dry creek bed, which looks like it could be running depending on the time of year.

2.4 Right before the trail takes a sharp jog north (right), reach an overlook with a view of a waterfall below.

3.1 Break above tree line.

3.4 Arrive at a shelf overlooking Lower Ice Lakes Basin, where there are a series of camping spots west (left) of the trail.

3.8 Continue west and cross a sizeable creek. Follow the loose, rocky trail as it curves south and climbs steeply toward the upper basin.

4.1 Pass another waterfall and follow the trail as it turns hard toward the north (right) and continues climbing.

4.6 Reach Upper Ice Lake (12,270 feet).

8.2 Arrive back at the trailhead.

Options: For a longer jaunt, continue another 0.7 mile on the trail past Upper Ice Lake to reach Island Lake, which is only 130 feet higher. Alternatively, turn this into a 2-day backpacking adventure by spending a night in the lower basin.

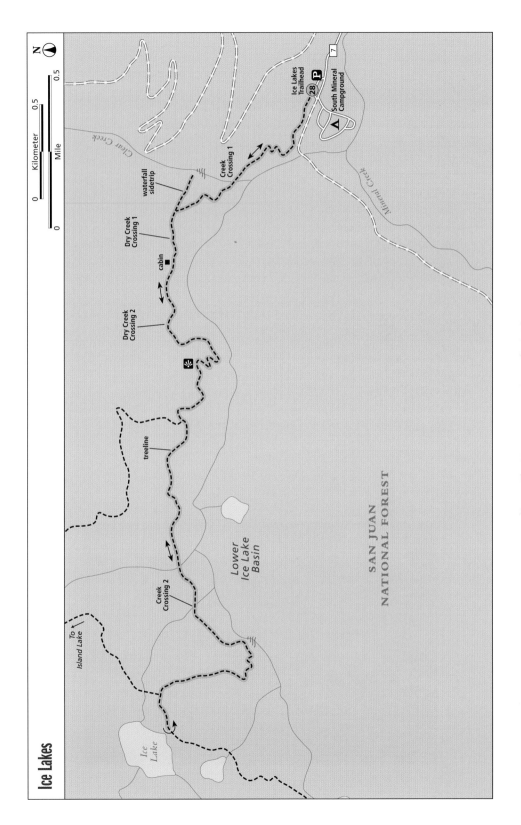

Hike Information

Local Information

Durango Area Tourism Office and Visitor Center: Durango; (970) 247-3500; durango.org

Silverton Area Chamber of Commerce: Silverton; (800) 752-4494 or (970) 387-5654; silvertoncolorado.com

Local Events/Attractions

Christ of the Miners Shrine: Silverton; (800) 752-4494 or (970) 387-5654

Durango &Silverton Narrow Gauge Railroad: Durango; (877) 872-4607 or (970) 247-2733; durangotrain.com

Mayflower Gold Mill Tour: Silverton; (970) 387-0294 (summer); http://www .sanjuancountyhistoricalsociety.org/mayflower-mill.html

Old Hundred Gold Mine Tour: Silverton; (800) 872-3009 or (970) 387-5444; minetour.com

Organizations

San Juan County Historical Society: Silverton; (970) 387-5838; sanjuancountyhistoricalsociety.org

San Juan Mountains Association: Durango; (970) 385-1210; sjma.org

Trails 2000: Durango; (970) 259-4682; trails2000.org—a 501(c)(3) organization that builds and maintains trails; educates trail users; and encourages connectivity on road, path, and trail.

Other Resources

Poe, Anne and Mike. 2013. *Southwest Colorado High Country Day Hikes: Ouray, Silverton, & Lake City.* Las Vegas, NV: Take a Hike Guidebooks.

Towering Jacob's ladder

29 Pass Creek Trail (#500)

Hiking enthusiasts of all levels will love this moderately challenging trail that climbs toward Engineer Mountain, a distinct and captivating peak dominating the San Juan skyline for miles along Hwy. 550. Gain relatively easy access to some of Colorado's most breathtaking scenery via a high-altitude route that passes through lush forest, meanders by ponds, and boasts an incredible and varied wildflower display. Unmatched vistas from meadows brimming with spectacular color reward hikers who push on to the end.

Start: From the Pass Creek Trailhead (10,600 feet)
Distance: 5.7 miles out and back
Hiking time: 3–5 hours
Difficulty: Moderate due to length, smooth terrain, and moderate elevation gain. *Note:* The entire hike is above 10,500 feet, which could make it more challenging.
Trail surface: Forested, dirt trail
Best season: June to October
Peak bloom: late July to mid-August
Flowers commonly found: alpine avens, Colorado columbine, mountain bluebells, yellow monkey-flower, heartleaf bittercress, Parry primrose, elephant heads, marsh marigold, subalpine Jacob's ladder, king's crown, corn lily, scarlet, western yellow, northern, and rosy paintbrush, Geyer's onion, American bistort, subalpine valerian, golden draba, aspen sunflower, orange sneezeweed, tall larkspur, Fremont geranium, northern goldenrod, parrot's beak lousewort, bracted lousewort, thick-bract senecio, queen's crown, Parry primrose, graceful buttercup, Colorado columbine, Gray's angelica, monkshood, triangularleaf senecio, wild rose, loveroot, glacial daisy, shrubby cinquefoil, Richardson's geranium, cowbane, subalpine arnica, mountain dandelion, mountain harebell, heartleaf arnica, death camas, yellow monkeyflower, alpine avens, cow parsnip, beautiful cinquefoil, triangularleaf senecio, monument plant, orange sneezeweed, Coulter's daisy, corn lily, western chainpod, golden aster, beautiful daisy, Whipple's penstemon, mountain parsley, black-tip senecio, yarrow, globeflower
Other trail users: Equestrians, mountain bikers
Canine compatibility: Dogs permitted
Land status: National forest
Nearest town: Silverton
Fees and permits: No fees or permits required
Schedule: Open all year, but often obstructed by snow from fall to early summer
Maps: USGS Engineer Mountain, CO; Trails Illustrated 141 Telluride, Silverton, Ouray, Lake City; Latitude 40 Durango Trails
Trail contacts: San Juan National Forest, Columbine Ranger District, 367 South Pearl St., PO Box 439, Bayfield, 81122; (970) 884-2512; www.fs.usda.gov/sanjuan

Finding the trailhead: From Silverton, travel south for 13.5 miles on Hwy. 550. After mile marker 57 and just before Coal Bank Pass, turn west (right) onto a spur road. Follow it for 500 feet to reach trailhead parking. **GPS: N37 41.954'/W107 46.744'**

The Hike

Head across a steep, grassy slope to find yourself enveloped in flowers taller than most of us. Cow parsnip, tall larkspur, mountain bluebells, beautiful cinquefoil, triangular-leaf senecio, Richardson's geranium, and aspen sunflower sway in the wind like trees.

Traverse this impressive first meadow, and lose yourself in towering specimens of monument plant, loveroot, orange sneezeweed, Coulter's daisy, and corn lily. Literally, everywhere you look, a different flower stares back. Brilliant clusters of the shrubby, intensely pink-purple western chainpod enliven the trail. Still only minutes from the trailhead, more blooms including scarlet paintbrush, golden aster, beautiful daisy, Whipple's penstemon, mountain parsley, black-tip senecio, yarrow, Geyer's onion, and parrot's beak lousewort greet you with a flurry of color.

The route ascends gently into the forest where spruce and fir trees offer welcome shade on a summer day. Monkshood and globeflower decorate a small intermittent pond. Scarlet and northern paintbrush, mountain dandelion, mountain harebell, heartleaf arnica, death camas, and parrot's beak dapple the forest floor. Absorb the beauty of periodic meadows overflowing with corn lily, shrubby cinquefoil, Richardson's geranium, cowbane, Gray's angelica, tall larkspur, mountain bluebells, bracted lousewort, scarlet and western yellow paintbrush, subalpine arnica, and Colorado columbine.

Switchbacks turn the trail westward through the forest where you discover wild rose, loveroot, glacial daisy, northern goldenrod, and more vibrant clusters of western chainpod. Continue weaving in and out of the forest where open areas teem with a rainbow of king's crown, monkshood, triangularleaf senecio, tall larkspur, and scarlet and rosy paintbrush. When the route mellows again, a wet area on the right supports graceful buttercup, mountain bluebells, heartleaf bittercress, subalpine Jacob's ladder, Colorado columbine, yellow monkeyflower, and Gray's angelica. Continue climbing gently through a healthy forest, which is home to lovely stands of mountain bluebells, king's crown, and Parry primrose. Arnicas, geraniums, paintbrush, and subalpine Jacob's ladder color the forest in brilliance. Leveling, the trail continues west through magnificent old growth to skirt the north shore of a small pond supporting elephant heads, queen's crown, and Parry primrose. Across the way, a meadow bursts with tall larkspur, aspen sunflower, parrot's beak, bracted lousewort, huge specimens of corn lily, and thick-bract senecio.

Flower-filled meadows guide the way to Engineer Mountain

The trail steepens slightly, meandering from forest to meadow and back again. Continue straight passing open areas full of aspen sunflower, orange sneezeweed, tall larkspur, Fremont geranium, and northern goldenrod. Look closely for sub-alpine valerian and golden draba, a tiny yellow bloom with small, cross-shaped flowers. As you ascend more gradually now, alpine avens, rosy paintbrush, marsh marigold, Geyer's onion, and American bistort dominate moist meadows. Subalpine

Subalpine Jacob's ladder

Jacob's ladder, king's crown, and corn lily appear before you pass through a stand of thick willows. The trail gets lusher with each step while heartleaf bittercress, Parry primrose, elephant heads, and marsh marigold foreshadow a hidden seep. Cross this tranquil trickle where attentive flower hunters can find yellow monkeyflower.

Break free from the trees to glimpse the spiny, rugged Engineer Mountain tower-ing ahead. Robust meadows burst with impressive displays of paintbrush in a rainbow of pinks, oranges, yellows, and reds while alpine avens, Colorado columbines, and mountain bluebells shimmer in the breeze.

Continue west through a field of vibrant magenta and gold to reach the Engi-neer Mountain Trail (#508) and Pass Trail junction. Walking toward the maroon crags of Engineer Mountain, reach a giant rock slab that marks the beginning of a steeper climb to the slender, exposed summit. At the base of this jagged peak, Mother Nature rewards you with brilliant panoramic views, making this a prime picnic locale. Retrace your route when you've absorbed all the beauty you can handle.

Miles and Directions

0.0 Start from the Pass Creek Trailhead. Pick up the gentle dirt path heading north.

1.0 Curve upward around a few switchbacks as the trail turns westward. When the route mellows again, a wet area on the right shelters a diverse array of flowers.

1.3 Leveling, the trail skirts the north shore of a small pond.

2.5 Break from tree line to get your first clear glimpse of Engineer Mountain.

2.8 Arrive at the Engineer Mountain Trail (#508) and Pass Trail intersection.

2.9 Reach a rocky slab marking your turnaround (11,800 feet).

5.8 Arrive back at the trailhead.

Options: Spirited hikers can continue on the strenuous Engineer Mountain Trail to reach the summit (12,968 feet). Take care on the progressively rockier, steep trail and especially while scrambling along the narrow, exposed summit ridge. Or, even if you are short on time or energy, it's worth just walking the first 10 minutes of this trail because the diversity of colors and species you see in the beginning is unmatched.

Pass Creek Trail

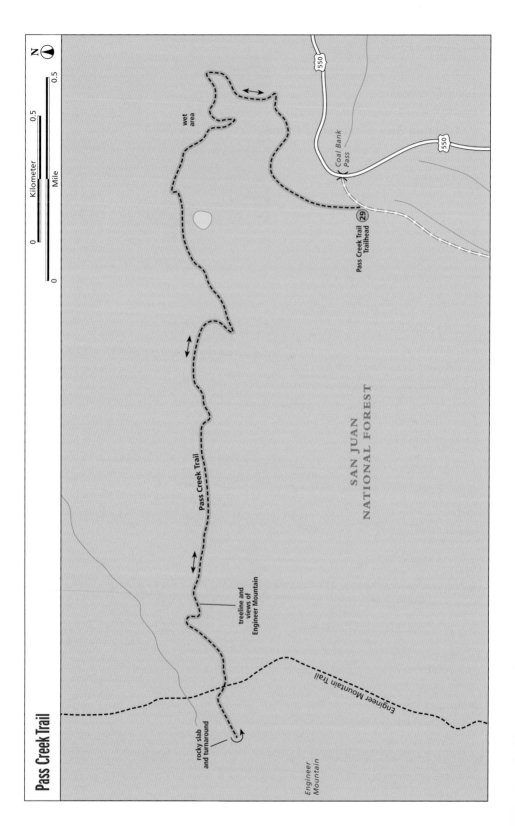

Hike Information

Local Information

Durango Area Tourism Office and Visitor Center: Durango; (970) 247-3500; durango.org

Silverton Area Chamber of Commerce: Silverton; (800) 752-4494 or (970) 387-5654; silvertoncolorado.com

Local Events/Attractions

Christ of the Miners Shrine: Silverton; (800) 752-4494 or (970) 387-5654

Durango & Silverton Narrow Gauge Railroad: Durango; (877) 872-4607 or (970) 247-2733; durangotrain.com

Mayflower Gold Mill Tour: Silverton; (970) 387-0294 (summer); http://www.sanjuancountyhistoricalsociety.org/mayflower-mill.html

Old Hundred Gold Mine Tour: Silverton; (800) 872-3009 or (970) 387-5444; minetour.com

Organizations

San Juan County Historical Society: Silverton; (970) 387-5838; sanjuancountyhistoricalsociety.org

San Juan Mountains Association: Durango; (970) 385-1210; sjma.org

Trails 2000: Durango; (970) 259-4682; trails2000.org—a 501(c)(3) organization that builds and maintains trails; educates trail users; and encourages connectivity on road, path, and trail.

Other Resources

Poe, Anne and Mike. 2013. *Southwest Colorado High Country Day Hikes: Ouray, Silverton, & Lake City.* Las Vegas, NV: Take a Hike Guidebooks.

A LESSON IN GEOLOGY

As you hike toward Engineer Mountain, its distinctive double-crested summit and steep, gray columnar cliffs likely pique your interest causing you to wonder, "How did this and many other mountains like it form?" Understanding this requires a trip back to the Pleistocene era, which spanned 2.6 million to 11,700 years ago, when the Animas Valley from Silverton to Durango underwent repeated glaciations.

Imagine glaciers with ice measuring 2,500 to 3,000 feet thick plowing south through the valley. Engineer Mountain towered above the San Juan Ice Field, so when the glacier arrived, it encircled Engineer, turning it into a nunatak, or a rock island surrounded by a sea of ice. As the glacier moved, it smashed into the part sticking out; this force, movement, and friction shaped the sides and carved the cliffs to create something similar to the prominent double cone that we see now.

Of course, at this time, the peak was nameless. This changed in 1873 when under the leadership of Lieutenant E. H. Ruffner, the Army Corps of Engineers began surveying the area. Legend has it that H. G. Prout, a civilian topographic assistant to Ruffner, earned the first-recorded summit of the 12,968-foot mountain. Though he originally wanted to name it after Ruffner, they ultimately chose a name that honored those working to map the area, instead of one man.

HONORABLE MENTIONS

Southwest

Here are a couple great hikes in the Southwest region that didn't make the A-list this time around but deserve recognition.

C. Meander and Lower Meander Trails

Primarily thought of as mountain bike routes, few explore the trails crisscrossing Crested Butte Mountain's Evolution Bike Park on foot. This is a shame since unmatched flower displays line these narrow, multiuse paths, especially those found on the backside like Lower Meander and Meander, which wind through aspen groves and conifer stands and offer breathtaking vistas of the East River Valley. Options abound for extending this flower-filled journey since you can reach Gothic Road, the Snodgrass Trailhead, and countless other trails, including favorites like Painter Boy and Prospector, which connect from the base of the mountain. From Crested Butte, travel north for 0.3 mile on Sixth Street. Continue north on Gothic Road for 2.2 miles. Turn right onto Snowmass Road to reach the resort base. Learn more from Crested Butte Mountain Resort at (877) 547-5143 or visit: http://bike.skicb.com/.

D. Petroglyph Point Loop

This 2.4-mile round-trip adventure through Mesa Verde National Park, world renowned for its distinctive cliff dwellings, begins from the Spruce Tree House Trail and continues below the edge of the plateau to a petroglyph panel. Rough at times, this path climbs to a mesa top, squeezes through gigantic rocks and skinny cracks, descends steep steps, and returns along the canyon rim. Along the way, enjoy views of Spruce and Navajo Canyons and a rainbow of wildflower blooms characteristic of the transition zone between mountains and desert. From Cortez, head east for 13 miles on Hwy. 160. Turn south (right) at the signed park turnoff. Stop at the Mesa Verde Headquarters to pay a fee and park at the trailhead, which is near the Chapin Mesa Archeological Museum. Registration at the trailhead or museum is required to hike this trail. Information: Call Mesa Verde National Park at (970) 529-4465 or visit: ww.nps.gov/meve.

South Central

D iversity. This defines Colorado's South Central region, which encompasses a plethora of fourteeners, the raging Rio Grande River, the expansive and flat 125-mile San Luis Valley, and Sand Dunes National Park, among other natural treasures. In the east, Colorado Springs, the state's second largest city, provides access to towering Pikes Peak (14,110 feet) and the Royal Gorge where the continent's highest suspension bridge spans a huge chasm. Further west and north sits Leadville, a mining town known for holding grueling running and biking endurance races made even tougher due to its position as the highest incorporated city in the United States (10,190 feet). From its nearby headwaters, the Arkansas River snakes south through Brown's Canyon, a newly named National Monument, and past the Collegiate Peaks, a series of imposing 14,000-foot summits. Buena Vista and Salida, quaint towns along the river, provide access to the Collegiates and offer a host of adventure opportunities including world-class rafting, mountain biking, and hiking. A long section of the Colorado Trail winds through the region, largely following the Continental Divide, whose spiny backbone dominates the horizon. Further south in the San Luis Valley, one of the highest alpine valleys in the world, lies Crestone, the spiritual center of the state. Here, the jagged crest of the Sangre de Cristo Mountains creates a breathtaking scene as snow-capped peaks tower over expansive ranchlands. Nearby, Great Sand Dunes National Park and Preserve encompasses a 30-square-mile area bursting with dramatic and undulating 700-foot-high dunes, the tallest in North America. This region, which extends all the way to New Mexico, has a rich history and deep cultural roots made even more interesting by the fact that Native American tribes, Spanish explorers, settlers, and miners all searched the area for riches. The Alamosa, Monte Vista, and Baca National Wildlife Refuges, San Luis Lakes State Park, and Blanca Wetlands provide welcome resting spots for migrating waterfowl and shorebirds.

30 Continental Divide Trail North

Enjoy an exceptional walk along the spine of the Rocky Mountains without having to exert a lot of effort. The famed Continental Divide Trail (CDT) heads north from the Lobo Overlook to meander through high-altitude forest and traverse rocky slopes with minimal climbing. Because there is no end goal or destination, you choose how far you walk, which means ample time to enjoy the vibrant colors at your feet. This exploration of subalpine and alpine environments boasts vistas that reach to New Mexico, meadows bursting with showy wildflowers and countless opportunities for wildlife encounters.

Start: From the trailhead sign near radio tower (11,700 feet)

Distance: 5.2 miles out and back

Hiking time: 2–4 hours

Difficulty: Moderate due to gradual, smooth terrain and moderate elevation gain. *Note:* The entire hike is above 11,000 feet, which could make it more challenging.

Trail surface: Dirt two-track, forested and dirt trail

Best season: mid-June to late September

Peak bloom: early to end of July

Flowers commonly found: Geyer's onion, fringed gentian, American bistort, king's crown, mountain bluebells, old man of the mountains, wild candytuft, loveroot, northern, scarlet, rosy and western yellow paintbrush, Whipple's penstemon, mountain parsley, pygmy bitter-root, queen's crown, cowbane, rosy pussytoes, beautiful cinquefoil, mountain dandelion, alpine sandwort, aspen sunflower, subalpine Jacob's ladder, yarrow, wild strawberry, valerian, black-tip senecio, western wallflower, Fremont geranium, tall larkspur, corn lily, mountain currant, Parry's lousewort, towering Jacob's ladder, moss campion, cushion phlox, slender-tubed phlox, Case's fitweed, plantainleaf buttercup, Hall's penstemon, mountain parsley, mountain harebells, subalpine buttercup, triangularleaf senecio, marsh marigold, black-headed daisy, globeflower, elephant heads, Gray's angelica

Other trail users: Equestrians, mountain bikers (until you enter Wilderness)

Canine compatibility: Leashed dogs permitted; dogs under verbal control permitted

Land status: National Forest, Wilderness

Nearest town: South Fork

Fees and permits: No fees or permits required

Schedule: Open all year, but often obstructed by snow from fall to summer

Maps: USGS Wolf Creek Pass, CO; Trails Illustrated 140 Weimnuche Wilderness; Latitude 40 Southwest Colorado Trails

Trail contacts: Rio Grande National Forest, Divide Ranger District, 13308 West Hwy. 160, Creede, 81132; (719) 658-2556; www.fs.usda.gov/riogrande

Special considerations: The trail is mostly downhill on the way out, and though gradual, you'll have to climb a couple hundred feet back to the trailhead. Keep this in mind as you determine how far to venture.

Finding the trailhead: From South Fork, follow US 160 southwest out of town toward Wolf Creek Pass. After 18.5 miles, just below Wolf Creek Pass, look for a blue sign indicating a scenic overlook and the Continental Divide. Turn north (right) here onto CR 402. Follow this gravel road for almost 3 miles as it winds upward to reach a fork. Head right at the fork and park on the north side of the radio tower. A left at the fork brings you to the Lobo Overlook, which we suggest you visit after your hike. **GPS: N37 29.577′ / W106 48.076′**

The Hike

Head west on the Lobo Trail (#878) through an open area where Geyer's onion, western yellow paintbrush, fringed gentian, American bistort, kings crown, and mountain bluebells greet you right away. Enjoy the stunning views as you meander along the well-worn dirt two-track that enters a sparsely forested section punctuated by a wealth of trees killed by bark beetles and fire.

Follow the road as it slopes downhill passing through meadows bursting with old man of the mountain, wild candytuft, loveroot, northern paintbrush, and Whipple's penstemon.

At the first junction, continue northwest (straight) on the CDT North to follow a ridge where mats of tiny white alpine sandwort bloom in the rocky soil. Break out into a moist meadow where you find mountain parsley, pygmy bitterroot, queen's crown, American bistort, cowbane, rosy pussytoes, beautiful cinquefoil, and mountain dandelion.

Travel deeper into the forest to find aspen sunflower, subalpine Jacob's ladder, yarrow, wild strawberry, valerian, scarlet paintbrush, loveroot, and Whipple's penstemon thriving amid taller trees. Continue cruising downhill to traverse a steep slope offering vistas of Treasure Mountain and teeming with black-tip senecio, Whipple's penstemon, western wallflower, mountain bluebells, and scarlet paintbrush. Incredible exhibitions of Fremont geranium, tall larkspur, mountain bluebells, loveroot, beautiful cinquefoil, and corn lily enliven the senses as you continue gradually descending. Huge bushes of mountain currant, with a plethora of dainty, hairy, pinkish-orange flared bells that turn to bright red berries, thrive. The sinuous trail is loose and rocky in

Paintbrush and loverroot line the trail while crags tower overhead

Old man of the mountain

spots, but look up every often to absorb the surrounding peaks and the slopes bursting with flowers.

When you intersect an unnamed trail, stay on the main trail as it curves southwest to continue traversing this magical slope, which passes through verdant meadows full of white, purple, blue, and yellow blooms. The forest feels alive here as gray jays flitter by busily, chipmunks scurry in the underbrush, and elk browse on the hillsides. The creamy-white-beaked flowers of Parry's lousewort complement the vibrant purple, towering Jacob's ladder as the trail opens up offering views of rock outcrops above. Here, find valerian, mats of moss campion, cushion phlox, and clusters of slender-tubed phlox. Black-tip senecio, tall larkspur, Fremont geranium, mountain currant, and loveroot create dazzling displays as the trail meanders through an exposed rock garden.

Weaving in and out of the trees, the path curves sharply away from the highway to reach a moist meadow or spring that explodes with huge flowering corn lily and towering clusters of Case's fitweed, whose brilliant pink and white spurred blooms add a vibrant splash of color amid countless shades of green. Interspersed within are Fremont geranium, plantainleaf buttercup, Hall's penstemon, and rosy and northern paintbrush.

Leaving this lush area, follow the trail west into a meadow with an impressive showing of northern paintbrush, valerian, mountain parsley, and beautiful cinquefoil. Soon you reach the Weimnuche Wilderness Boundary. Meander downhill through meadows and trees dappled with mountain harebells, bluebells, American bistort, subalpine buttercup, marsh marigold, subalpine Jacob's ladder, Geyer's onion, triangularleaf senecio, and blackheaded daisy. Break free from the trees to enter a series of meadows full of rosy and scarlet paintbrush, corn lily, American bistort, mountain parsley, globeflower, and shocking pink elephant heads.

Reach another magical spring bursting full of elephant heads. This magical spot is worth a stop and some photos before following the trail back into the forest where bluebells, arnica, Gray's angelica, and cow parsnip adorn the trail. Continue north to

Continental Divide Trail North

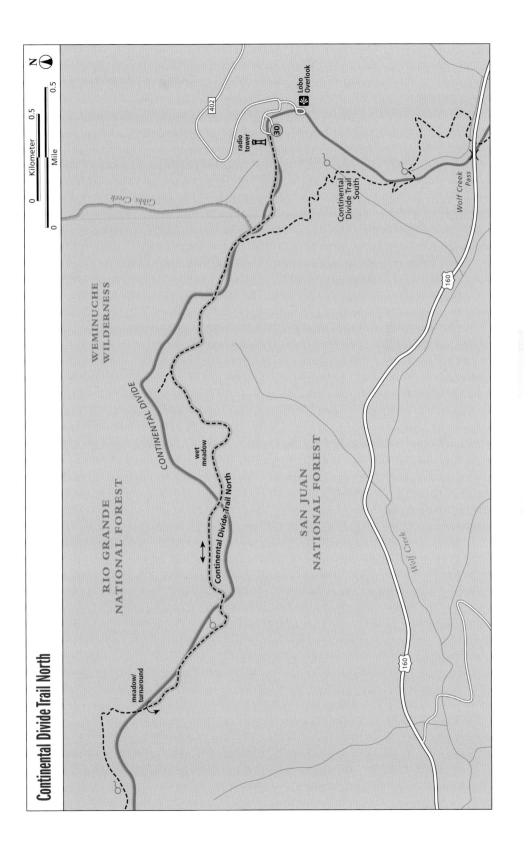

reach a meadow full of bistort, buttercups, and tiny blue violet. Spend time soaking in the view and listening for working woodpeckers before retracing your steps.

Miles and Directions

0.0   Start from the trailhead sign west of the microwave tower.

0.5   Turning north, reach a signed junction with the CDT (813). Continue northwest (straight) on CDT North.

1.0   Encounter a junction with an unnamed trail. Continue left (west) to stay on the main trail.

1.5   Reach a moist meadow.

1.7   Arrive at the signed Weminuche Wilderness Boundary.

2.2   Reach tree line and continue to reach a spring.

2.6   Continue north until you reach a vast open meadow—our turnaround point.

5.2   Arrive back at the trailhead.

Options: Shorten or lengthen this hike by turning around at any point. For a brief side trip, from the trailhead, wander or drive over to the Lobo Overlook for a picnic in a stunning setting with expansive vistas of the San Juan Mountains and Pagosa Springs to the west. Dine amid an incredibly dense array of flowers including old man of the mountain, cutleaf daisy, Hall's penstemon, Geyer's onion, alpine clover, and alpine chiming bells.

Hike Information

Local Information

South Fork Visitor Center: South Fork; (800) 571-0881 or (719) 873-5512; southfork.org

Pagosa Springs Visitor Center: Pagosa Springs; (800) 252-2204; pagosasprings.com

Local Events/Attractions

Logger Days Festival: South Fork; (800) 571-0881 or (719) 873-5512

Silver Thread Scenic Byway: Creede; (800) 571-0881 or (719) 873-5512; http://www.southfork.org/silver-thread-scenic-byway

Wildflower & Mushroom Forays: South Fork; (800) 571-0881 or (719) 873-5512

Wolf Creek Ski Area: Pagosa Springs; (970) 264-5639; wolfcreekski.com

Hot Springs: Pagosa Springs boasts three unique hot springs facilities that can soothe muscles sore from days of hiking and tracking down wildflowers.

Organizations

Continental Divide Trail Coalition: 710 10th St., Ste. 200, Golden ; (303) 996-2759; continentaldividetrail.org

Continental Divide Trail Society: Baltimore, MD; (410) 235-9610; cdtsociety.org

Silverthread Outdoor Recreation Club: South Fork; (719) 203-7117; silverthreaders.org This diverse group of locals, part-timers, and visitors exists to preserve multiuse trails. They organize weekly hikes and many other activities. Ask for a copy of their recreation map from the Visitor Center (above).

HIKING THE DIVIDE

The Continental Divide National Scenic Trail (CDT), a footpath that spans 3,100 miles between Mexico and Canada, traverses five states and offers access to many of the most wild, remote, and scenic spots left in the states and, possibly, the planet. This hike—and others like the Green Mountain Trail (part of the Green Mountain-Onahu Loop hike)—follows short portions of the highest, most grueling, and most remote of the National Scenic Trails. But, what does it mean when we say the trail works its way along the spine of the Rockies, also known as the Continental Divide, through Montana, Idaho, Wyoming, Colorado, and New Mexico? Well, a continental divide is a naturally occurring boundary or ridge separating a continent's river systems. Generally, precipitation that falls on one side of the divide flows to one basin and precipitation that falls on the other side flows to another basin. In the United States, the Western Continental Divide is an imaginary line sitting atop a continuous ridge of mountain summits that divide the continent into two main drainage areas: West of the Divide, water flows into the Pacific Ocean, and east of the Divide, it heads to the Mississippi River drainage and Atlantic Ocean. The Continental Divide Coalition estimates that about 150 people set out to through-hike the entire length of the route each year (and a handful set out to mountain bike most of it via the Tour Divide, a self-supported bike race), while many more set out to hike or bike large chunks each summer. Though you are only hiking a small part today, it's still an interesting glimpse of one of the greatest and most significant long-distance trails in the world. If you're feeling really motivated, continue north all the way to Canada!

31 Big Meadows Loop

Enjoy a short, peaceful meander through several habitats on a beautiful trail that pops in and out of the delightful forests, meadows, and marshes as it circumnavigates Big Meadows Reservoir. Teeming with waterfowl, birds, chipmunks, and a wide range of flower species, this largely flat hike provides a chance to enjoy the serenity of nature. Though the reservoir is popular with anglers, you'll still find solitude amid the excellent mountain views and plentiful blooms prevalent along this mellow trail.

Start: From Big Meadows Reservoir (9,300 feet)

Distance: 2.8-mile loop

Hiking time: 1–3 hours

Difficulty: Easy due to minimal elevation gain and smooth terrain

Trail surface: Dirt trail

Best season: June to September

Peak bloom: late June to mid-July

Flowers commonly found: shrubby and beautiful cinquefoil, mountain parsley, northern goldenrod, pearly everlasting, Parry's harebell, scarlet and northern paintbrush, nodding onion, yarrow, beautiful daisy, cow parsnip, wild rose, subalpine arnica, mountain bluebells, Fremont geranium, twinberry, black-tip senecio, monkshood, northern green bog orchid, littleflower penstemon, prairie smoke, mountain dandelion, alpine bistort, elephant heads, monkshood, fringed gentian, red columbine, spotted coralroot orchid, Rocky Mountain pussytoes, rattlesnake plantain orchid, Fendler's meadow rue, scarlet gilia, twisted

stalk, fireweed, heartleaf bittercress, baneberry, corn lily, monument plant, twinflower, death camas, orange sneezeweed, wild strawberry, queen's crown, valerian, yellow monkeyflower, loveroot, wild raspberry, Colorado columbine, American vetch, marsh marigold

Other trail users: Equestrians, anglers, mountain bikers

Canine compatibility: Dogs permitted

Land status: National Forest

Nearest town: South Fork

Fees and permits: No fees or permits required. Must have a fishing license for streams and lakes.

Schedule: Open all year, but often obstructed by snow from fall to late spring.

Maps: USGS Mount Hope; Trails Illustrated 140 Weimnuche Wilderness

Trail contacts: Rio Grande National Forest, Divide Ranger District, 13308 West Hwy. 160, Del Norte, 81132; (719) 657-3321; www.fs.usda.gov/riogrande

Finding the trailhead: From South Fork, travel west for 11 miles on Hwy. 160. Turn west (right) onto FR 410 (also known as Big Meadows Road) and continue straight for 1.4 miles to a "Y" intersection with FR 430. Bear left to stay on FR 410 for 0.3 mile. Take the right fork below the reservoir to the Boat Ramp. Park here. **GPS: N37 32.503'/W106 48.162'**

The Hike

In just the first few feet, Rocky Mountain penstemon, beautiful cinquefoil, yarrow, mountain parsley, fireweed, and northern goldenrod greet your arrival. Brilliant displays of scarlet gilia line the open slopes below. Enter spruce forest where wild roses, northern bedstraw, and Fremont geranium blossom.

Dropping toward the reservoir, continue past vibrant yellow blooms of shrubby cinquefoil, mountain parsley, and northern goldenrod and pinkish-white pearly everlastings and pussytoes. The very delicate but vibrant Parry's harebell makes a strong showing amid grassy fields dappled with northern paintbrush, nodding onion, yarrow, and clusters of beautiful daisy.

The trail oscillates, bringing you to the water's edge and then darting back into the shady, cool spruce forest. A footbridge provides a perch above the stream where you can revel in the water's soothing sound. From here, enjoy a bird's-eye view of huge cow parsnip, wild rose, subalpine arnica, mountain bluebells, Fremont geranium, twinberry, black-tipped senecio, and monkshood. Continue south, enjoying the shady spots that punctuate this easy, flat walk. Northern green bog orchid joins with northern paintbrush, littleflower penstemon, prairie smoke, yarrow, mountain dandelion, and shrubby cinquefoil to create a colorful display.

Heading out into an open meadow that showcases wildlife utilizing the reservoir, the character of the hike changes dramatically. Lines of baby ducks cruise along the water behind their dutiful parents. Geese take flight overhead. Distant peaks rise as Parry's harebell, beautiful cinquefoil, alpine bistort, and yarrow thrive in this moist meadow.

Gentle pink elephant heads, monkshood, and fringed gentian poke upward from this flat, marshy area. Shrubby cinquefoil bushes add a tantalizing golden glow to the sun-kissed meadow.

When the trail shoots back into the forest, look closely to find red columbine sprouting from rocky soil. Those with an exceptionally keen eye will be able to spot two tiny orchids amid the underbrush: the spotted coralroot orchid and rattlesnake plaintain orchid. Fendler's meadow rue, Fremont geranium, scarlet gilia, twinberry, and an exotic known as shepherd's purse grow amid the pines.

At the Archuleta Trail junction, head east (left) toward the South Fork of the Rio Grande, whose swiftly flowing waters speak from a distance. Relish in the colorful trailside display of scarlet gilia, mountain parsley, twisted stalk, and fireweed as the trail parallels the shady creek providing a welcome respite on a hot summer day.

Cross the South Fork on a footbridge and note the plethora of heartleaf bittercress, twinberry, and baneberry nearby. Enter an open field full of corn lily, monument plant, and Rocky Mountain pussytoes. Another tiny bridge brings northern paintbrush, cow parsnip, monkshood, and arnica. Back in the woods, notice dainty single delight, twinflower, and death camas hiding in the underbrush.

Popping out to curve along the meadow's edge, enjoy views of the reservoir complemented by brilliant orange sneezeweed and creeping wild strawberry. Down

Big Meadows Reservoir

by the brook, look for elephant heads, queen's crown, mountain dandelion, loveroot, valerian, and a little clan of yellow monkeyflower. The trail skirts the water's edge and a series of beaver dams before climbing into the forest where we have the best of both worlds; from up here we can see water-loving flowers below like yellow monkeyflower while walking amid arnica, geranium, and wild raspberry bushes.

Pearly everlasting

A talus slope gives life to clumps of Colorado columbine, tall scarlet paintbrush, and wild rose. The last meadow delivers an array of Parry's harebells, yarrow, shrubby cinquefoil, northern paintbrush, prairie smoke, American vetch, and wild rose.

Two tiny bridges deliver you to an impressive display of monkshood, marsh marigold, and prairie smoke. Head back to the parking lot by contouring around the water to cross the dam where a waterfall rages.

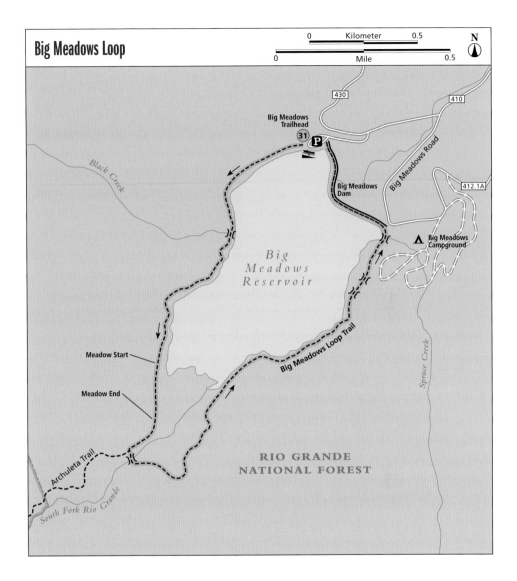

Miles and Directions

0.0 Start at Big Meadows Reservoir. Follow the trail straight past the restrooms as it traverses a gradient above the water.

0.5 Cross Black Creek on a wooden footbridge. Continue straight along the trailthrough forest.

0.8 The trail travels out into a wide-open meadow.

1.1 The meadow ends, and the trail travels back into the forest.

1.2 At a junction with the Archuleta Trail, follow the sign pointing you east (left) toward the South Fork of the Rio Grande.

1.3 Cross the South Fork of the Rio Grande on a footbridge.

2.2 Cross a small stream on a tiny wooden bridge.

2.3 Cross another footbridge and stay straight on the main trail. A trail to the campground comes in from the east (right).

2.7 Reach Big Meadows Dam.

2.8 Arrive back at the parking lot.

Options: For a longer, more adventurous hike, continue straight at the junction with the Archuleta Trail, which travels approximately 7 miles along Archuleta Creek and the South Fork of the Rio Grande River and joins the Continental Divide Trail at Archuleta Lake.

Hike Information

Local Information

South Fork Visitor Center: South Fork; (800) 571-0881 or (719) 873-5512; southfork.org

   Pagosa Springs Visitor Center: Pagosa Springs; (800) 252-2204; pagosasprings.com

Local Events / Attractions

Logger Days Festival: South Fork; (800) 571-0881 or (719) 873-5512

   Silver Thread Scenic Byway: Creede; (800) 571-0881 or (719) 873-5512; http://www.southfork.org/silver-thread-scenic-byway

   Wildflower & Mushroom Forays: South Fork; (800) 571-0881 or (719) 873-5512

   Hot Springs: Pagosa Springs boasts three unique hot springs facilities that can soothe muscles sore from days of hiking and tracking down wildflowers.

Organizations

Silverthread Outdoor Recreation Club: South Fork; (719) 203-7117; silverthreaders. org. This diverse group of locals, part-timers, and visitors exists to preserve multiple uses of trails. They organize weekly hikes and many other activities. Ask for a copy of their recreation map from the Visitor Center (above).

32 Dry Lakes

An imposing jagged crest of stone—the Sangre de Cristo Mountains—unfolds in front of your eyes, and this is just on the drive to the trailhead. Imagine what happens when you leave the car behind! Take your time on this stout climb following a creek up a narrow, forested valley so you can enjoy every moment and surprise that awaits. Pass a waterfall, wander by a moraine, and walk through a profusion of wildflowers to reach a series of shallow alpine lakes nestled in a superb glacially carved amphitheater encased by steep rock walls.

Start: From the Horn Creek Trailhead (9,220 feet)

Distance: 9.5 miles out and back

Hiking time: 4–6 hours

Difficulty: Strenuous due to distance, altitude, and elevation gain

Trail surface: Forested, dirt trail

Best season: June to September

Peak bloom: early to late July

Flowers commonly found: northern bedstraw, heartleaf arnica, Parry clover, yarrow, star Solomonplume, Rocky Mountain pussytoes, orange sneezeweed, blanketflower, mountain harebell, wild strawberry, wild rose, red elderberry, cow parsnip, pinedrops, Fremont geranium, Wyoming paintbrush, lambstongue groundsel, fireweed, mountain bluebells, nodding onion, monkshood, triangularleaf senecio, tall larkspur, shrubby cinquefoil, Rocky Mountain penstemon, elephant heads, death camas, bog pyrola, shooting star, American bistort, beautiful cinquefoil, corn lily, mountain dandelion, aspen sunflower, Colorado columbine, alpine bistort, dwarf golden aster, Whipple's penstemon, mouse-ear chickweed, fringed gentian, mountain harebells, Parry's lousewort, queen's crown, northern and rosy paintbrush, yellow stonecrop, edible valerian, bracted lousewort, mountain thistle

Other trail users: Equestrians

Canine compatibility: Leashed dogs permitted

Land status: National Forest, Wilderness

Nearest town: Westcliffe

Fees and permits: No fees or permits required

Schedule: Open all year, but often obstructed by snow from winter to summer.

Maps: USGS Horn Peak, CO; Trails Illustrated 138 Sangre de Cristo Mountains

Trail contacts: San Isabel National Forest, San Carlos Ranger District, 3028 East Main St., Canon City 81212; (719) 269-8500; www.fs.usda.gov/psicc

Finding the trailhead: Drive south from Westcliffe on Hwy. 69 for 3.4 miles. Turn west (right) on CR 140 (Schoolfield Lane) and follow it for 0.9 mile. Turn south (left) onto CR 129 (Colfax Road) and continue for 2.0 miles. Turn west (right) onto CR 130 (Horn Creek Road) and follow it for 2.2 miles. Veer left and follow signs for Horn Creek Ranch. When you enter the ranch, stay right, and follow CR 130 for another 0.2 mile to the Horn Creek Trailhead. **GPS: N38 03.276'/W105 32.121'**

The Hike

From the Horn Creek Trailhead, follow the gradual and open trail west. The route brings you near Dry Creek for a moment, but then darts south away from the water to a signed junction with the Rainbow Trail (#1336). Turn right (north), cross the creek, and reach an intersection with the Dry Creek Trail (#1343), where a "Motor Vehicles Prohibited" sign reminds us we are nearing Wilderness. Turn west (left) here and follow the trail as it curves to the left, passes a trail register, and climbs through a mixed montane forest comprised of ponderosa, spruce, and aspen. Northern bedstraw, heartleaf arnica, Parry clover, yarrow, star Solomonplume, Rocky Mountain pussytoes, orange sneezeweed, blanketflower, and mountain harebell add glitters of color to the forest floor. Wild strawberry vines creep across the ground while wild rose bushes, red elderberry, and cow parsnip adorn the trailside. Pinedrops, a plant that lacks chlorophyll, the photosynthetic pigment that gives plants their green color, adds a unique accent to the brush.

As you cross the creek, notice a change in vegetation. Aspens dominate here, as do Fremont geranium, Wyoming paintbrush, lambstongue groundsel, rose, and fireweed. Follow the rocky trail as it leaves the water behind and climbs arduously into a cool, shady forest where cliffs hide torrents roaring in the distance. Grasses proliferate, but colorful bits of mountain bluebells, nodding onion, monkshood, triangularleaf senecio, tall larkspur, shrubby cinquefoil, and Rocky Mountain penstemon shine through nonetheless. Wetter spots give rise to elephant heads, death camas, bog pyrola, and the aptly named shooting star, all blooms that stand out in contrast to the plentiful and varied green hues.

Flowers line the shores of Dry Lake, an alpine lake set in a cirque surrounded by rugged ridges.

The trail winds south and back toward the water. Heartleaf arnica, American bistort, triangularleaf senecio, and beautiful cinquefoil line the way. Enter a huge meadow where huge, deep purple blooms of monkshood join forces with corn lily, blanketflower, mountain dandelion, aspen sunflower, Colorado columbine, shrubby cinquefoil, Fremont geranium, and yarrow to create a dazzling display. Absorb breathtaking views of the giant granite slabs towering above and the moraine filling the southern edge of the valley.

After passing into the Sangre de Cristo Wilderness, the trail turns nasty and loose as it climbs steeply to the right and dives back into dense forest. Break free from the forest, trading bushes and trees for sweeping valley vistas. Little Horn Peak towers to the left and Horn Peak rises to the right. Alpine bistort, dwarf golden aster, Whipple's penstemon, mouse-ear chickweed, and fringed gentian adorn the willow-lined trail. A spectacular cascade pours over a magnificent rock chasm to the left of the trail.

From here, climb to the first lake, whose shoreline explodes with color. The delicate purple blooms of mountain harebells join with dazzling rosy paintbrush, brilliant shrubby cinquefoil, and the uniquely shaped Parry's lousewort to create a picturesque vision. Elephant heads, yarrow, queen's crown, Parry clover, Rocky Mountain penstemon, and a host of grasses full of tiny yellow and white blooms round

▶ **TIDBIT—Similar in appearance to larkspurs, monkshood (*Aconitum columbianum*) lacks the spurred sepal. The generic name *Aconitum* is loosely translated as "unconquerable poison." All parts of this plant are poisonous.**

Bog pyrola

Dry Lakes

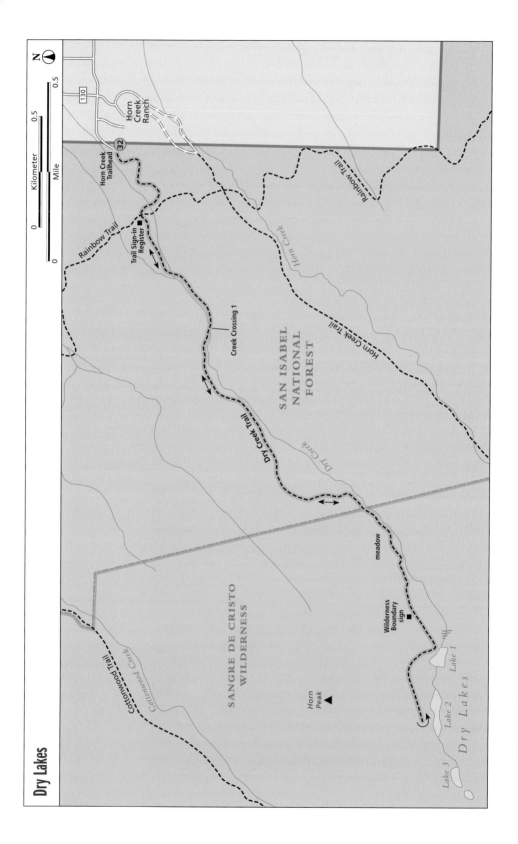

out the experience. This dazzling display of flowers is as impressive as the jagged rock formations forming the steep cirque encircling this scene, which includes Fluted Peak (13,554 feet), Little Horn Peak (13,143 feet) to the east, and Horn Peak (13,450 feet) to the west. Continue to the second lake on a faint trail skirting the rocky slope above the right side of the first lake. Here find northern and rosy paintbrush, yellow stonecrop, beautiful cinquefoil, yarrow, edible valerian, mountain harebells, bracted lousewort, and mountain thistle, a native species with white, yellow, or purple blooms and a large terminal cluster that often nods to one side. Retrace your steps back to the trailhead.

Miles and Directions

0.0 Start at the Horn Creek Trailhead.
0.5 Reach a signed junction with the Rainbow Trail (#1336) and turn right (north) onto it.
0.6 At a signed intersection turn west (left) to stay on the Dry Creek Trail (#1343).
0.7 Sign in at the trail register.
1.4 Cross to the north side of Dry Creek.
3.3 Enter a huge flower-filled meadow.
3.8 Reach the Sangre de Cristo Wilderness boundary.
3.9 Pass a waterfall on the left of the trail.
4.0 Reach the first lake.
4.7 Arrive at the second lake.
9.4 Arrive back at the trailhead.
Options: From the second lake, you can navigate talus slopes to the right of the second lake to reach the smaller third lake.

Hike Information

Local Information
Custer County Visitor Center: Westcliffe; (719) 783-9163; custercountyco.com/visitor-center.

Local Events/Attractions
Mission: Wolf: Gardner; (719) 859-2157; www.missionwolf.org
　　　Bishop Castle: Wetmore; bishopcastle.org.
　　　Great Sand Dunes National Park & Preserve; Mosca; (719) 378-6395; www.nps.gov/grsa

Other Resources
Hart, Lee. 2016. *Hiking Colorado's Sangre de Cristos and Great Sand Dunes: A Guide to the Area's Greatest Hiking Adventures,* 2nd Edition. Guilford, Connecticut: Globe Pequot Press.

33 Lost Lake

Immerse yourself into the splendor of the high country with this popular, beginner-friendly hike to a sparking lake perched near the Continental Divide. Starting at tree line, this short, easy hike immediately explores open hillsides buzzing with a kaleidoscope of color and delivers stunning, snow-capped peak views in all directions. Take a swim, bring a fishing pole, spend the night, or just revel in discovering all this rugged, wild landscape has to offer.

Start: From the Lost Lake Trailhead off Cottonwood Pass Road (12,126 feet)
Distance: 2.6-miles out and back
Hiking time: 2–3 hours
Difficulty: Easy due to gradual, smooth terrain and minimal elevation gain. *Note:* The entire hike is above 11,500 feet, which could make it more challenging.
Trail surface: Dirt two-track
Best season: July to October
Peak bloom: July
Flowers commonly found: subalpine and heartleaf arnica, bracted lousewort, shrubby and beautiful cinquefoil, pygmy bitterroot, king's crown, wild strawberry, subalpine Jacob's ladder, fireweed, parrot's beak, dotted saxifrage, sulphur flower, rosy pussytoes, Canada violet, yarrow, rosy, western yellow paintbrush, American bistort, alpine fleabane, narcissus

anemone, elephant heads, yarrow, Geyer's onion, heartleaf bittercress, cowbane, mountain bluebells, spring beauty, marsh marigold, cutleaf daisy, blue violet, thickleaf ragwort, Whipple's penstemon, alpine and mountain avens, Parry's lousewort, mountain dandelion
Other trail users: Equestrians
Canine compatibility: Dogs permitted
Land status: National Forest
Nearest town: Buena Vista
Fees and permits: No fees or permits required
Schedule: The Cottonwood Pass Road is closed by snow from late November to May.
Maps: USGS Tincup, CO; Nat Geo Trails Illustrated 129 Buena Vista/Collegiate Peaks; Latitude 40° Maps: Salida / Buena Vista
Trail contacts: San Isabel National Forest, Salida Ranger District, Salida; (719) 539-3591; www.fs.usda.gov/psicc

Finding the trailhead: From the traffic light in Buena Vista, turn west onto CR 306 toward Cottonwood Pass. Continue for 18 miles. There is a small parking area on the right, and the trail starts across the road on the west (left) side. **GPS: N38 49.073' / W106 24.360'**

The Hike

Just shy of Cottonwood Pass (12.126 feet), a discrete but well-worn path travels southwest away from the highway. With just a few steps, it dives deep into the forest to pass heartleaf arnica, bracted lousewort, beautiful cinquefoil, pygmy bitterroot, king's crown, wild strawberry, subalpine Jacob's ladder, and fireweed. Break from the trees and hop over a small trickle lined with a dazzling display of color; parrot's beak, dotted saxifrage, and sulphur flower await on the other side. Continue traversing a grassy slope to find rosy pussytoes, Canada violets, yarrow, shrubby cinquefoil, and thickleaf

Spectacular scenery and fields of flowers en route to Lost Lake

ragwort dappling the hillside. Breaths may come sparsely as you walk high above it all, so take your time, and enjoy the rugged snow-capped peaks, the fresh cool air, and the ground below you springing forth with bud after bud.

A high, lush meadow rewards hikers with western yellow paintbrush, American bistort, subalpine arnica, dotted saxifrage, sulphur flower, alpine fleabane, and bracted lousewort. Creating an idyllic scene, these flowers bloom against the backdrop of the Collegiate Peaks.

Climb a bit further to intersect with North Fork Cottonwood Creek, a small waterway giving rise to a lush spot bursting with blooms. Before crossing, explore its banks to discover rosy paintbrush, bracted lousewort, narcissus anemone, elephant heads, alpine speedwell, yarrow, arnica, and Geyer's onion. While hopping rocks to reach the other side, pause to find heartleaf bittercress, cowbane, king's crown, and mountain bluebells hiding amid the verdant vegetation lining this sweet-sounding creek.

Ascending a bit, the trail brings you to an open area with jaw-dropping vistas and a new assortment of flowers including pygmy bitterroot, spring beauty, beautiful cinquefoil, marsh marigold, cutleaf daisy, and blue violet. Stunted and mangled trees welcome you to a level spot with incredible vistas of the Continental Divide, a snow-spotted ridge towering overhead.

Continue walking south (straight) along an undulating trail passing through tiny willow bushes where thickleaf ragwort, western yellow paintbrush, and Whipple's

Parry's lousewort

penstemon add unexpected bits of color. Reach a peaceful lake surrounded by impressive amounts of paintbrush, elephant heads, and American bistort. Follow the well-defined two-track road lined with more uniquely shaped pines and onion, bistort, cinquefoil, and paintbrush. While ascending, look back periodically for a bird's-eye view of this lake and the mountains rising behind it. Climb the hill above the lake to reach another moist meadow teeming with rosy paintbrush, elephant heads, shrubby and beautiful cinquefoil, and alpine fleabane. Alpine avens, American bistort, and mountain avens burst from the ground in bits of yellow and white. Keep an eye out for the exquisite, but easy-to-miss, Parry's lousewort whose tiny clusters of creamy white, yellowish, or pinkish beaked flowers adorn the top of smooth stems that stretch only 4–16 inches from the ground.

Curving left, the trail heads downhill into a thicker stand of trees. Follow the trail through this shaded section past sulphur flower, mountain dandelion, rosy and western yellow paintbrush, and narcissus-flowered anemone. Just after crossing a drainage, begin climbing slightly to reach Lost Lake, a brilliant turquoise lake nestled in a rocky basin. Explore its shores for familiar flowers and absorb the powerful views in every direction—including those overhead. Retrace your steps to the trailhead, pausing often to enjoy the epic vistas of rugged ridges and precarious summits like Turner Peak (13,232 feet) to the northeast.

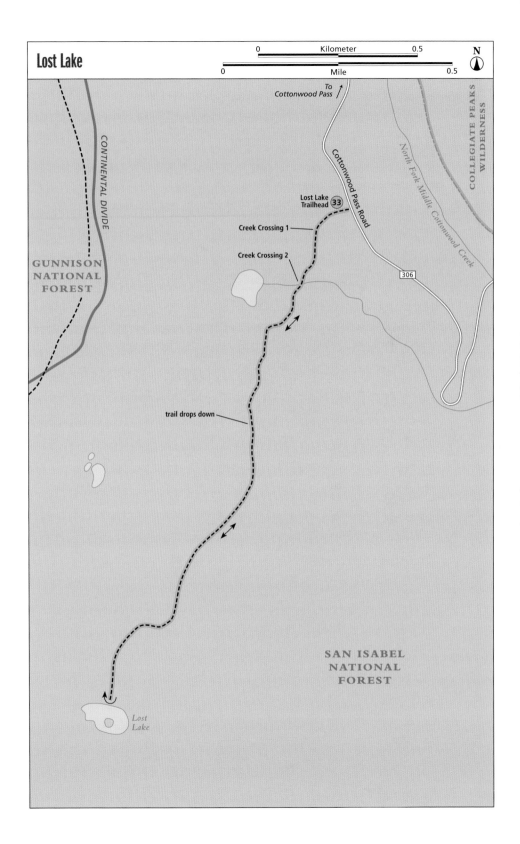

Miles and Directions

0.0 Start from the Lost Lake Trailhead on Cottonwood Pass Road.

0.1 Travel southwest on a well-worn path through the forest to cross a small stream.

0.2 Continue climbing south to cross North Fork Cottonwood Creek.

0.4 Follow the rolling trail to reach a small lake on the west (right) of the trail.

0.7 Climb away from the small lake on the well-defined two-track, passing a wet meadow until the trail begins dropping down into the forest.

1.3 Reach Lost Lake (11,891 feet) after a short climb.

2.6 Arrive back at the trailhead.

Hike Information

General Information

Buena Vista Chamber of Commerce: Buena Vista; (719) 395-6612; buenavistacolorado.org

Buena Vista Heritage: Buena Vista; (719) 395-8458; buenavistaheritage.org

34 Crystal Lake via Hoosier Pass

This route, accessible right from the highway, begins in the subalpine forest, which means that no matter what your ability or fitness level you can explore the subalpine and alpine ecosystems almost immediately and with very little effort. Because the trail follows an easily navigable road with a gentle grade, all of your energy goes to enjoying each blossom and absorbing the expansive mountain views surrounding you. Discover old mining remnants, watch an array of flittering birds, spy on a colony of busy marmots, and spend time wandering around a serene high mountain lake (11,720 feet). This short jaunt is perfect for those who are short on time or who are looking to explore the high country without busting a lung to get to altitude.

Start: From the Continental Divide road sign on the west side of Hoosier Pass (11,542 feet)

Distance: 3.3 miles out and back

Hiking time: 1–3 hours

Difficulty: Easy due to gradual, smooth terrain and minimal elevation gain. *Note:* The entire hike is above 11,000 feet, which could make it more challenging.

Trail surface: Two-track dirt road

Best season: July to September

Peak bloom: mid to late July

Flowers commonly found: subalpine Jacob's ladder, Whipple's penstemon, heartleaf arnica, narcissus anemone, Parry's lousewort, glacial daisy, elephant heads, yarrow, alpine avens, Rocky Mountain pussytoes, shrubby cinquefoil, mountain bluebells, Gray's angelica, wild candytuft, mountain-ear chickweed, tall larkspur, pygmy bitterroot, alpine clover, blue violet, western yellow and scarlet paintbrush, snowball saxifrage, mountain parsley, beautiful cinquefoil, globeflower, marsh marigold, snow buttercup, Parry clover, beautiful daisy, death camas, monkshood, sky pilot, old man of the mountains, Geyer's onion, king's crown, triangularleaf senecio, alpine primrose, Colorado columbine, alpine bistort.

Other trail users: Equestrians and mountain bikers; highway legal vehicles permitted from 5/21 to 11/22

Canine compatibility: Dogs permitted

Land status: National Forest

Nearest town: Breckenridge

Fees and permits: No fees or permits required

Schedule: Open to nonmotorized use all year, but often obstructed by snow from fall to summer

Maps: USGS Hoosier Pass West CO; Trails Illustrated 109 Breckenridge, Tennessee Pass; Latitude 40 Summit County Colorado Trails

Trail contacts: White River National Forest, Dillon Ranger District, 680 Blue River Pkwy., Silverthorne 80498; (970) 468-5400; www.fs.usda.gov/whiteriver

Special considerations: Don't confuse this hike with the Crystal Lakes hike (not in this book) that begins off of Spruce Creek Road and shares the same trailhead with Lower Mohawk Lake (see the Lower Mohawk Lake hike).

Finding the trailhead: From Breckenridge, take Hwy. 9 south for 9.7 miles to the top of Hoosier Pass. Park in the large dirt parking area on the west (right) side of the road and marked by the Continental Divide sign. **GPS: N39 21.710' / W106 03.795'**

The Hike

From the dirt parking area, a few paths head west. All wander through the forest, pass a campground, and climb to the four-wheel-drive road (FR 849). Enjoy walking through this spot of forest characterized by giant spruces, where plentiful amounts of subalpine Jacob's ladder, Whipple's penstemon, and heartleaf arnica blossom. Look closely to find narcissus anemone and Parry's lousewort, with clusters of creamy white, yellowish, or pinkish beaked flowers hiding along the forest floor. From the junction with FR 2, absorb views of Montgomery Reservoir, Mount Lincoln (14,286 feet), and Mount Bross (14,172 feet) towering to the southwest (ahead). Shortly after turning north (right) to stay on FR 849, trade the trees for a slope thick with willows that opens wide above you revealing a rainbow of blooms including glacial daisy, elephant heads, yarrow, scarlet paintbrush, alpine avens, Rocky Mountain pussytoes, shrubby cinquefoil, mountain bluebells, arnica, and Parry's lousewort.

Climbing gradually, the trail reveals lacy Gray's angelica, wild candytuft, mountain-ear chickweed, and cinquefoil. Large stands of tall larkspur explode in a burst of purple, while tinier buds like pygmy bitterroot, alpine clover, and blue violet dapple the ground with small bits of color.

The trail levels and Quandary Peak (14,265 feet) looms large to the northwest. Enjoy the prolific blooms of western yellow paintbrush, mountain bluebells,

Flowers and views abound at Crystal Lake

snowball saxifrage, mountain parsley, yarrow, and beautiful cinquefoil populating the field ahead. Note that winter never truly leaves the Continental Divide; patches of snow persist through summer. It is here at the edge of summer and winter that globeflower, marsh marigold, and snow buttercup often blossom.

Note a flurry of bird activity amid the willows. Even if you aren't inclined to identify these constantly moving creatures, take a moment to soak in their songs and observe their frenzied movement. Also, notice that even though you are merely a mile from the car, this hike feels isolated. Cinquefoil lines the road while tall larkspur, mountain bluebells, scarlet paintbrush, wild candytuft, and both Parry and alpine clover paint the hillsides.

Monkshood

Moving on, come to a water-filled drainage coming in from the west (left). Though the moisture may not always be flowing depending on the year, the plethora of larkspur, beautiful daisy, death camas, marsh marigold, and paintbrush imply a life-giving seep underfoot.

From here, the road loses elevation, turns left, and heads into a tiny stand of trees. You emerge, and thick willows line the trail, but periodically you catch a glimpse of debris on the hillside that reminds us of those who came here searching for fortune. The spine of the Continental Divide, a craggy ridge high above and to the west, parallels our route as it leads to the summit of North Star Mountain.

In a lush, open rocky basin, monkshood stands tall in stately blooms amid overwhelming stands of the brilliant red scarlet paintbrush. A tiny trail to your left cuts through a field of multicolored paintbrush, sky pilot, old man of the mountain, and Geyer's onion to reach the southeastern edge of the Crystal Lake.

Returning to the main road, follow as it curves northeast (left) to reach the signed National Forest Boundary and the north end of Crystal Lake, which rests on an open shelf below an imposing ridge. Find remnants from the Crystal Mine scattered about and multicolored tailing piles dotting hillsides above the lake. Enjoy a break here watching marmots scurry back and forth, absorbing the soothing sound of water rushing over rocks, and exploring the lakeside. King's crown, triangularleaf senecio, elephant heads, alpine primrose, Colorado columbine, shrubby cinquefoil, and alpine bistort color this tranquil scene. Retrace your route to the trailhead.

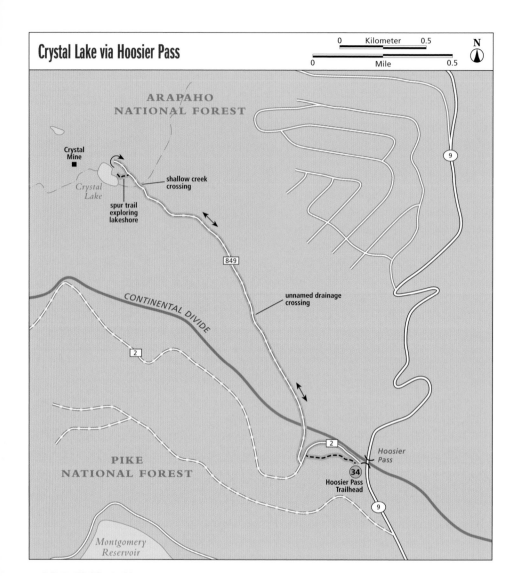

Crystal Lake via Hoosier Pass

Crystal Mine

Crystal Lake

shallow creek crossing

spur trail exploring lakeshore

ARAPAHO NATIONAL FOREST

849

unnamed drainage crossing

CONTINENTAL DIVIDE

2

PIKE NATIONAL FOREST

2

Hoosier Pass

34
Hoosier Pass Trailhead

9

9

Montgomery Reservoir

0   Kilometer   0.5

0   Mile   0.5

N

Miles and Directions

0.0   Start from the parking area on the west side of Hoosier Pass. Follow FR 849 west.

0.3   At the junction with FR 2, turn north (right) to stay on FR 849.

0.7   Cross an unnamed drainage coming in from the west.

1.3   Cross the shallow creek to reach an open rocky basin.

1.4   Veer from the main trail to reach the southeastern edge of the lake and explore its shores.

1.5   Reach Crystal Lake at the National Forest boundary.

3.2   Arrive back at the trailhead.

Hike Information

Local Information

Breckenridge Resort Chamber: Breckenridge; (970) 453-2918 or (888) 251-2417; gobreck.com

Local Events/Attractions

Country Boy Mine: 0542 French Gulch Rd., Breckenridge; (970) 453-4405; countryboymine.com

Town of Frisco: Frisco; (970) 668-5276 or (800) 424-1554; townoffrisco.com

Historic Walking Tour; (970) 453-9767; http://www.breckheritage.com/historic-walking-tour

Hike Tours

Guided Hiking Tours: Breckenridge; (970)453-5000; http://www.breckenridge.com/summer-breck-treks.aspx;townofbreckenridge.com/index.

Organizations

Friends of the Dillon Ranger District: (970) 262-3449; fdrd.org

HONORABLE MENTIONS

South Central

Here is a great hike in the South Central region that didn't make the A-list this time around but deserves recognition.

E. Boss and Hunt Lakes

This tranquil, moderately challenging 4-mile out-and-backhike touches two tranquil lakes and reaches just below the Continental Divide providing stunning vistas. Starting in the forest and breaking out into the rocky subalpine, this adventure offers the opportunity to see a range of colorful wildflowers from the end of June to August. From Poncha Springs, take US 50 west for about 12 miles to the town of Monarch. Turn right on FR 230 (Middle Fork). This road is located on the north side of Hwy. 50, across from the Monarch Mountain Lodge. If you have a four-wheel-drive vehicle, drive the next 1.1 miles to the Boss Lake Trailhead. If not, walk this section and add 2.2 miles to the round-trip journey. Information: San Isabel National Forest at (719) 539-3591 or www.fs.usda.gov/psicc.

Front Range

Technically, the Front Range encompasses the eastern boundary of Colorado's Rocky Mountains spanning the entire area from the Wyoming border to Pueblo or even further south. However, "Front Range" is also a colloquial term used often—and in this book—to describe the most populated portion of Colorado. Geographically, this region encompasses a narrow corridor of plains, foothills, and high mountains that offer an unmatched range of venues for exploring the outdoors year-round since altitudes range from 5,000 to 14,264 feet (Grays Peak).

Foothills near Fort Collins, Denver, and Boulder offer thrilling hiking and biking trails with amazing views, interesting geology, and a range of early wildflowers. Horsetooth Reservoir, near Fort Collins, lures hikers, bikers, anglers, and climbers, while the iconic Flatirons, angled rock fins rising sharply from the Boulder foothills, draw hikers and climbers from around the world. Further south, similar fins rise from Red Rocks Park and Roxborough State Park, a gem designated as a Colorado Natural Area and a National Natural Landmark. The Peak-to-Peak Highway, a scenic byway northwest of Boulder, meanders through a rugged canyon to provide access to bountiful forest, alpine lakes, and funky towns like Nederland and Ward.

The Front Range also acts as a gateway to Rocky Mountain National Park, a Colorado treasure located just outside Estes Park. Glacially sculpted peaks, high alpine lakes, pristine tundra, and awesome wildlife-viewing opportunities make it a crown jewel of the National Park system. Trail Ridge Road, the highest continuous road in the United States, cuts from one side of the park to the other, bringing you from forest to the "land above the trees" and back again. The Rocky Mountain Conservancy (formerly the Rocky Mountain Nature Association) offers great classes in all aspects of the region's natural history. Rocky, as locals call the park, contains an expansive trail network allowing adventurers to explore flower-filled meadows, mountaintops, the Colorado River, the Continental Divide, historic sites, and delicate tundra.

35 Staunton Ranch/Davis Ponds Loop

Explore Colorado's newest state park on this easy loop through verdant forest. Brilliant vistas of the mountains and Staunton's prominent Lions Head outcropping abound, as do colorful blossoms. This peaceful loop through a range of habitats and steeped in history passes an old homestead and stocked ponds popular for fishing, which means it has something for everyone.

Start: From the Staunton Ranch Trailhead south of the upper parking lot (8,300 feet)
Distance: 3.4-mile loop
Hiking time: 1.5–2.5 hours
Difficulty: Easy due to length, gradual, smooth terrain, and moderate elevation gain
Trail surface: Dirt, forested trail
Best season: June to September
Peak bloom: mid to late June
Flowers commonly found: golden banner, showy daisy, lanceleaf chiming bells, rosy pussytoes, mouse-ear chickweed, miner's candle, mountain parsley, western wallflower, wild rose, chokecherry, mountain beard-tongue, silverweed and beautiful cinquefoil, lambstongue groundsel, kinnikinnick, sticky geranium, star Solomonplume, silvery lupine, wild candytuft, wild strawberry, scarlet paintbrush, mountain harebell, Colorado locoweed, blanketflower, black-eyed Susan, mariposa lily, wild iris, sugar bowl, pearly everlasting

Other trail users: Mountain bikers and equestrians on the Staunton Ranch Trail; hikers only on the Davis Ponds Trail
Canine compatibility: Leashed dogs permitted
Land status: State park
Nearest town(s): Conifer/Pine
Fees and permits: Daily fee or annual parks pass required; available at the park entrance station, the Visitor Center, or the self-service station.
Schedule: Open all year; summer hours: 7 a.m. to 9 p.m.
Maps: USGS Meridian Hill, Conifer, Pine, Bailey; Trails Illustrated 100 Boulder/Golden; Colorado Parks and Wildlife Pocket Trail Map #50: Staunton State Park Trail Use Map (available on website)
Trail contact: Staunton State Park, Pine; (303) 816-0912; http://www.cpw.state.co.us/placestogo/parks/staunton

Finding the trailhead: From Conifer, take US 285 south for 6 miles. Take the Elk Creek Road exit and turn north (right) onto Elk Creek Road. Follow signs 1.5 miles to the parkentrance. **GPS: N39 29.992'/W105 22.741'**

The Hike

From the parking lot, pick up the Staunton Ranch Trail heading north. At the Mason Creek Trail intersection, turn north (left) to curve west through forest dominated by ponderosa pine, Douglas fir, and blue spruce, Colorado's state tree. Golden banner, showy daisy, lanceleaf chiming bells, rosy pussytoes, mouse-ear chickweed, miner's candle, and mountain parsley adorn the forest floor in yellow, purple, blue, pink, and white.

The trail passes through an open, sunny forest with patches of brilliant green, quaking aspen trees. Western wallflowers brighten the scene with bursts of yellow and wild rose blooms in a flurry of pink. Sweet-smelling white blossoms arranged in cylindrical clusters alert you to the presence of chokecherry, a shrub that produces sour reddish-purple to black cherries.

Mountain beardtongue, golden banner, lanceleaf chiming bells, beautiful cinquefoil, and lambstongue groundsel add bits of color as the path cruises through forest. Breaks in the forest allow views of impressive rock cliffs towering overhead. Kinnikinnick turns the ground a shiny green hue while wild rose, sticky geranium, and star Solomonplume burst forth in bits of vibrant white and pink.

Staying straight at an intersection, climb along mild switchbacks. Inhale the vanilla-scented pines as you head toward more unique geologic formations. Most of Staunton sits on a large granite formation called the Pikes Peak batholiths, created as the earth's crust was pushed up from below its hot liquid core. Ages of uplift exposed the granite and eroded away most of the Precambrian rocks to create the jaw-dropping outcrops you see including Lions Head, Chimney Rock, Elk Creek Spires, and Staunton Rocks.

▶ **GREEN TIP—Pack out what you pack in, even food scraps because they can attract wild animals.**

Draw your eyes away from these captivating cliffs periodically to catch a glimpse of silvery lupine, golden banner, wild candytuft, silverweed cinquefoil, wild strawberry, scarlet paintbrush, and mountain harebell scattered along the trail as it meanders through towering pines, firs, and aspen trees.

Golden banner set against interesting rock formations at Colorado's newest state park

Turn onto the Chase Meadow Trail (newly completed, may not be on all maps) and head downhill through a meadow punctuated by Colorado locoweed, wild rose, lupine, blanketflower, black-eyed Susan, harebells, and the more brilliant golden banner.

Descending through the pine-laden meadows of the Staunton Cabin District, reach a historic structure reminiscent of the homestead created by Doctors Rachel and Archibald Staunton in 1905. In 1986, three years before her death, their daughter Frances Hornbrook Staunton willed the 1,720-acre ranch to the state and required they preserve it as a "natural Wilderness-type park." It took years to realize her dream, but in 2013 Staunton opened and various preserved cabins remain on site.

Cross a service road to find mariposa lilies, wild irises, and golden banner painting an open meadow. Pause periodically to look back; being further away from the rugged granite cliffs offers impressive vistas. An aspen grove lines the trail to the left and guides you to a bend in the trail where you will find a pile of rusting cans and other debris providing a glimpse into the lives of those brave and enduring people who settled in the area.

After an intersection, climb gently through aspens passing golden banner, sugar bowls, pearly everlasting, and rosy pussytoes. Explore Davis Ponds and then follow the easy grade through a forested meadow with incredible views of jagged cliffs in the distance. Cross a creek and find cow parsnip, sugar bowls, lupine, and

Silvery lupine

paintbrush lining the trail in a dazzling display of purple and red. Enjoy breathtaking vistas across the meadow to your left as you cruise toward an informational kiosk and a spur trail. Turn north (left) passing rose, strawberry, parsley, and golden banner to make your way back.

Miles and Directions

0.0 From the east edge of the upper parking lot, pick up the Staunton Ranch Trail heading north passing the Mason Creek Trail junction.

0.5 Cross a signed road intersection to continue east and stay on the Staunton Ranch Trail.

1.1 Turn south (left) onto the Chase Meadow Trail.

1.4 Pass a cabin and continue straight to cross a service road.

1.6 Stay southwest (straight) at two consecutive service road crossings to remain on the trail.

1.8 Reach a historic spot with a pile of rusting cans and other debris marked by a cross and a sign reading "Staunton's Secrets."

2.0 Turn southwest (right) onto the Davis Ponds Trail.

2.2 Reach a signed junction and head southwest (straight) through the intersection toward Davis Ponds.

2.5 At the next junction, explore the ponds via a spur trail to your right. Next, head east (left) on the main trail.

2.8 Come to another junction, go east (right), and cross a bridge over the brook.

3.2 Turn north (left) at an informational kiosk.

3.3 Go east (right) at a junction with the Ranch Hand Picnic Area.

3.4 Arrive back at the trailhead.

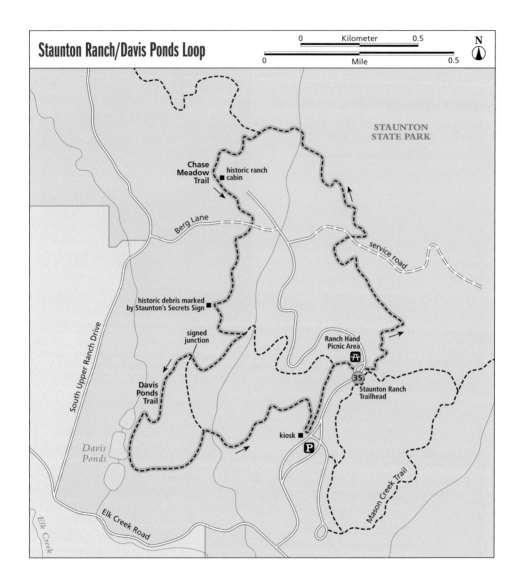

Staunton Ranch/Davis Ponds Loop

0   Kilometer   0.5

0   Mile   0.5

N

STAUNTON
STATE PARK

Chase Meadow Trail

historic ranch cabin

Berg Lane

service road

historic debris marked by Staunton's Secrets Sign

signed junction

Ranch Hand Picnic Area

35

Davis Ponds Trail

Staunton Ranch Trailhead

South Upper Ranch Drive

Davis Ponds

kiosk

P

Mason Creek Trail

Elk Creek Road

Elk Creek

Hike Information

General Information

Conifer Area Chamber of Commerce: (303) 838-5711; goconifer.com

Clubs and Organizations

Friends of Staunton State Park: Preserve, protect, and promote the park; Pine; http://www.friendsofstauntonstatepark.org/

36 Mount Falcon Loop

Escape to nature with this easy exploration of Mount Falcon Park, an oasis just a short drive from the city. Rolling meadows and forested hills along a 3-mile lollipop bring you through an area rich in human and natural history. Rewards include spectacular views of the Continental Divide, Denver, Red Rocks, and snow-capped peaks from a historic cabin and fire tower and a journey back in time as you explore the remains of a magnificent mansion built by John Walker, a tycoon who settled in the area in the early 1900s.

Start: From the West Trailhead of Mount Falcon Park (7,800 feet)
Distance: 3.0-mile lollipop
Hiking time: 1.5–2.5 hours
Difficulty: Easy due to gradual, smooth terrain and moderate elevation gain
Trail surface: Dirt and forested trail
Best season: May to September
Peak bloom: June
Flowers commonly found: low and sidebells penstemon, salsify, Fremont geranium, lance-leaf chiming bells, whiskbroom parsley, wild rose, yellow stonecrop, spiderwort, sulphur flower, wax currant, blue flax, boulder raspberry, golden corydalis, Wyoming paintbrush, butter 'n' eggs, beautiful cinquefoil, Nuttall's larkspur, tuber starwort, mountain bluebells, Oregon grape, false Solomon's seal, pussytoes, Britton skullcap, mountain harebell, monument plant, sugar bowls, yarrow, golden aster, mountain dandelion

Other trail users: Mountain bikers, equestrians
Canine compatibility: Leashed dogs permitted
Land status: Jefferson County Open Space
Nearest town: Morrison
Fees and permits: No fees or permits required
Schedule: Open all year; one hour before sunrise to one hour after sunset
Maps: USGS Morrison; Trails Illustrated 100 Boulder/Golden; Latitude 40° Colorado Front Range
Trail contact: Jefferson County Open Space, Golden; (303) 271-5925; www.jeffco.us/open-space/parks

Finding the trailhead: From Morrison, take US 470 south to US 285. Head southwest on US 285 for 4.5 miles. Take the Indian Hills turnoff and turn north (right) onto Parmalee Gulch Road. Follow Parmalee Gulch for 2.7 miles, then turn right at the Mount Falcon sign onto Picutis Road. Follow the curvy, well-signed road, which turns to Mount Falcon Road, for another 1.8 miles to reach the parking lot on the right. **GPS: N39 38.166' / W105 14.347'**

The Hike

Head east on Castle Trail to pass restrooms, an information kiosk, and a junction with Parmalee Gulch Trail. The wide, treed trail continues straight to pass low penstemon, salsify, Fremont geranium, lanceleaf chiming bells, and whiskbroom parsley. Moving into the open, low penstemon, sidebells penstemon, yellow stonecrop, spiderwort, sulphur flower, and wild rose adorn the hillside. Expansive vistas abound out to the south (right) where a burn scar gives rise to saplings and speckles of brilliant color. Wax currant, blue flax, and boulder raspberry thrive along the wide, well-worn road.

Stay straight at Meadow Trail junction to take this aptly named path through an open meadow bursting with golden corydalis, yellow stonecrop, butter 'n' eggs, low penstemon, salsify, Wyoming paintbrush, and beautiful cinquefoil. Catch a glimpse of Denver to your left and snow-capped peaks to the right.

Just after entering the shade of ponderosa pines, stay straight on Tower Trail, which narrows now to curve through the forest. Continue climbing along the rocky path keeping an eye out for wax currant, wild rose, low penstemon, pussytoes, Nuttall's larkspur, and tuber starwort. Reach the Eagle Eye Shelter, a historic structure formerly used as a private summer cabin. Take a breather to absorb the unfettered and unmatched views of the Continental Divide before continuing upward to reach the fire tower, which also offers incredible vistas out to the Divide and back toward the city. Notice the multitude of tiny multicolored sparkles that light up the ground below; this perch offers perspective on the sheer number of blooms bursting in the vicinity.

Now the trail cruises downhill through ponderosa pines and scrub oak where mountain bluebells, boulder raspberry, Oregon grape, false Solomon's seal, pussytoes, and larkspur thrive. Continue downward to find deep purple Britton's skullcap, mountain harebell, and low penstemon interspersed among huge clumps of golden banner shining like the sun.

Views from Mount Falcon, an urban escape into nature

Head straight (east) through the Parmalee-Meadow Trail junction to remain on Meadow Trail through an open area painted with the purples, yellows, blues, and whites of lupine, golden banner, whiskbroom parsley, golden banner, shrubby cinquefoil, monument plant, sidebells penstemon, and sugar bowls, whose one purplish to dull reddish flower hangs like an inverted jug from a single slim stem. Cross the water to find

Stonecrop

common evening primrose, wild rose, and western wallflower adding splashes of pink and yellow to the lush vegetation in this section. Yarrow, golden aster, mountain dandelion, and sulphur flower adorn the trail through an open hillside before it returns to the shade of the pines.

At the Castle Trail junction, go straight to explore the ruins of Walker Home, a magnificent chalet built by John Walker, a successful businessman whose vision for protecting large tracts of land laid the foundation for Denver Mountain Parks and Jefferson County Open Space. As you wander the grounds, notice the

▶ **TIDBIT—A noxious weed, like yellow toadflax or butter 'n' eggs, which you find at Mount Falcon, is a nonnative plant which, having no natural checks in our environment, damages grazing land, crops, the environment, ecosystems, humans, or livestock.**

range of flowers—penstemon, wild rose, boulder raspberry, paintbrush, Nuttall's larkspur—and all the humming birds buzzing busily about overhead.

Leaving the ruins, hop back on Castle Trail headed south and then west to tackle a steady climb through an open area blooming with blue flax, golden banner, cinquefoil, salsify, penstemon, parsley, and monument plant. At the top of the hill, reach a familiar junction where Castle and Meadow Trails collide and a short spur trail heads west toward a bench and a viewpoint. If you bypassed this on the way in, take a few moments to explore the rocky outcrop and to revel in the view of Mount Evans (14,264 feet). Return to the main trail, turn northwest (left), and retrace your steps back to the trailhead.

Miles and Directions

0.0 From the trailhead, head east on Castle Trail.

0.4 Stay straight at the Meadow Trail junction to head south through an open area.

0.6 At the intersection between Tower Trail and Meadow Trail, stay south (straight) on the Tower Trail.

0.7 Reach the Eagle Eye Shelter, a historic structure formerly used as a private summer cabin.

0.9 Climb the fire tower steps to get amazing views out to the Continental Divide.

1.3 After descending, head straight (east) through the Parmalee-Meadow Trail junction to stay on the Meadow Trail.

1.4 At an intersection with the Ute Trail, turn north (left) to pass through a lush open area on Meadow Trail.

1.6 Cross a tiny brook on a little wooden bridge before climbing out of the meadow.

1.8 At an intersection with the Castle Trail, go north (straight) to explore the Walker Home ruins. Return to the main trail and turn south (right).

2.4 At the top of a long hill, reach a familiar junction where Castle and Meadow Trails collide and a short spur trail heads west toward a bench and a viewpoint.

2.5 Go west to explore this viewpoint offering awesome vistas and countless blooms. Return to the main trail, turn northwest (left), and retrace your steps.

3.0 Arrive back at the trailhead.

Hike Information

General Information
Conifer Area Chamber of Commerce: (303) 838-5711; goconifer.com

Local Events/Attractions
Red Rocks Park and Amphitheater: Morrison; (303) 697-4939; (720) 865-2494; redrocksonline.com. Tours available May through October or by appointment, (303) 697-6910

Clubs and Organizations
Jefferson County Open Space Volunteers: Golden; (303) 271-5922; www.jeffco.us/open-space/volunteer

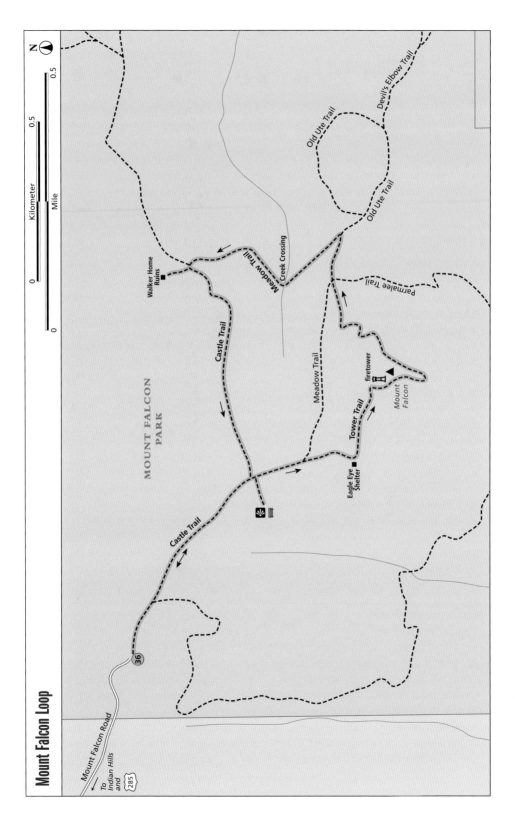

Mount Falcon Loop

37 Fountain Valley

Discover a wealth of interesting geological features on this easy adventure through Roxborough State Park, an often-overlooked gem resting south of Denver. This trail, which offers two must-do side trips to overlooks, illuminates the best of Roxborough: ecological diversity, scenic beauty, and unmatched views. Pass through a range of different communities—from those dominated by scrub oak to wet meadows—and walk in wonder under the shadow of giant red sandstone fins thrusting upward from the earth as you explore this unique 2.5-mile lollipop trail. Other highlights include a visit to a historic cabin and a meadow where striped chorus frogs may be heard singing.

Start: From the Fountain Valley Trailhead (6,160 feet)

Distance: 2.5-mile lollipop

Hiking time: 1–2 hours

Difficulty: Easy due to gradual, smooth terrain and moderate elevation gain

Trail surface: Dirt trail

Best season: May to September

Peak bloom: mid-May to mid-June

Flowers commonly found: Chokecherry, wild plum, mountain currant, golden banner, northern bedstraw, Nuttall's larkspur, northern bedstraw, silvery lupine, rosy pussytoes, boulder raspberry, peavine, mullein, yucca, mouse-ear chickweed, yarrow, narrowleaf puccoon, prickly pear cactus, yellow prairie violets, spring beauty, lanceleaf chiming bells, Onesided penstemon, leafy cinquefoil, lambstongue groundsel, yellow stonecrop, kinnikinnick, Fendler's waterleaf, spring beauty, Canada violet, wild licorice, American yellowrocket, horsemint, mariposa lily, Oregon grape

Other trail users: Runners; trails closed to horses and bicycles

Canine compatibility: Dogs not permitted

Land status: State park

Nearest town: Littleton

Fees and permits: Daily fee or annual parks pass required; available at the park entrance station, the Visitor Center, or the self-service station.

Schedule: Open all year; summer hours: 5 a.m. to 9 p.m.

Maps: USGS Kassler; Trails Illustrated 135 Deckers, Rampart Range Trail Map; Colorado Parks and Wildlife Pocket Trail Map #47: Roxborough State Park Trail Use Map (available on website)

Trail contact: Roxborough State Park, Roxborough; (303) 973-3959; http://www.cpw.state.co.us/placestogo/parks/Roxborough/

Special considerations: The park is day-use only.

Finding the trailhead: From Denver, take Wadsworth Boulevard (CO 121) south. Continue 4.5 miles past Wadsworth's intersection with CO 470 to turn south (left) on Waterton Road (just before the entrance to Lockheed Martin). Continue on Waterton Road for 1.6 miles until it ends. Turn south (right) on North Rampart Range Road, continuing south for 2.3 miles past Roxborough Village and the Foothills Water Treatment Plant. At the intersection of North Rampart Range Road and Roxborough Park Road (just before the entrance to Arrowhead golf course), turn left onto Roxborough Park Road. Take the next, almost immediate right on Roxborough Drive to enter the park. Pay the fee and continue following the road as it curves west to the end of the road and a parking lot on the right. If this is full, backtrack a few hundred feet to reach one of the other two overflow parking lots. **GPS: N39 25.779' / W105 04.175'**

The Hike

From Roxborough State Park Visitor Center, follow the wide dirt road that climbs northwest through thickets of scrub oak, one of the most common plants in the park. Chokecherry, wild plum, and mountain currant offer a fragrant introduction to this easy route. Take a quick detour down Fountain Valley Overlook Trail to pass an impressive display of golden banner, northern bedstraw, and Nuttall's larkspur en route to an overlook with an alluring bird's-eye perspective on the unique geology of the area you are about to explore. A band of rocks—pushed up during the uplift that formed the Rocky Mountains—rises from the ground at a dramatic angle. Red fins, formed from the Fountain Formation (also seen in Garden of the Gods and Red Rocks Park), lord over the verdant valley below while further north (right) the yellow-orange Lyons Formation forms a chunkier banded ridge. The younger, more rugged Dakota Hogback dominates the eastern skyline.

Return to the main trail where golden banner, northern bedstraw, silvery lupine, Nuttall's larkspur, rosy pussytoes, boulder raspberry, and peavine color the trail. At the junction, go right through an open area where mullein, yucca, mouse-ear chickweed, yarrow, golden banner, and narrowleaf puccoon brighten the scene. Passing through a grassland community, note wildlife signs include fresh dirt mounds made by pocket gophers and mountain mahogany browsed by mule deer. Yucca, prickly pear cactus, and yellow prairie violets add subtle bits of color to this section of trail.

View from the Lyons Overlook

Canada violet

At the Lyons Overlook Trail junction, turn left to head southwest for a short but worthy side trip that climbs past Nuttall's larkspur, spring beauty, yellow prairie violets, lanceleaf chiming bells, chokecherry, Onesided penstemon, leafy cinquefoil, and lambstongue groundsel. Wind downward through rocky soil harboring yellow stonecrop and kinnikinnick to reach the Lyons Overlook, an observation deck that rewards you with vistas of the Fountain Formation's otherworldly fins, Carpenter Peak, and Longs Peak way in the distance. Follow a spur lined with larkspur, Fendler's waterleaf, spring beauty, and Canada violet bursting from lush green vegetation. Meet the main trail and continue cruising downhill through a section of road characterized by mullein and thistle, plants that thrive in disturbed sites. Pass a shaded bench and soon Persse Place comes into view. In the early 1900s, Henry S. Persse built this as a summer home. He wanted to develop the land into a resort, causing Denver mayor R.W. Speer to write, "The area should be owned by the city for the free use of the people." It would be decades before this materialized, but in 1975, Colorado purchased the first 500 acres of Roxborough State Park, which now stands at 3,300 acres. Cross Little Willow Creek, an intermittent stream that acts as an important water source for wildlife. Wild licorice and wild plum bloom near the edge of a meadow bounded by red sandstone fins and covered in American yellow-rocket. Skirt this wet meadow blooming with sunshine to reach Signpost 15 (part of the self-guided nature trail). The frog picture alerts you to listen for striped chorus frogs, tiny amphibians with a big song. Pause to listen and look back at the brilliant yellow meadow set against alien rock formations.

Climb ever so slightly through juniper and ponderosa pine. Pass a bench and continue walking along the path looking for horsemint, mariposa lily, and Onesided penstemon, pausing often to enjoy the fins towering overhead. An open field supports a dazzling display of lupine and larkspur, while Canada violets, Oregon grape, and northern bedstraw hiding in the scrub oak underbrush guide you back to the end of the loop. Turn south (right) and retrace your steps to the trailhead.

Miles and Directions

0.0   Head northwest along the wide dirt road from the trailhead behind the Visitor Center.

0.1   Follow a short spur trail west (left) to the Fountain Valley Overlook.

0.3   At a trail junction signaling the start of the loop, head northeast (right).

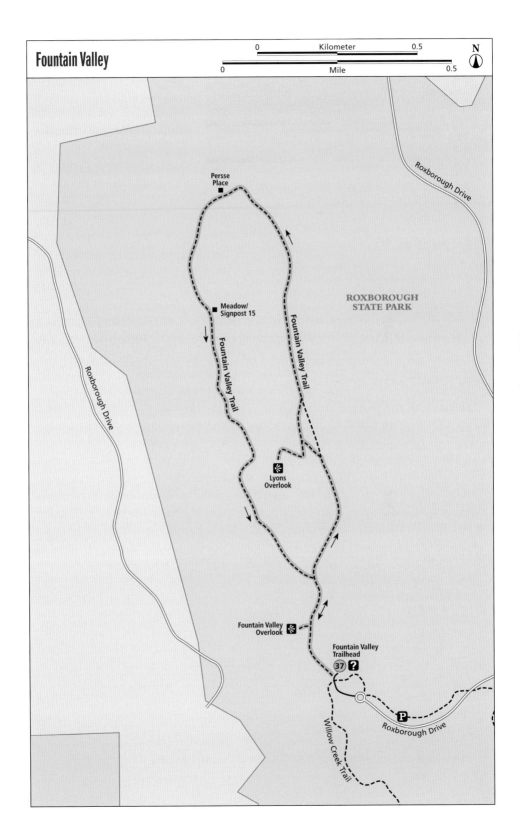

Fountain Valley

ROXBOROUGH
STATE PARK

Persse
Place

Meadow/
Signpost 15

Fountain Valley Trail

Fountain Valley Trail

Lyons
Overlook

Fountain Valley
Overlook

Fountain Valley
Trailhead
37 ?

Roxborough Drive

Roxborough Drive

Willow Creek Trail

P

N

Kilometer

0   0.5

Mile

0   0.5

0.6 At a junction with the Lyons Overlook Trail, turn west (left) toward the overlook.

0.7 Reach the Lyons Overlook.

0.8 Retrace your steps along this spur until you reach a junction. Veer left at the signed fork for a shortcut back to the main trail.

0.9 Reach the main trail. Turn north (left).

1.4 Arrive at Persse Place. Follow the trail southwest (left) through the meadow.

1.7 Midway through the meadow, reach Signpost 15. Pause and listen for striped chorus frogs.

2.3 Reach a familiar junction signaling the end of the loop. Turn south (right).

2.5 Arrive back at the trailhead.

Hike Information

General Information

South Metro Denver Chamber of Commerce: Littleton; (303) 795-0142; bestchamber.com

Local Events/Attractions

Chatfield State Park: Littleton; (303) 791-7275; http://www.cpw.state.co.us/placestogo/Parks/Chatfield

Accommodations

Chatfield State Park Campgrounds: Littleton; (303) 791-7275; http://www.cpw.state.co.us/placestogo/Parks/Chatfield

Clubs and Organizations

Friends of Roxborough:volunteer naturalists/stewards; Roxborough State Park, Littleton; (303) 973-3959; http://www.cpw.state.co.us/placestogo/parks/Roxborough/Pages/Friends Of Roxborough.aspx

Hike Tours

Roxborough State Park: Littleton; (303) 973-3959; http://www.cpw.state.co.us/placestogo/Parks/roxborough

DISCOVERING WILD PLANTS: FIELD GUIDE TO MEDICINAL AND HISTORIC USES

Cultures past and present have revered plants for their healthful, curative, and protective properties. Whether steeping leaves into tea, crushing petals into a poultice, making a cream from various plant parts, or eating a berry off the branch, for centuries, humans have been using plants and wildflowers as much more than beautiful decorations. Learn about the historic and medicinal uses of the following common wildflowers (in addition to a few other fun facts) and you'll begin seeing each trail—and the pharmacy it contains—in a different way.

Note: Meant solely for educational purposes, this is not a definitive guide for plant use. Many plants, including those used medicinally or historically, are toxic and can cause harm or death. In addition, countless edible plants have poisonous counterparts that look similar. Because of the difficulties and uncertainties associated with plant identification, do not eat, use, or attempt to create medicine out of any of the plants or fruits you find.

Green-Flower Pyrola (*Pyrola chlorantha*)

Also called shinleaf because the leaves were used as a poultice to lessen the pain of bruised shins. The active ingredient in wintergreen leaves is *methyl salicylate*, a compound similar to aspirin that acts as a natural painkiller. The leaves can be chewed, brewed into a tea, or applied to wounds as a poultice to relieve overall pain, soothe muscles, and ease headaches.

Greenflower pyrola

Alpine Sorrel (*Oxyria digyna*)

The name *Oxyria* is derived from a Greek word meaning "sour." It refers to the taste of the leaves, which are high in oxalate and vitamin C. The young greens make a thirst-quenching snack and add life to salads and dressings. They can also be added to casseroles or dried and sprinkled on grains

Alpine sorrel

King's crown

for added flavor. It is best to consume only small amounts, to stick with the young leaves, and to boil or dry the leaves before eating because they contain oxalates, which can be toxic in large quantities.

King's Crown (*Rhodiola integrifolia, Syn: Sedum rosea, Tolmachevia integrifolia*)

Also called Roseroot. Juicy leaves can provide water in an emergency, while both leaves and shoots provide a tasty, vitamin-packed snack when eaten raw or cooked. The plant looks similar to rose crown (*R. rhodantha*), which has flowers ranging from deep pink to light pink to whitish. *R. rhodantha*'s flower cluster forms a rounded column whereas *R. integrifolia*'s inflorescence is flat.

Nodding Onion (*Allium cernuum*)

Nodding onion

A. cernuum is the most widespread North American species of the genus, but we also find Geyer's onion (*A. geyeri*) and textile onion (*A. textile*) along some of these hikes. In North America, scientists discovered evidence of indigenous people using a variety of wild onions as food 6,000 years ago. Native Americans ate the young leaves and bulbs raw or cooked. Explorers from both Stephen Long's and Prince Maximilian's nineteenth-century expeditions ate wild onion leaves to cure an illness that probably was scurvy.

Mountain Harebell (*Campanula rotundifolia*)

Also called Bluebell of Scotland. This circumboreal plant is also found in Eurasia. *Campanula* means "small bell" and *rotundifolia* refers to the leaf shape. The Navajo rubbed harebell on their bodies for protection from injury while hunting and for protection from witches.

Mountain harebell

Kinnikinnick (*Arctostaphylos uva-ursi*)

Kinnikinnick

Also called Bearberry. In Greek, *Arctos* means "bear" and *staphyle* means "grape," while *uva* means "grape" and *ursus* means "bear." Bears, along with a host of other animals, enjoy feasting on this berry. Deer and bighorn sheep also browse on the evergreen leaves and twigs in winter. Native Americans smoked the dried leaves of Kinnikinnick on their own or mixed with tobacco. When cooked slowly, the bland berries pop like popcorn.

Wild Rose (*Rosa woodsia*)

Wild rose

Also called Wood's rose after Joseph Woods, an architect, botanist, and scholar. Rose hips, extremely rich in vitamin C, make a delectable trail snack and often taste best after the first frost. Just be sure to remove the inner seeds and hairs because these can irritate the digestive tract. Roses hybridize, so species may be hard to tell apart.

Loveroot (*Ligusticum porteri*)

Loveroot

Also called Osha, wild parsnip, Porter's lovage, and wild celery. Various Native American groups have used roots to ward off rattlesnakes, soothe sore throats, and cure various illnesses especially respiratory infections like colds, coughs, pneumonia, and flu. Wild populations are declining because collectors continue digging up the plant for its medicinal roots. Because conservationists are concerned about its long-term viability, it has been ranked as a rare plant in the United States and has also been ranked as "vulnerable."

Yarrow

Yarrow (*Achillea millefolium, Syn: A. lanulosa*)

Yarrow has many medicinal properties. Taken internally, yarrow tea treats colds and fevers. When applied externally, it relieves burns, sores, pimples, and, perhaps most notably, acts as a styptic—a substance that stops bleeding. Legend has it that Achilles, a hero in Greek mythology, applied yarrow to soldiers' wounds in the battle of Troy, thereby saving the lives of many.

Heartleaf arnica (*Arnica cordifolia*)

Also called Leopard's Bane. Colonists applied a tincture made from this plant to soothe sprains and cuts. Today, arnicas are often used in creams for sore muscles. Some children who have ingested this plant have gone into comas.

Shrubby cinquefoil (*Dasiphora fruticosassp. floribunda, Syn: Pentaphylloides floribunda, D. floribunda*)

Also called yellow rose (formerly *Potentilla fruticosa*), varieties of this plant are popular in yards and gardens. Native American tribes have used various parts of this plant for medicinal and ceremonial purposes, including drinking tea made from the leaves. *Potentilla* comes from the Latin "potens" for "powerful" and may denote the medicinal value of some species.

Heartleaf arnica

Shrubby cinquefoil

38 Willow Creek-South Rim Loop

Traverse a shady hillside, cross flower-filled meadows, and follow a tranquil stream on a delightful journey through Roxborough State Park, a natural wonderland located in the transition zone between Colorado's plains and mountains. This short, lollipop trail rolls over undulating terrain lined with shrubs and trees and dotted with colorful blooms. Expect sublime vistas of otherworldly red rock fins across the valley and the opportunity to spot a range of birds and colorful blooms.

Start: From the Willow Creek Trailhead at the first parking area on your left after you enter Roxborough State Park (6,120 feet)

Distance: 2.9-mile lollipop

Hiking time: 1.5–2 hours

Difficulty: Easy due to gradual, smooth terrain and moderate elevation gain

Trail surface: Dirt and forested trail

Best season: May to September

Peak bloom: mid-May to late June

Flowers commonly found: aromatic sumac, golden currant, Canada violet, lanceleaf chiming bells, Fendler's waterleaf, poison hemlock, Nuttall's larkspur, golden banner, orange paintbrush, leafy cinquefoil, sulphur flower, sand lily, Drummond's milkvetch, blue flax, yellow prairie violet, Oregon grape, short's milkvetch, yucca, mouse-ear chickweed, Colorado locoweed, western wallflower, sprawling daisy, Easter daisy, Britton skullcap, white peavine, spring beauty, chokecherry, leafy cinquefoil, heartleaf arnica, silvery lupine, boulder raspberry, monument plant, wild plum, wild licorice, scorpionweed

Other trail users: Runners; trails closed to horses and bicycles

Canine compatibility: Dogs not permitted

Land status: State park

Nearest town: Littleton

Fees and permits: Daily fee or annual parks pass required; available at the park entrance station, the Visitor Center, or the self-service station.

Schedule: Open all year; summer hours: 5 a.m. to 9 p.m.

Maps: USGS Kassler; Trails Illustrated 135 Deckers, Rampart Range Trail Map; Colorado Parks and Wildlife Pocket Trail Map #47: Roxborough State Park Trail Use Map (available on website)

Trail contact: Roxborough State Park, Roxborough; (303) 973-3959; http://www.cpw .state.co.us/placestogo/parks/Roxborough/

Special considerations: The park is day-use only.

Finding the trailhead: From Denver, take Wadsworth Boulevard (CO 121) south. Continue 4.5 miles past Wadsworth's intersection with CO 470 to turn south (left) on Waterton Road (just before the entrance to Lockheed Martin). Continue on Waterton Road for 1.6 miles until it ends. Turn south (right) on North Rampart Range Road, continuing south for 2.3 miles past Roxborough Village and the Foothills Water Treatment Plant. At the intersection of North Rampart Range Road and Roxborough Park Road (just before the entrance to the Arrowhead golf course), turn left onto Roxborough Park Road. Take the next, almost immediate right on Roxborough Drive to enter the park. Pay the fee and continue following the road as it curves west to reach a small parking area on the left. If this is full, continue another 750 feet to reach two parking lots on your right. **GPS: N39 25.768′/ W105 03.824′**

The Hike

Head downhill on the Willow Creek Trail past aromatic sumac, willow, and golden currant to reach a bridge that crosses over Willow Creek. Climbing into the shade of scrub oak, look closely to find whitish-purple Canada violets bursting from the undergrowth. Revel in the sound of the bubbling rivulet as you move past lanceleaf chiming bells, Fendler's waterleaf, poison hemlock, and Nuttall's larkspur. Reach an open slope where a breathtaking scene awaits to your right: brilliant yellow golden banner and bright blue lanceleaf chiming bells bloom against a backdrop of red angled sandstone fins jutting dramatically from the earth.

At an intersection, go left to pick up the South Rim Trail, which cruises through a dazzling display of orange paintbrush, leafy cinquefoil, sulphur flower, sand lily, Drummond's milkvetch, and blue flax. Yellow prairie violets and Oregon grape add bursts of yellow to the shrubby trailside while Nuttall's larkspur, short's milkvetch, and chiming bells add sparkles of blue, pink, and purple. Continue climbing steadily but gradually through a shrubby scrub oak community where aromatic sumac, yucca, mouse-ear chickweed, and brilliant magenta Colorado locoweed add bits of brilliant color.

As the trail switchbacks upward, look across the verdant valley for unique vistas of geologic marvels and rugged sandstone ridges and fins formed from the Fountain, Lyons, and Dakota Hogback formations. The hillside above grows thick with scrub oak, and ahead, views of forested foothills abound. Undulating between sunny spots

View from the South Rim trail

and shady groves, each step reveals new blooms including western wallflower, leafy cinquefoil, Nuttall's larkspur, golden banner, Drummond's milkvetch, sprawling daisy, and Colorado locoweed. Though not as obvious, Easter daisy, Britton's skullcap, yellow prairie violet, Canada violet, sand lily, and white peavine add smaller but equally captivating bursts of white, purple, yellow, and pink.

Easter daisy

Follow more switchbacks past spring beauty, chokecherry, larkspur, and chiming bells. Periodically tiny tunnels of oak offer a respite from the sun. Leveling, the trail reaches an overlook with far-reaching vistas in every direction where lambstongue groundsel blooms. From here, cruise along the rim decorated in shades of yellow from leafy cinquefoil, prairie violets, and more groundsel. An unmarked spur on the left ends at a shaded bench where a break rewards visitors with yet another awesome view.

Return to the main trail and head downhill through a shady forest of conifers and taller scrub oak giving life to Easter daisy, heartleaf arnica, spring beauty, and larkspur. A shaded bench dedicated in loving memory of two Roxborough naturalist guides offers a sweet place to rest in the shade of a giant Douglas fir. Cruise through the forest past a plethora of yellow, purple, and pink blooms to reach an open meadow with another shaded bench. Curving through a field of silvery lupine, the trail seems to head right for the alluring red sandstone formations at the heart of Roxborough.

Calling you toward it, the creek sings a melodic song. Cross a bridge that brings you past stately cottonwoods to reach the Carpenter Peak Trail intersection. Turn right to find boulder raspberry, chokecherry, larkspur, and hillsides covered in sunshine thanks to golden banner. Turn right again at the next signed junction to join the Willow Creek Trail as it descends through a cool forest and then passes through an open spot where monument plants flourish. Cross the brook again into a fragrant mixture of chokecherry, wild plum, and wild licorice. Chiming bells, Canada violet, and scorpionweed blossom nearby. Climb briefly to rejoin the South Rim Trail. Turn north (left) and retrace your steps back to the trailhead.

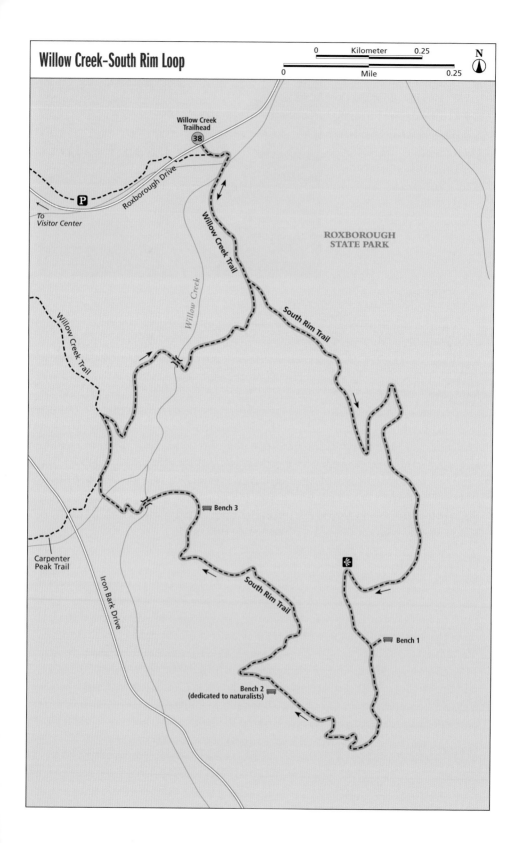

Willow Creek-South Rim Loop

0   Kilometer   0.25

0   Mile   0.25

N

Willow Creek
Trailhead
38

Roxborough Drive

P

To
Visitor Center

Willow Creek Trail

Willow Creek

ROXBOROUGH
STATE PARK

South Rim Trail

Willow Creek Trail

Bench 3

Carpenter
Peak Trail

Iron Bark Drive

South Rim Trail

Bench 1

Bench 2
(dedicated to naturalists)

Miles and Directions

0.0 Start from the Willow Creek Trailhead.

0.2 Reach a signed trail junction. Go southeast (straight) on the South Rim Trail.

1.0 Arrive at a viewpoint offering vistas of angled red rocks lining the valley.

1.1 Near the top of a long hill climb, a spur heads left. A short side trip brings you to a shaded bench with astounding vistas. Return to the main trail and continue south along the can yon rim.

1.5 Heading downhill, pass a shaded bench dedicated to the memory of two Roxborough naturalist guides.

1.9 Reach an open meadow with another shaded bench. Follow the winding trail through a field.

2.0 Curving west (left) through an open meadow, cross a small bridge over the creek.

2.1 At the Carpenter Peak Trail intersection, turn north (right).

2.2 Turn right at the next signed junction to head south on the Willow Creek Trail.

2.4 Turning east, cross the water and follow the trail upward.

2.7 Reach a familiar junction and turn north (left) to rejoin the South Rim Trail.

2.9 Arrive back at the trailhead.

Hike Information

General Information
South Metro Denver Chamber of Commerce: Littleton; (303) 795-0142; bestchamber.com

Local Events/Attractions
Chatfield State Park: Littleton; (303) 791-7275; http://www.cpw.state.co.us/placestogo/Parks/Chatfield

Accommodations
Chatfield State Park Campgrounds: Littleton; (303) 791-7275; http://www.cpw.state.co.us/placestogo/Parks/Chatfield.

Clubs and Organizations
Friends of Roxborough: volunteer naturalists/stewards; Roxborough State Park, Littleton; (303) 973-3959; http://www.cpw.state.co.us/placestogo/parks/Roxborough/Pages/FriendsOfRoxborough.aspx

Hike Tours
Roxborough State Park: Littleton; (303) 973-3959; http://www.cpw.state.co.us/placestogo/Parks/roxborough

39 Green Mountain-Hayden Loop

This easy loop hike around Green Mountain, complete with superb mountain views and fields a wash in colorful blossoms, is a perpetual favorite of locals and visitors alike. Though perched on the city outskirts, this trail offers the chance for full immersion into nature. Perfect as an early morning or late evening adventure, journey through open space and enjoy a respite from the everyday.

Start: From the Florida Trailhead (William Frederick Hayden Park) (6,080 feet)
Distance: 3.4-mile loop
Hiking time: 1.5-2.5 hours
Difficulty: Easy due to distance, gradual, smooth terrain, and minimal elevation gain
Trail surface: Dirt two-track, rocky in spots
Best season: April to July
Peak bloom: mid-May to late June
Flowers commonly found: yucca, whiskbroom parsley, salsify, silvery lupine, Drummond's milkvetch, orange paintbrush, blue flax, wax currant, wild rose, many-stem pea, mountain bluebells, Colorado locoweed, prickly poppy, sand lily, small-flowered alyssum, double bladderpod, golden banner, western wallflower, magenta locoweed, yarrow, mouse-ear chickweed, prairie violet, tall larkspur blanketflower, yellow stonecrop, sulphur flower, Fremont geranium, butter 'n' eggs, Britton skullcap, beautiful cinquefoil, copper globemallow, double bladderpod

Other trail users: Equestrians, mountain bikers
Canine compatibility: Leashed dogs permitted
Land status: City of Lakewood park
Nearest town: Lakewood
Fees and permits: No fees or permits required
Schedule: Open all year; summer hours: 5 a.m. to 10 p.m.
Maps: USGS Riley Canyon, Beaty Canyon, O V Mesa; US Forest Service Comanche National Grassland
Trail contact: William Frederick Hayden Park, Lakewood; (303) 697-6159; lakewood.org/HaydenPark

Finding the trailhead: From Lakewood, head west for 2.8 miles on W Alameda Avenue. Veer south (left) onto W Alameda Parkway and follow it for 1.7 miles. Just after you pass Florida Drive on your left, turn right into the William F. Hayden Green Mountain Park parking lot across from the Green Mountain Recreation Center. **GPS: N39 41.440' / W105 09.134'**

The Hike

From the trailhead, take the right fork of the Green Mountain Trail to begin climbing steadily on an old jeep road that passes through an open slope teeming with yucca, whiskbroom parsley, salsify, silvery lupine, Drummond's milkvetch, orange paintbrush, and blue flax. After one large switchback the trail levels and wax currant, wild rose, many-stem pea, sulphur flower, and mountain bluebells arrive on the scene in a flurry of color.

Ascend to pass an old gate climbing through a rainbow of blooms including Colorado locoweed, orange paintbrush, blue flax, silvery lupine, and prickly poppy.

Views of snow-capped fourteeners, red rock features the foothills loom large from the Green Mountain trail.

Leveling again, the trail moves across a green grassy slope punctuated by sand lilies, small-flowered alyssum, double bladderpod, golden banner, and Drummond's milkvetch. Reach a junction with the Hayden Trail, which heads south (left), but continue past it to traverse a hill teeming with wild roses, western wallflower, brilliant magenta locoweed, orange paintbrush, and salsify. Looking across the valley to your left gives a glimpse of where the trail will eventually lead you.

Pass a Trail Closed sign and continue along the rising path to find a slope dappled with yarrow, bluebells, sand lily, mouse-ear chickweed, wallflower, and yellow prairie violet, an alluring and hardy plant with bright yellow flowers and purple stripes that act as nectar guides. Near the radio tower to find tall larkspur and a multitude of other orange, magenta, yellow, white, blue, and purple blossoms. Before cruising past the tower, pause to look back for a stunning view of Denver and the Dakota Hogback, a unique jutting geologic formation. Continue along a leveling trail where distant views of Mount Evans, Pikes Peak, and Longs Peak, three snow-capped summits rising above 14,000 feet, dominate the skyline in all directions.

When you come to a junction with the Summit Loop Trail, which heads off to the northeast (right), turn left to follow the Green Mountain Trail. Soon reach an intersection with the Hayden Trail, an obvious path that cuts across the hillside. Turn left and begin curving southeast. Across the valley, awesome vistas of unique red

Britton skullcap

rock features reward your efforts. Begin your descent through a rainbow of wildflowers including yellow prairie violets, whiskbroom parsley, orange paintbrush, blanketflower, yellow stonecrop, sulphur flower, Fremont geranium, blue flax, bluebells, wallflower, and butter 'n' eggs, a noxious and invasive weed with yellow and goldish-orange blooms.

Curve left to pass another Trail Closed sign. Continue around the bend heading downhill passing more brilliant magenta Colorado locoweed, parsley, and wallflower. Overwhelming views in every direction—frosty peaks, red rocks, forested foothills—draw your attention upward. Pikes Peak stands like a sentinel straight ahead. Turn another corner and the trail snakes back into the wild making you feel much further away from civilization. Tiny but radiant Britton's skullcap pushes through rocky soil amid orange paintbrush, beautiful cinquefoil, copper globemallow, and double bladderpod. At a junction with the Green Mountain Trail, stay straight and continue downhill passing blanketflower, wild rose, and many-stem pea. Reach another junction and go left, heading downhill before the trail climbs once again to pass through an intoxicatingly sweet-smelling grove of chokecherry. Beautiful displays of Drummond's milkvetch, bluebells, Colorado locoweed, tall larkspur, and Britton's skullcap divert your attention from the road as you return to the parking area.

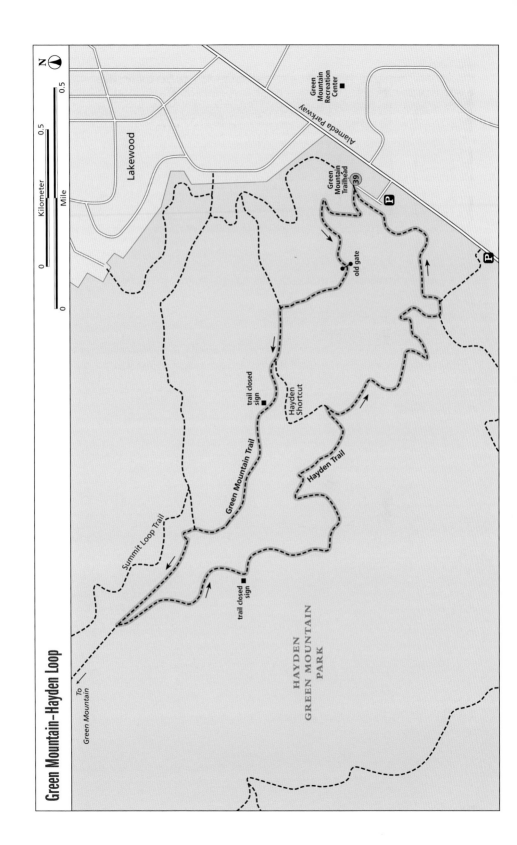

Green Mountain–Hayden Loop

Lakewood

Green Mountain Recreation Center

Alameda Parkway

Green Mountain Trailhead

39

P

P

old gate

trail closed sign

Hayden Shortcut

Hayden Trail

Green Mountain Trail

Summit Loop Trail

trail closed sign

To Green Mountain

HAYDEN GREEN MOUNTAIN PARK

N

Kilometer
0   0.5

Mile
0   0.5

Miles and Directions

0.0 From the parking lot, climb steadily on the Green Mountain Trail, an old road heading steeply up the hill in front of you.

0.4 Pass an old metal gate.

0.6 At an intersection with the Hayden Trail, continue straight to stay on the Green Mountain Trail.

0.8 Pass a Trail Closed sign and continue along the rising trail.

1.1 At a junction with the Summit Loop Trail, veer left to follow the Green Mountain Trail and pass the radio tower.

1.4 Turn southeast (left) at a junction with the Hayden Trail, which sharply angles back as it heads downhill.

1.8 Curve left to pass another Trail Closed sign before heading downhill.

2.5 At a junction with the Green Mountain Trail, stay straight and continue downhill on the Hayden Trail.

3.0 Reach an unsigned junction. Go east (left).

3.4 Arrive back at the trailhead.

Options: For a shorter journey, turn left at the first intersection with the Hayden Trail. For a longer adventure, continue on the Green Mountain Trail or explore the Summit Loop.

Hike Information

General Information

Colorado Tourism: Denver; 1-800-COLORADO; colorado.com

Visit Denver: Denver; (800) 233-6837; denver.org

The West Chamber: Lakewood; (303) 233-5555; westchamber.org

40 Caribou Ranch Loop

Caribou Ranch Open Space, a 2,151-acre parcel of protected land perched in the shadow of the Continental Divide, rests in the montane zone between 8,300 and 10,000 feet. Located a few miles north of Nederland, an easy 4.9-mile meander along a tranquil, well-defined trail visits forest, meadows, and wetlands, offering first-class wildflower viewing and the opportunity to see a range of wildlife from moose to mountain lion. Along this picturesque route, discover the area's rich history by exploring a homestead and historic mining complex.

Start: From the Caribou Ranch Trailhead (8,600 feet)
Distance: 4.9-mile lollipop (includes two short side trips)
Hiking time: 2–3 hours
Difficulty: Easy due to distance, gradual, smooth terrain, and minimal elevation gain
Trail surface: Dirt two-track and forested trail
Best season: July to October
Peak bloom: July
Flowers commonly found: Scarlet paintbrush, beautiful and shrubby cinquefoil, yellow stonecrop, whiskbroom parsley, kinnikinnick, Onesided penstemon, rosy pussytoes, golden banner, aspen and annual sunflower, mountain harebell, Fremont geranium, western wallflower, spotted coralroot orchid, wild rose, wax currant, sulphur flower, blanketflower, Colorado locoweed, cutleaf daisy, silvery lupine, yarrow, northern bedstraw, loveroot, blanketflower,

Colorado columbine, monument plant, globeflower, cow parsnip, shooting star, scarlet gilia, white fairy trumpets, boulder raspberry, fireweed, false Solomon's seal, black-eyed Susans, mountain bluebells
Other trail users: Equestrians
Canine compatibility: Dogs prohibited
Land status: County parks and open space
Nearest town: Nederland
Fees and permits: No fees or permits required
Schedule: Closed April 1–June 30 to protect migratory birds and calving and rearing elk. Open July 1–March 31; sunrise to sunset.
Maps: USGS Nederland; Trails Illustrated 102 Indian Peaks, Gold Hill; Latitude 40 Boulder County; Caribou Ranch Trail Map
Trail contact: Boulder County Parks & Open Space, 5201 St. Vrain Road, Longmont, 80503; (303) 441-4444; www.bouldercountyopenspace.org

Finding the trailhead: From the roundabout in Nederland, head west on CO 72 for 2 miles. At the sign for Caribou Ranch Open Space, turn left onto CO 126. Follow this dirt road for 0.9 mile, then turn right into the obvious parking lot. **GPS: N39 58.946' / W105 31.159'**

The Hike

From the start, this tranquil trail through ponderosa pine really delivers. Scarlet paintbrush, shrubby cinquefoil, yellow stonecrop, and whiskbroom parsley colorfully greet your arrival into the forest as you climb to a bench perched where views abound. Catch your breath and descend through healthy stands of delicate aspens and sturdy pines anchored in a ground covered with plentiful kinnikinnick and juniper.

Visit the Delonde Homestead, a highlight of this journey

Leveling, find Onesided penstemon, rosy pussytoes, golden banner, annual sunflower, mountain harebell, Fremont geranium, and western wallflower painting the forest floor with speckles of color. Wild rose, wax currant, shrubby cinquefoil, and sulphur flower lead the way to an aspen-encased meadow bursting with blanketflower, yellow stonecrop, Colorado locoweed, mountain harebell, and cutleaf daisy. Walk through a mini-aspen grove to find silvery lupine, harebell, wild rose, rosy pussytoes, yarrow, northern bedstraw, geranium, and paintbrush blossoming with a flourish.

Head back into a pine grove sheltering spotted coralroot orchids. Spitting you out into the open where more magenta, yellow, purple, blue, and red blooms await, the trail intersects with an old road that was once part of the Switzerland Trail of America, the 26.1-mile narrow gauge railroad that traveled from Boulder to Ward via sublime mountain scenery, comparable to any in Europe.

Various blossoms—paintbrush, lupine, blanketflower, shrubby cinquefoil, locoweed, Onesided penstemon, and sulphur flower—thrive on the roadside lined with conifers and aspens. Descending slightly, catch a glimpse of foothill peaks and find Colorado columbine and monument plant thriving here.

Reaching the Bluebird Loop, head north (right) to drop down past beautiful cinquefoil, blanketflower, Colorado locoweed, and wild rose. Nearing the homestead, the road parallels a creek supporting globeflower, cow parsnip, and loveroot. Look closely to find shooting stars in the vicinity before following the path to reach the DeLonde Homestead, a structure with a storied past that involves being used as an Arabian horse ranch, a movie set for *Stagecoach*, and a recording studio for legends like Elton John.

Monument plant

Pick up a narrow path that passes some new flowers including scarlet gilia, white fairy trumpets (a subspecies of scarlet gilia), and boulder raspberry. Continue meandering through this lusher, forested riparian corridor to reach a set of stairs heading down to the brook where fireweed, wild rose, false Solomon's seal, and geranium await.

At a signed junction with the Bluebird Mine Complex Trail, turn right and follow this short but steep spur trail lined with gold and magenta (senecio and Colorado locoweed) to reach the spot that drew many optimistic miners in the 1870s. Named

▶ **TIDBIT—Though Caribou Ranch is home to many animals, there are no caribou here. Legend has it that a prospector who had been mining in British Columbia's Cariboo Range came to the area and saw a connection between the two places that led to the name.**

for blue azurite, a mineral often found in silver ore, the Blue Bird remained in action until the 1960s. Interpretive signs guide your exploration of the remains, which include a bunkhouse, mining company house, smoke house, and mine shafts. While imagining what life was like centuries ago, notice plentiful blossoms—rose, geranium, cinquefoil, daisies, locoweed, and blanketflower—proliferating amid the structures. Continue past the last outbuilding to a private picnic table resting next to a cascade on North Boulder Creek.

Regain the main trail, which gradually descends through an aspen grove. The road opens up to a stunning meadow where blanketflower, black-eyed Susans, and Colorado locoweed provide a colorful foreground for views of the homestead and foothills. Weaving in and out of open montane meadows bursting with blooms, the

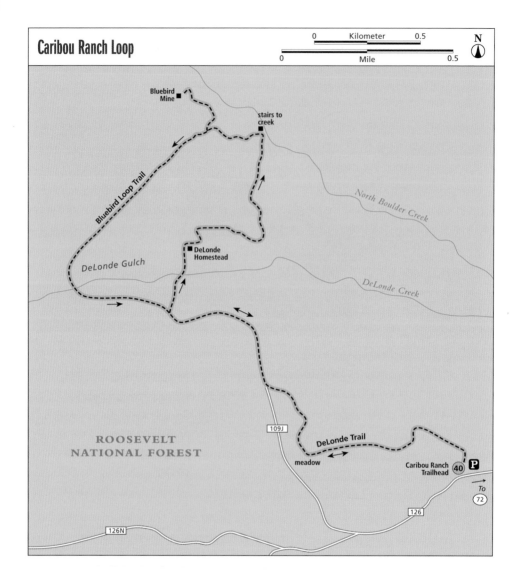

Caribou Ranch Loop

0   Kilometer   0.5

N

0   Mile   0.5

Bluebird Mine

stairs to creek

North Boulder Creek

Bluebird Loop Trail

DeLonde Gulch

DeLonde Homestead

DeLonde Creek

ROOSEVELT NATIONAL FOREST

109J

DeLonde Trail

meadow

Caribou Ranch Trailhead   40

To 72

126

126N

rose-lined road crosses DeLonde Creek to reveal mountain bluebells, golden banner, aspen sunflower, and globeflower. Continue straight to reach the end of the loop. Retrace your steps back to the trailhead keeping an eye out for elk, black bears, coyote, bobcats, moose, and mountain lions—just some of the animals who call Caribou Ranch home.

Miles and Directions

0.0   Head northwest on the DeLonde trail from the trailhead.

0.5   Reach a meadow bursting with every color of the rainbow.

0.8   Curving west (left), intersect with an old road. Turn north (right) onto the road.

1.2 Reach a junction with the Bluebird Loop where you turn north (right).

1.5 Arrive at the DeLonde Homestead. Explore and then turn east (right).

2.1 After following a narrow path through the forest, reach a set of stairs that head down to the creek. Return to the main trail and head northwest from here.

2.3 Turn right at a signed junction with the Bluebird Mine complex trail.

2.5 A short steep climb brings you to the Bluebird Mine. Return to the main trail and follow it downhill.

3.4 Turn east (left), cross DeLonde Creek, and continue straight.

3.7 Come to the end of the loop where the Bluebird and DeLonde Trails intersect. Travel east on the DeLonde Trail to return the way you came.

4.9 Arrive back at the trailhead.

Options: Even if you decide to turn around at the first meadow, the sheer density of blooms, variety of species, and moment of solitude make it all worth it.

Hike Information

General Information

Boulder Chamber of Commerce: Boulder; (303) 442-1044; boulderchamber.com/
Boulder Convention & Visitors Bureau: Boulder; (303) 938-2098; http://www .bouldercoloradousa.com/cvb/
Nederland Area Chamber and Visitors Center; Nederland; (303) 258-3936

Local Events/Attractions

Frozen Dead Guy Days: Nederland; (303) 763-0267; frozendeadguydays.org

41 Lichen Loop

Heil Valley Ranch, a 5,000-acre protected parcel near Boulder, encompasses the transition zone where the Great Plains meet the Rockies. Traveling along a rocky, forested, pedestrian-only path through the foothills, the short, easy Lichen Loop Trail offers the ideal introduction to the region's grasslands and forests, not to mention the wildflowers and wildlife that thrive here. Highlights include periodic breaks in the forest that reward your efforts with vistas of surrounding foothills and open meadows and hillsides teeming with colorful blossoms.

Start: From the main trailhead at Heil Valley Ranch (6,000 feet)
Distance: 1.6-mile lollipop
Hiking time: 1–1.5 hours
Difficulty: Easy due to distance, gradual, smooth terrain, and minimal elevation gain
Trail surface: Dirt and forested trail
Best season: April to October
Peak bloom: mid-May to early June
Flowers commonly found: sulphur flower, Fremont geranium, curly dock, onesided and low penstemon, Colorado locoweed, tall and plains larkspur, miner's candle, sand lily, yucca, prickly pear cactus, prickly poppy, spiderwort, spiked gilia, creamtips, blanketflower, yucca, blue flax, tall coneflower, scarlet gaura, mullein, western wallflower, shrubby cinquefoil, mariposa lily, mountain harebells, mountain bluebells, mouse-ear chickweed, spotted coralroot orchid, Oregon grape, whiskbroom parsley, wild rose, silvery lupine, chokecherry, boulder raspberry, aromatic sumac, Rocky Mountain loco

Other trail users: Hikers only
Canine compatibility: Dogs prohibited
Land status: County parks and open space
Nearest town: Boulder
Fees and permits: No fees or permits required
Schedule: Open all year; sunrise to sunset
Maps: USGS Boulder; Trails Illustrated 100 Boulder/Golden; Latitude 40 Boulder County; Heil Valley Ranch Trail Map
Trail contact: Boulder County Parks & Open Space, 5201 St. Vrain Road, Longmont 80503; (303) 441-4444; www.bouldercountyopenspace.org

Finding the trailhead: From Boulder, take US 36 north for 4.7 miles. Turn west (left) onto Left Hand Canyon Drive for 0.7 mile. Turn north (right) at a sign for Heil Valley Ranch onto Geer Canyon Road. Continue for 1.3 miles to reach a parking area on the right. **GPS: N40 08.964'/W105 18.006'**

The Hike

Lichen Loop, marked by a map and information sign, begins on the north side of the parking area where you can find sulphur flower, Fremont geranium, curly dock, and low penstemon. Cross a seasonal stream on a small footbridge to reach a trail junction. Turn left on the trail that heads up through an open meadow blooming with Colorado locoweed, plains larkspur, miner's candle, and sand lily.

Reach a signed junction for the Lichen Loop. You can go either direction here, but to follow our path turn east (right). Head into sparse forest, popping in and out of open meadows to find yucca, prickly pear cactus, and prickly poppy. The wide rocky dirt trail rises gradually through the forest where spiderwort, spiked gilia, Onesided penstemon, and creamtips add speckles of bright purple, pink, and yellow to the landscape.

Hugging a vast oak- and pine-lined meadow frequented by turkeys, find blanketflower, yucca, blue flax, Onesided penstemon,

Yucca with meadow Lichen Loop

and a multitude of white daisies. Curving right at the edge of the meadow, the trail climbs gradually past tall coneflower, scarlet gaura, mullein, and aromatic sumac to reach a big boulder that would make a good bench if you need a resting spot. Continue climbing gently through the forest past western wallflower and plains paintbrush to reach a shaded bench perfect for a pause so you can rejoice in the beauty and all the buzzing birds. Leveling, the trail passes through another meadow bursting with shrubby cinquefoil, daisies, and mariposa lilies. Peer through openings in the trees to snag impressive views of forested foothill peaks towering across the ravine.

Skirt the rest of the meadow and return to the shady forest where yarrow, mullein, and thistle thrive. Abert's squirrels scurry through the pines as you pass mountain harebells, mountain bluebells, spotted coral root orchid, mouse-ear chickweed, miner's candle, mullein, and prickly pear cactus blooming in brilliant yellow. Zigzag down

through the trees via a few gradual switchbacks that reveal spotted coralroot orchids and Oregon grape creeping along the forest floor. When you reach an intersection with the Waipiti Trail, turn south (left) to stay on the Lichen Loop as it heads out into a sunny meadow teeming with tall larkspur, whiskbroom parsley, and Fremont geranium. Wild rose, prickly pear cactus, blanketflower, geranium, larkspur, silvery lupine, and penstemon paint the hillsides in a flurry of color as you continue down-valley. Chokecherry, boulder raspberry, and aromatic sumac bloom upslope. Though flowers light up the trail, be sure to catch the stunning vistas of Green Mountain and Bear Peak in the distance behind Boulder.

Blanketflower

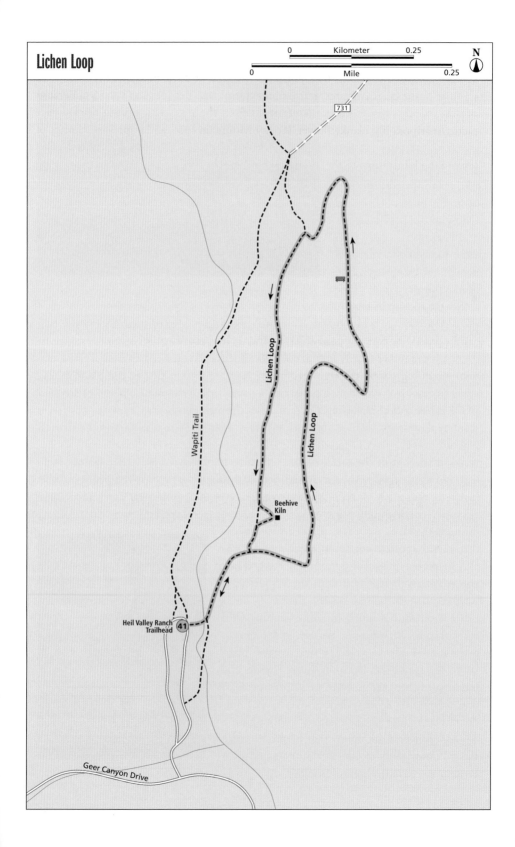

Just as the trail levels, find a turnoff to the left that brings you to the remains of a beehive kiln used to make quicklime and charcoal, products used by early settlers for a number of reasons. An interpretive sign explains that this location was ideal because of the natural limestone deposits nearby. Rejoin the main trail passing prickly pear cactus, mariposa lily, blanketflower, Rocky Mountain loco, and impressive clumps of plains larkspur that light up the meadow with their creamy white spires. Shortly after leaving the kiln, return to the intersection where the loop started. Head south to pick up the stem of the "lollipop." Retrace your steps back to the trailhead via this trail.

Miles and Directions

0.0 From the trailhead, head north, cross a seasonal creek on a small footbridge, and immediately go north (left) at a signed trail junction.

0.2 Pass through an open meadow to reach a signed junction for the Lichen Loop. To follow our path, turn east (right).

0.7 Continue meandering gently through the forest to reach a shaded bench perfect for a pause.

1.0 Reach the Waipiti Trail junction. Turn south (left) to stay on the Lichen Loop.

1.3 After descending through the forest, the trail levels to reach a historic beehive kiln.

1.4 Return to the intersection where the loop started. Head south (right) to retrace your steps back to the trailhead.

1.6 Arrive back at the trailhead.

Hike Information

General Information

Boulder Chamber of Commerce: Boulder; (303) 442-1044; boulderchamber.com/ Boulder Convention & Visitors Bureau: Boulder; (303) 938-2098; http://www .bouldercoloradousa.com/cvb/

42 Ouzel Falls Trail

This 5.4-mile out-and-back hike through Rocky Mountain National Park's lush Wild Basin follows a raging brook to visit three waterfalls of varying power and size. Experience varied and dazzling wildflower displays as you discover this verdant forest. Well-worn and easy to navigate, this moderate trail, which is steep, rocky, and rugged in spots, rewards adventurers with beautiful river-valley scenery.

Start: From the Wild Basin Trailhead (8,520 feet)
Distance: 5.4-mile out and back
Hiking time: 2–4 hours
Difficulty: Moderate due to elevation gain, rocky terrain, and steep sections
Trail surface: Rocky, dirt and forestedtrail
Best season: June to October
Peak bloom: early to mid-July
Flowers commonly found: yarrow, northern bedstraw, western yellow paintbrush, golden banner, Gray's angelica, northern goldenrod, beautiful daisy, yellow stonecrop, sulphur flower, mountain harebell, aspen sunflower, blanketflower, Colorado columbine, Richardson's geranium, mountain bluebells, beautiful cinquefoil, bog pyrola, twinflower, pearly everlasting, rosy pussytoes, yellow monkeyflower, monkshood, twisted stalk, white bog orchid, scarlet and Wyoming paintbrush, Geyer's onion, mouse-ear chickweed, heartleaf arnica, wild strawberry, wild rose, cow parsnip, spotted coralroot orchid, greenflower pyrola, One-sided wintergreen, kinnikinnick, Whipple's penstemon, heartleaf bittercress, brook saxifrage, triangularleaf senecio, false Solomon's seal, single delight, green mitrewort, fairy slipper, golden banner, fireweed
Other trail users: Equestrians
Canine compatibility: Dogs prohibited
Land status: National Park
Nearest towns: Estes Park
Fees and permits: Entrance fee required. Wilderness permits are required for overnight camping (970-586-1242); a fee is charged. Download the Wilderness Camping Guide from the park website.
Schedule: Open all year, though Trail Ridge Road is closed from Many Parks Curve to Colorado River Trailhead from mid-October to Memorial Day.
Maps: USGS Allenspark; Nat Geo Trails Illustrated 200 Rocky Mountain National Park & 301 Longs Peak: Rocky Mountain National Park [Bear Lake, Wild Basin]; Latitude 40 Front Range Trails; Rocky National Park Map
Trail contacts: Rocky Mountain National Park; 1000 Hwy. 36, Estes Park, 80517; (970) 586-1206; www.nps.gov/romo

Finding the trailhead: From Estes Park, drive 12.6 miles south on CO 7 to the Wild Basin Road junction and turn right. After 0.4 mile, turn right, pay the fee at the entrance station, and continue into the park. After 2.2 miles on a narrow, well-maintained gravel road, reach the Wild Basin Trailhead on the left. This is a popular area which can be very busy and congested. Plan ahead for a more enjoyable visit. In summer, the park's busiest times are between 9 a.m. and 3 p.m. Expect congestion, including full parking lots, busy roads, and crowded trails.
GPS: N40 12.506' / W105 33.660'

The Hike

Just after leaving the trailhead, cross two small wooden bridges into a tranquil forest where wild rose, green mitrewort, and spotted coralroot orchid bloom amid the pines. Yarrow, northern bedstraw, western yellow paintbrush, golden banner, Gray's angelica, and northern goldenrod make an appearance early in your walk.

Quaking aspens give the wide, well-defined trail an ethereal look while beautiful daisies, stonecrop, sulphur flower, mountain harebells, aspen sunflower, and blanket-flower add bursts of color to the forest floor. Nearby, impressive clusters of Colorado columbine, Richardson's geranium, mountain bluebells, and beautiful cinquefoil adorn the route.

Soon, a wetter spot gives rise to bog pyrola and twinflower, tiny delicate pinkish blooms that draw your eye downward. Pearly everlasting and rosy pussytoes bloom in a flurry of creamy white before you hop a few rocks to cross the creek where yellow monkeyflower, bog pyrola, and more mountain bluebells thrive.

Cross a small bridge to find monkshood, twisted stalk, and white bog orchid. Off to the left, a spur trail lined with yarrow and scarlet paintbrush leads to Copeland Falls, a pretty cascade lined with granite boulders. The main trail reveals Geyer's onion, mouse-ear chickweed, and more brilliant yellow in the form of beautiful cinquefoil.

Calypso cascades roars through the forest

Ouzel Falls Trail

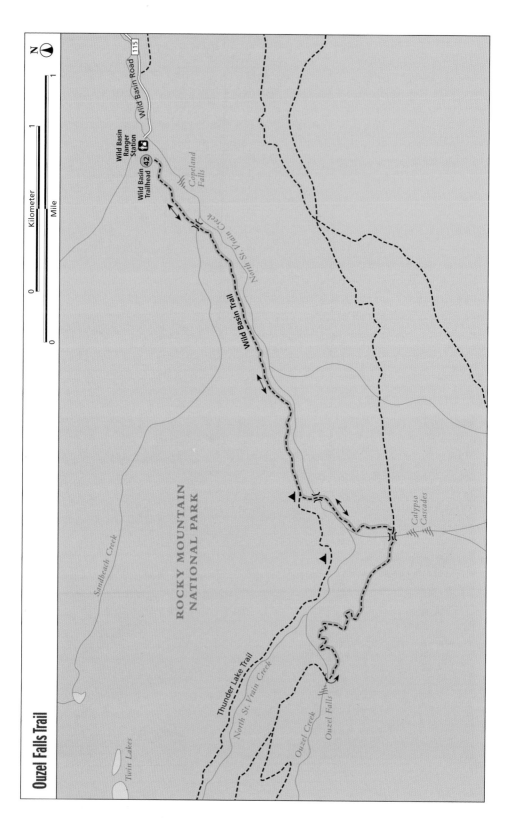

Sulphur flower, northern bed-straw, heartleaf arnica, and aspen sunflower dapple the trailside.

Reveling in the rushing water sound, meander past wild strawberry, Colorado columbine, wild rose, cow parsnip, mountain bluebells, and feathery blooms of Gray's angelica. The bright purple buds of monkshood make an occasional appearance here. Remain observant as you continue climbing to discover spotted coralroot orchid, bog pyrola, and green-flower pyrola hiding in the undergrowth.

Colorado columbine

A rock ledge affords splendid views of dense trees and cliffs across the way. Cross the brook to find One-sided wintergreen, bog pyrola, kinnikinnick, and rosy pussytoes awaiting. Steepening and becoming increasingly rugged, the trail moves toward Calypso Cascades, which announces its existence with a thundering roar. Whipple's penstemon, heartleaf bittercress, brook saxifrage, and triangularleaf senecio join others to create a colorful garden. Just below the falls, false Solomon's seal and twisted stalk appear.

Reach Calypso Cascades, where three small bridges carry you across its length. Look closely in the moist, shady, evergreen forest to find more twinflower, pyrola, single delight, green mitrewort, and perhaps even fairy slippers, an orchid with delicate and fragrant rose-purple to pink flowers with a slipper-shaped lip. The trail levels briefly, passing Wyoming paintbrush and golden banner before crossing the creek via some well-placed boulders. Rosy pussytoes and wild roses greet you on the other side amid an array of lush vegetation. The increasingly rocky and rugged trail climbs more steeply now, passing rocky outcrops harboring yellow stonecrop. Breaks in the trees, largely due to the Ouzel Fire of 1978, offer spectacular summit vistas and a glimpse of fireweed's bright magenta racemes. Large steps and switchbacks ease the ascent as do the rainbow of blooms of paintbrush, golden banner, mountain harebells, pearly everlasting, and Colorado columbine. Enter a more shaded canopy of pines to find the mighty Ouzel Falls, adorned with heartleaf bittercress and thick clusters of mountain bluebells, awaiting your arrival. Revel in the power of the falls, enjoying a well-earned rest here before heading back to the trailhead the way you came.

Miles and Directions

0.0 Start from the Wild Basin Trailhead and Ranger Station.

0.3 Cross the creek on a small bridge.

0.4 Off to the left, take a spur trail south to Copeland Falls. Return to the main trail and continue southwest along the creek.

1.5 Continue south past a junction with a trail heading north to reach campsites.

1.6 Cross the water on a big bridge and begin climbing more steeply over rocky terrain.

1.9 Pass a sign and a spur trail for a privy and hitch rack to reach Calypso Cascades. Turn west (right) crossing three tiny bridges to head away from the brook.

2.7 After climbing more steeply over rugged terrain, arrive at Ouzel Falls. Retrace your path when ready.

5.4 Arrive back at the trailhead.

Hike Information

General Information
Visit Estes Park: Estes Park; (970) 577-9900; (800) 443-7837; visitestespark.com

Local Events/Attractions
Estes Park Area Historical Museum: Estes Park; (970) 586-6256; estesparkmuseumfriends.org/our-museum

Longs Peak Scottish/Irish Highland Festival: Estes Park; (970) 586-6308, 800-90ESTES (800-903-7837); scotfest.com

MacGregor Ranch Museum: Estes Park; (970) 586-3749; macgregorranch.org

Clubs and Organizations
Rocky Mountain Conservancy: Estes Park; (970) 586-0108; rmconservancy.org

Hike Tours
Rocky Mountain Conservancy: Estes Park; (970) 586-0108; rmconservancy.org

Rocky Mountain National Park offers park-wide ranger-led programs like bird walks, nature walks, and talks on many interesting topics. Find the schedule in the park newspaper, available at the entrance stations and visitor centers, or check: www.nps .gov/romo/planyourvisit/ranger_led_activities.htm.

43 Gem Lake

This moderately challenging hike to spectacular Gem Lake may feel a lot longer than 3.2 miles, but it's worth every step. Breathtaking views, tiny wildflowers bursting with color, crazy rock formations, and the shallow emerald waters of the lake itself reward those who spend time cruising upward through aspen and ponderosas across the aptly named, boulder-strewn Lumpy Ridge, a massive granite rock area teeming with numerous types of raptors and opportunities for topnotch climbing. Accessible year-round, it's especially suited for those seeking a peek at early season blooms since it's often snow-free well before the rest of the Rocky Mountains.

Start: From the Lumpy Ridge Trailhead (7,840 feet)

Distance: 3.2 miles out and back

Hiking time: 2–3 hours

Difficulty: Moderate due to elevation gain and steep sections

Trail surface: Rocky, dirt and forested trail

Best season: March to October

Peak bloom: June and July

Flowers commonly found: Onesided pentemon, blanketflower, wild iris, black-eyed Susan, chokecherry, heartleaf arnica, yellow stonecrop, waxflower, pasqueflower, wild rose, northern bedstraw, silvery and shrubby cinquefoil, cutleaf daisy, miner's candle, Wyoming paintbrush, sulphur flower, boulder raspberry, shooting star, mountain bluebells, dogbane, rock clematis, fireweed, Fremont geranium, bracted alumroot, dotted saxifrage

Other trail users: Equestrians

Canine compatibility: Dogs prohibited

Land status: National Park

Nearest towns: Estes Park

Fees and permits: Entrance fee required. Wilderness permits are required for overnight camping (970-586-1242); a fee is charged. Download the Wilderness Camping Guide from the park website.

Schedule: Open all year

Maps: USGS Estes Park; Nat Geo Trails Illustrated 200 Rocky Mountain National Park; Latitude 40 Front Range Trails; Rocky National Park Map

Trail contacts: Rocky Mountain National Park; 1000 Hwy. 36, Estes Park, 80517; (970) 586-1206; www.nps.gov/romo

Finding the trailhead: From the intersection of US 34 and US 36 in Estes Park, drive north on Wonderview Avenue (the US 34 Bypass Road) until it meets MacGregor Avenue. Turn north (right) on MacGregor Avenue and follow it for 1.2 miles as it makes a sharp right turn and turns into Devils Gulch Road. The well-marked Lumpy Ridge Trailhead will be on your left. **GPS: N40 23.790'/ W105 30.787'**

The Hike

From the west side of the parking lot, head right past a National Park Service information kiosk and map to pick up the Gem Lake Trail that begins ascending the southeastern part of the massive granite rock outcropping known as Lumpy Ridge.

Views from Gem Lake hike

Almost 2 billion years of wind, erosion, and weathering have sculpted the spectacular blocks, bumps, and lumps that characterize this unique area. Shortly after you start climbing, find Onesided penstemon, blanketflower, wild iris, and black-eyed Susans in a dry, grassy field. Chokecherry and heartleaf arnica bloom in the shade of ponderosa pines and Douglas firs that dominate the trailside as it curves right toward Lumpy Ridge's spectacular granite features. Pass rocky outcrops where yellow stonecrop and waxflower thrive.

After climbing a bit, reach a junction with the Black Canyon Trail. Veer east (right) to enter an aspen-lined section of trail that passes pasqueflower, wild rose, northern bedstraw, shrubby cinquefoil, cutleaf daisy, miner's candle, and Wyoming paintbrush.

While ascending, you'll find many points where the forest breaks to afford panoramic vistas of Estes Park, Mount Meeker, the Twin Sisters, the looming Longs Peak (14,259 feet), and the many other snow-capped peaks of the Continental Divide. Rocky ledges bursting with the yellow of sulphur flower and stonecrop offer amazing views. Take time to catch your breath and explore a few stony perches where you can soak in all the stunning beauty of this landscape. In addition to wide-ranging views, pass through some spots with giant boulders, balanced rocks, and odd stone formations. Explore as you like!

The views only quit once the trail—which can get quite hot in summer—winds into a welcoming, cool canyon lined with steep walls and a tiny trickle of a stream where waxflower, boulder raspberry, shooting stars, mountain bluebells, spreading dogbane, and rock clematis thrive. Climb a couple of small, short, and steep switchbacks past fireweed, silvery cinquefoil, and Fremont geranium to emerge from this oasis. Just as you reach the top, take note of Paul Bunyan's Boot, a rock formation that lives up to its name almost exactly. Grab a photo here and continue climbing along rocky ledges where you find bracted alumroot and dotted saxifrage growing in cracks and crevices. Tackle one more series of steep switchbacks—complete with spectacular views and stone steps—before the grade mellows and you finally reach Gem Lake (8,880 feet), a tiny but unique body of water carved out of the base of granite cliff walls surrounding it. Gem Lake lacks an inlet or outlet since it is not fed by a stream, but rather receives water from the snowmelt and rainwater that is trapped, collected, and steered into the small basin by surrounding rock. Enjoy a picnic on the beach-like west shore of the lake or explore the vertical granite walls that flank the north and east shores. Keep an eye out

Miner's candle

for aggressive chipmunks after your lunch and giant raptors—who call these cliffs home—soaring overhead.

Miles and Directions

0.0 Start from the Lumpy Ridge Trailhead.

0.5 Reach an intersection with the Black Canyon Trail. Turn right to carry on to Gem Lake.

1.1 While ascending, reach a few open rock slab areas offering panoramic views.

1.3 Follow the trail into a cool steep-walled canyon complete with a tiny trickle of a stream.

1.4 Reach Paul Bunyan's Boot, a rock shaped like a hiking boot with a hole in the sole.

1.7 Leveling, the trail reaches Gem Lake (8,880 feet), a small body of water surrounded by granite cliffs.

3.5 Arrive back at the trailhead.

Options: If you'd like more adventure, follow the trail past Gem Lake to complete the Twin Owls Loop or to visit Bridal Veil Falls.

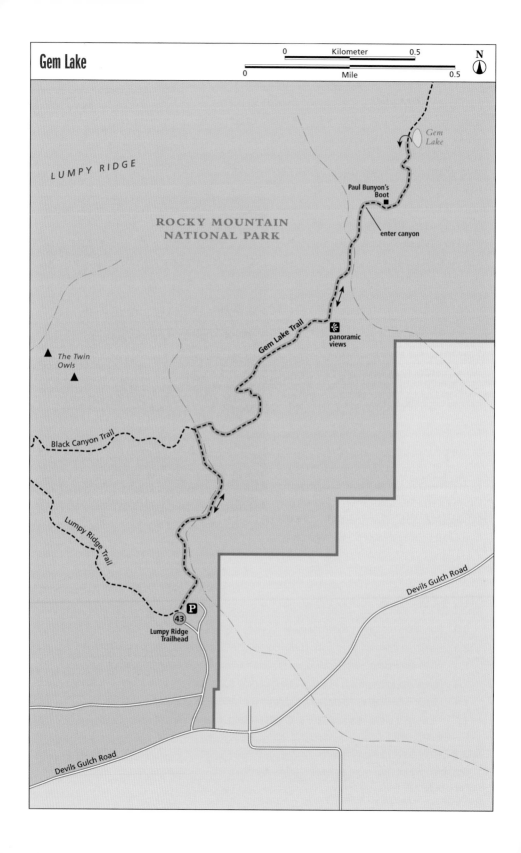

Gem Lake

Kilometer
0   0.5

Mile
0   0.5

N

Gem Lake

Paul Bunyon's Boot

enter canyon

LUMPY RIDGE

ROCKY MOUNTAIN
NATIONAL PARK

panoramic views

Gem Lake Trail

The Twin Owls

Black Canyon Trail

Lumpy Ridge Trail

Devils Gulch Road

P
43
Lumpy Ridge Trailhead

Devils Gulch Road

Hike Information

General Information

Visit Estes Park: Estes Park; (970) 577-9900, (800) 443-7837; visitestespark.com

Local Events/Attractions

Estes Park Area Historical Museum: Estes Park; (970) 586-6256; estesparkmuseum-friends.org/our-museum

Longs Peak Scottish/Irish Highland Festival: Estes Park; (970) 586-6308, 800-90ESTES (800-903-7837); scotfest.com

MacGregor Ranch Museum: Estes Park; (970) 586-3749; macgregorranch.org

Clubs and Organizations

Rocky Mountain Conservancy: Estes Park; (970) 586-0108; rmconservancy.org

Hike Tours

Rocky Mountain Conservancy: Estes Park; (970) 586-0108; rmconservancy.org

Rocky Mountain National Park offers park-wide ranger-led programs like bird walks, nature walks, and talks on many interesting topics. Find the schedule in the park newspaper, available at the entrance stations and visitor centers, or check: www.nps .gov/romo/planyourvisit/ranger_led_activities.htm.

44 Cub Lake Loop

From your very first steps across the Big Thompson River and around the edge of Moraine Park, where enormous elk herds may wander, this 6.6-mile adventure through Rocky Mountain National Park delivers. Wander through moist grassy meadows and cool dense forest past beaver ponds and streams to reach Cub Lake, where mats of yellow pond lilies adorn blue waters. Further highlights of this loop that passes through a variety of habitats include a visit to the turbulent waters of "The Pool," expansive views of rocky crags, and an array of jaw-dropping wildflowers that will not disappoint. Start early to enjoy a few moments of solitude along the way.

Start: From the Cub Lake Trailhead (8,080 feet)
Distance: 6.6-mile loop
Hiking time: 3–4 hours
Difficulty: Moderate due to length, some steep sections, and moderate elevation gain
Trail surface: Rocky, dirt, and forested trail
Best season: May to October
Peak bloom: July
Flowers commonly found: mouse-ear chickweed, shooting star, cow parsnip, beautiful and shrubby cinquefoil, mountain bluebells, sulphur flower, Fremont geranium, mountain harebell, golden banner, yarrow, wild rose, black-eyed Susan, Parry's harebell, horsemint, low penstemon, yellow evening primrose, northern bedstraw, Geyer's onion, western and Wyoming paintbrush, meadow anemone, blanketflower, yellow stonecrop, wax currant, chokecherry, western wallflower, rosy pussytoes, wood lily, tall coneflower, fireweed, heartleaf arnica, red elderberry, dogbane, wild raspberry, strawberry blite, One-sided wintergreen, twinberry, bog

pyrola, pearly everlasting, Colorado columbine, scorpionweed, bracted alumroot
Other trail users: Equestrians
Canine compatibility: Dogs prohibited
Land status: National Park
Nearest towns: Estes Park
Fees and permits: Entrance fee required. Wilderness permits are required for overnight camping (970-586-1242); a fee is charged. Download the Wilderness Camping Guide from the park website.
Schedule: Open all year
Maps: USGS McHenrys Peak; Nat Geo Trails Illustrated 200 Rocky Mountain National Park; Latitude 40 Front Range Trails; Rocky National Park Map
Trail contacts: Rocky Mountain National Park; 1000 Hwy. 36, Estes Park, 80517; (970) 586-1206; www.nps.gov/romo
Special considerations: Arrive early. This area is very popular so arrive early to ensure a parking spot and tranquility.

Finding the trailhead: From Estes Park, head west on US 36/Trail Ridge Road for 2.8 miles to reach the Beaver Meadows Entrance Station. Pay a fee and travel 0.1 mile west to turn left onto Bear Lake Road. Follow Bear Lake Road 1.2 miles to Moraine Park Road and turn right (look for signs for Moraine Park Campground). Continue for 0.5 mile to another junction. Turn left (south) toward the Fern Lake and Cub Lake Trailheads. After 1.2 miles, reach the Cub Lake Trailhead on your left. This is a popular area which can be very busy and congested. Plan ahead for a more enjoyable visit. In summer, the park's busiest times are between 9 a.m. and 3 p.m. Expect congestion, including full parking lots, busy roads, and crowded trails. **GPS: N40 21.369'/W105 36.950'**

The Hike

Magnificent vistas of craggy distant peaks abound as you cross the Big Thompson River. Lush riparian vegetation gives rise to mouse-ear chickweed, shooting stars, and cow parsnip. Shrubby cinquefoil, mountain bluebells, sulphur flower, Fremont geranium, mountain harebell, golden banner, and yarrow blossom as you cut across an expansive meadow frequented by large herds of elk.

Skirt the meadow's edge where wild rose, black-eyed Susan, horsemint, mountain harebell, low penstemon, and yellow evening primrose burst from the ground. Periodically, the violet bell-shaped flowers of Parry's harebell appear. Curving away from the meadow, revel in the views ahead and the melodic brook giving rise to rose, shooting stars, horsemint, northern bedstraw, nodding onion, western yellow and Wyoming paintbrush, and meadow anemone.

Climbing to a drier, rockier slope, the trail moves past blanketflower, yellow stonecrop, sulphur flower, and wax currant. Mountain harebells, Fremont geranium, chokecherry, western wallflower, and currant adorn the trail as it heads downhill and curves around a beaver pond. Move onward to find rosy pussytoes and wood lily, a rare flower whose showy, orange-red blossoms surely catch your eye.

As you climb, you will see beautiful granite slabs, boulders, and cliffs lining the trail's right side, while the willow-lined left side comes alive with fireweed and tall coneflower proudly displaying its showy drooping ray flowers. Ascend the increasingly rocky, rugged, but lush trail brimming with ferns, yarrow, cow parsnip, heartleaf arnica, beautiful cinquefoil, and asters to reach another, more defined beaver pond.

Move steadily upward through rock slabs adorned in a splash of yellow—sulphur flower and stonecrop. Switchbacks ease the ascent as you cruise through a sea of purple punctuated by pink and white harebells, bluebells, paintbrush, asters, red

Mountain views offer a backdrop for pond lilies filling the tranquil Cub Lake

elderberry, cow parsnip, fireweed, tall coneflower, and wild rose blooming enthusiastically. The soothing sound of the water guides you to a signed junction pointing north (right) toward a hitch rack and Wilderness campsites. Continue straight along the leveling trail to pass dogbane and wallflower. Catch your first glimpse of Cub Lake, a dark blue body of water covered in a mass of brilliant yellow pond lilies.

Follow the trail lined with fireweed, wild raspberry, paintbrush, horsemint, yarrow, and tiny aspens as it skirts the right side of the lake and offers views of craggy peaks in the distance. Rising along the lakeside, your path reveals low penstemon, mariposa lily, and a greater perspective on the astounding amount of lilies floating in the water. Tackle a steep rocky section through some small aspens and pine trees to leave the lake.

Wood lily

Descending on rocky, loose terrain toward "The Pool," pass Wyoming paintbrush, wild rose, strawberry blite, bracted alumroot, heartleaf arnica, and dogbane. Dropping steeply into the forest, find One-sided wintergreen, twinberry, bog pyrola, and pearly everlasting. Just beyond a lush cascade, a tiny seep gives life to fireweed, heartleaf arnica, Colorado columbine, and Wyoming paintbrush.

After a long descent, go straight to cross a bridge over the Pool, a

Crossing the Big Thompson River to start the journey to Cub Lake

Cub Lake Loop

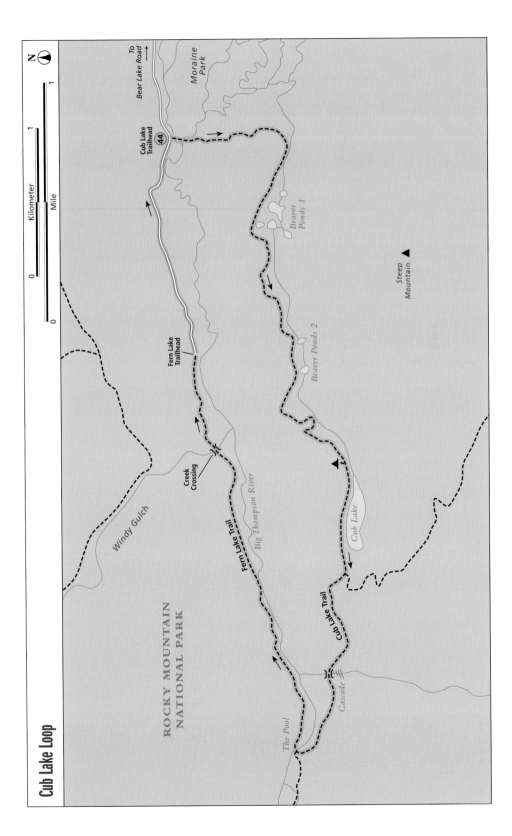

turbulent wide spot in the Big Thompson River. Below the bridge, rolling terrain undulates next to the roaring river past a rainbow of colors created by an array of blooms including scorpionweed, paintbrush, harebell, and arnica. Alternating between open and forested areas, get periodic glimpses of rock cliffs to the left and beaver ponds to the right before crossing a tiny bridge over a stream. Continue heading in the same direction past mariposa lily, asters, and sulphur flower to get even better vistas of the giant cliffs bordering the path. At the Fern Lake Trailhead, turn right and walk back along the road peppered with aspens, wild rose, and sulphur flower to reach the spot where this adventure started.

Miles and Directions

0.0 Start from the Cub Lake Trailhead. Follow the trail heading south along the edge of Moraine Park.

0.6 Turn west (right) away from Moraine Park to enter a wet meadow.

1.0 After a small downhill, pass beaver ponds on the south (left) side of the trail.

1.7 The trail weaves in and out of the forest to reach a grassy spot where a second beaver pond rests.

2.4 After switchbacks, continue west (straight) through a signed junction pointing north (right) to Wilderness campsites.

2.6 Reach Cub Lake and follow the trail skirting its north (right) side.

3.0 Leveling, the trail reaches a signed junction. Go west (right) toward "The Pool."

3.6 Arrive at a lush cascade spanned by a small bridge.

4.0 At a junction where trails head west toward Fern Lake, continue east (straight) to cross a bridge over "The Pool."

5.3 Cross a small bridge over a stream. Continue east along the river.

5.7 Reach the Fern Lake Trailhead. Turn right and walk east along the road.

6.2 Arrive back at the trailhead.

Hike Information

General Information

Visit Estes Park: Estes Park; (970) 577-9900, (800) 443-7837; visitestespark.com

Local Events/Attractions

Estes Park Area Historical Museum: Estes Park; (970) 586-6256; estesparkmuseumfriends .org/our-museum

Longs Peak Scottish/Irish Highland Festival: Estes Park; (970) 586-6308, 800-90ESTES (800-903-7837); scotfest.com

MacGregor Ranch Museum: Estes Park; (970) 586-3749; macgregorranch.org

Clubs and Organizations

Rocky Mountain Conservancy: Estes Park; (970) 586-0108; rmconservancy.org

Hike Tours

Rocky Mountain Conservancy: Estes Park; (970) 586-0108; rmconservancy.org

Rocky Mountain National Park offers park-wide ranger-led programs like bird walks, nature walks, and talks on many interesting topics. Find the schedule in the park newspaper, available at the entrance stations and visitor centers, or check: www.nps .gov/romo/planyourvisit/ranger_led_activities.htm

45 Tundra Communities Trail

This short, easy meander along a paved interpretive trail gives you the opportunity to experience the tundra. Learn about the native plants and animals of the alpine environment and see a multitude of dazzling blooms that adorn the grassy alpine slopes with swatches of yellow, red, pink, blue, purple, and white. You must stay on the trail here, which is a Tundra Protection Area, to protect the fragile alpine tundra from damage caused by walking on it. Though the air is in short supply up here, this short hike requires a relatively small amount of effort and comes with a big payoff for those willing to huff and puff their way to the end.

Start: From the Tundra Communities Trailhead (12,110 feet) at Rock Cut overlook
Distance: 1.1 miles out and back
Hiking time: 20–30 minutes
Difficulty: Short, but moderate due to altitude
Trail surface: Paved trail
Best season: July to September
Peak Bloom: July
Flowers Commonly Found: alpine paintbrush, lanceleaf chiming bells, Parry clover, alpine sorrel, alpine spring beauty, sky pilot, old man of the mountain, alpine avens, alpine clover, yellow western yellow paintbrush, American bistort, moss campion, alpine sandwort, alpine phlox, alpine forget-me-not, dwarf clover, alplily, king's crown, wild candytuft, yellow stonecrop
Other trail users: Hikers only
Canine compatibility: Dogs prohibited
Land status: National Park
Nearest towns: Estes Park, Grand Lake

Fees and permits: Entrance fee required. Wilderness permits are required for overnight camping (970-586-1242); a fee is charged. Download the Wilderness Camping Guide from the park website.
Schedule: Open all year, though access is limited because Trail Ridge Road is closed from Many Parks Curve to the Colorado River Trailhead from mid-October to Memorial Day
Maps: USGS Trail Ridge; Nat Geo Trails Illustrated 200 Rocky Mountain National Park; Latitude 40 Front Range Trails; Rocky National Park Map
Trail contacts: Rocky Mountain National Park; 1000 Hwy. 36, Estes Park, 80517; (970) 586-1206; www.nps.gov/romo
Special considerations: Despite the hike being short, bring layers because the weather can turn from summer to winter in an instant. Alpine tundra is very fragile. You must stay on the Tundra Communities Trail.

Finding the trailhead: From Estes Park, head west on US 36/Trail Ridge Road for 2.8 miles to reach the Beaver Meadows Entrance Station. Pay a fee and travel another 19 miles along Trail Ridge Road to reach the Rock Cut and a signed parking area on the right. This is a popular area which can be very busy and congested. Plan ahead for a more enjoyable visit. In summer, the park's busiest times are between 9 a.m. and 3 p.m. Expect congestion, including full parking lots, busy roads, and crowded trails. **GPS: N40 24.732'/W105 43.975'**

The Hike

Visiting Rocky Mountain National Park offers an unmatched opportunity to access the tundra, or "the land above the trees," with very little effort thanks to Trail Ridge Road, the main artery through Rocky Mountain and the highest road in any National Park. Topping out at 12,183 feet, Trail Ridge transports you above tree line with ease. Stroll at the top of the world and discover a multitude of wonders by picking up the paved path that rises gradually through open tundra teeming with tiny blooms. Pushing forth amid dwarf green grass, find alpine paintbrush, lanceleaf chiming bells, Parry clover, alpine sorrel, and alpine spring beauty, also called big-rooted spring beauty because of its thick, long taproot that retains water in tundra's drying winds.

Summer often lasts only forty days here, yet flowers paint the tundra in a rainbow of color. Their ability to survive is largely due to adaptations. Some have dense hairs for wind protection while others utilize red-colored pigments called anthocyanins to convert the sun's rays into heat. Above tree line, each incredible tiny flower has its own particular niche, whether on wind-blown slopes or next to sheltering rocks.

Continue upward passing dazzling displays of sky pilot, old man of the mountain, alpine avens, alpine clover, and yellow western yellow paintbrush. Brilliant yellows, magenta, purples, and blues bring this otherwise harsh alpine environment to life. American bistort, whose tiny white or pinkish flowers blossom in a tight, oblong

Hardy flowers flourish in the land above the trees

cluster (raceme) atop a slender stem, stands much taller—in a relative sense—than many other flowers up here.

Pause periodically to catch your breath, which may be short this high up, and to take in the increasingly outstanding scenery. Enjoy commanding views of mountains in all directions, including the Never Summer range standing tall to the west and the sentinels of the Mummy Range—Mount Chapin, Mount Chiquita, and Ypsilon Mountain—to the east.

Drawing your attention downward once again, an array of cushion plants including moss campion, alpine sandwort, and alpine phlox light up the scene with brilliant bursts of hot pink, white, and light purple. Cushion plants, which look like clumps of moss, hug the ground to avoid strong winds, and long taproots extend deep into rocky soil to reduce erosion.

More than halfway up, a spur trail on the right brings you to the aptly named Mushroom Rocks, whose "mushroom" appearance arose because the granite stem eroded faster than the schist cap. Take the short side trip to stand in their shadow; rewards include a glimpse of brilliant pink alpine primrose and an unfettered view of Longs Peak (14,259 feet), Forest Canyon, and meadows frequented by elk.

Continuing upslope, alpine forget-me-nots, dwarf clover, old man of the mountain, alplily, alpine avens, bluebells, and sky pilot merge to form lush, intensely colored gardens.

A rock outcrop, known as the Toll Memorial (12,319 feet), marks the trail's end. Here, a bronze plaque honors Roger Wolcott Toll, an avid mountaineer who served as

The Tundra Communities Trail offers easy access to the land above the trees

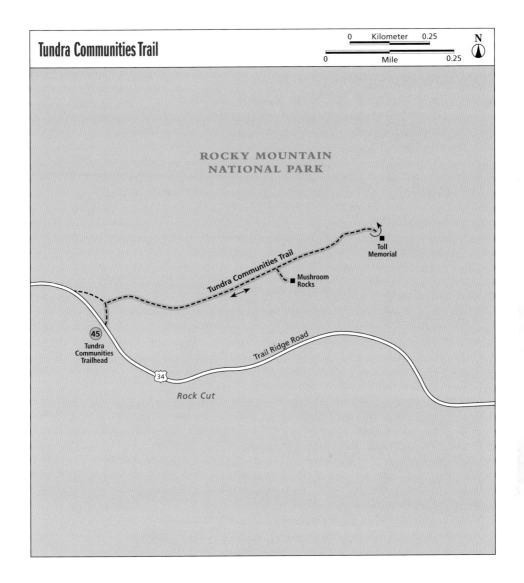

Rocky Mountain's superintendent and ran Mount Rainier and Yellowstone National Parks. Nearby, king's crown, wild candytuft, yellow stonecrop, and alpine phlox bloom.

Take care climbing to the top of this rocky outcrop (if you'd like) to find an elevation marker (12,304 feet) and a circular metal marker that points to other mountain ranges in the park and delineates distances to other National Parks including Yellowstone, Yosemite, and the Grand Canyon. From your perch above, pause to enjoy the vistas and absorb the grandeur of life. Scan for pikas, marmots, ptarmigans, and bighorn sheep. Retrace your steps to the trailhead, remembering that this entire area is a Tundra Protection area and you must stay on the paved trail.

Miles and Directions

0.0 Start from the Tundra Communities Trailhead.

0.4 Reach a spur trail that leads southeast (right) to Mushroom Rocks. Take this worthy side trip to visit unique geologic features that resemble their name.

0.6 Come to the trail's end at the Toll Memorial (12,319 feet). If you want to, climb the rock pillar for better views.

1.1 Arrive back at the trailhead.

Hike Information

General Information

Visit Estes Park: Estes Park; (970) 577-9900, (800) 443-7837; visitestespark.com

Local Events/Attractions

Estes Park Area Historical Museum: Estes Park; (970) 586-6256; estesparkmuseumfriends.org/our-museum

Longs Peak Scottish/Irish Highland Festival: Estes Park; (970) 586-6308, 800-90ESTES (800-903-7837); scotfest.com

MacGregor Ranch Museum: Estes Park; (970) 586-3749; macgregorranch.org

Alpine forget-me-not

Clubs and Organizations

Rocky Mountain Conservancy: Estes Park; (970) 586-0108; rmconservancy.org

Hike Tours

Rocky Mountain Conservancy: Estes Park; (970) 586-0108; rmconservancy.org

Rocky Mountain National Park offers park-wide ranger-led programs like bird walks, nature walks, and talks on many interesting topics. Find the schedule in the park newspaper, available at the entrance stations and visitor centers, or check: www.nps.gov/romo/planyourvisit/ranger_led_activities.htm.

THE LAND ABOVE THE TREES

Stunted vegetation and the thin, rocky soil of the tundra characterize the alpine zone. On the tundra, intense cold and drying winds forbid the growth of trees, except for occasional dwarf willows. As a result, mountaintops look like forbidding fortresses of rock and snow from afar. However, for those willing to practice "belly botany," a closer examination reveals a medley of plants hugging the ground to conserve heat. These hardy specimens have adapted to extreme cold and high winds. For instance, plants like moss campion survive arctic temperatures by growing in the curved shape of a cushion, which allows icy windblasts and scouring snow to flow over them.

Spring usually arrives to the tundra, or "the land above the trees," in June. Through August, robust plants like the tiny cushion phlox, brilliant alpine primrose, and bright old man of the mountain transform the tundra into a colorful kaleidoscope.

Because snow can fall and frost can come any day of the year, the growing season lasts only about six weeks. This is hardly enough time for plants to grow from seed, reproduce, and make seeds. Consequently, most alpine plants are perennials, or plants that live for more than one year.

Life at the top of the world can be tough, but a number of animals like American pikas, Rocky Mountain bighorn sheep, and yellow-bellied marmots require the alpine environment for survival.

Alpine

46 Well Gulch Loop

Escape from the fast-paced modern world with this short, easy foothills loop hike overlooking Horsetooth Reservoir in Lory State Park, a refuge near Fort Collins. Designated for foot traffic only, the Well Gulch Nature Trail climbs gently through tranquil forest adorned with a host of wildflowers. As you traverse life zones, soak in the soothing sounds of water rushing past, discover blooms in the lush riparian corridor, marvel at steep rock walls, look for wild turkeys and Abert's squirrels, and enjoy sweeping views of the reservoir.

Start: From the Well Gulch Nature Trailhead across the road from the South Eltuck Picnic Area (5,480 feet)

Distance: 2.0-mile loop

Hiking time: 1–1.5 hours

Difficulty: Easy due to distance and moderate elevation gain

Trail surface: Rocky, dirt trail

Best season: April to September

Peak bloom: end of May to late June

Flowers commonly found: yucca, wild plum, Boulder raspberry, aromatic sumac, tall coneflower, horsemint, spiderwort, chokecherry, wild rose, showy milkweed, Fremont geranium, silvery lupine, Nuttall's larkspur, smooth goldenrod, prickly pear cactus, Oregon grape, Canada violet, spring beauty, mouse-ear chickweed, leafy cinquefoil, Fendler's waterleaf, golden banner, lanceleaf chiming bells, whiskbroom parsley, mountain ninebark, lambstongue groundsel, spotted coralroot, Parry's milkvetch, virgin's bower clematis, mountain bladderpod, four-nerve daisy, sand lily, golden aster, rosy pussytoes, Geyer's larkspur, scarlet beeblossom, Colorado locoweed, northern bedstraw, death camas, sprawling daisy, sugar bowls, mountain harebell, Drummond's milkvetch

Other trail users: Foot traffic only

Canine compatibility: Leashed dogs permitted

Land status: State park

Nearest town: Fort Collins

Fees and permits: Daily fee or annual parks pass required; available at the park entrance station, the Visitor Center, or the self-service station.

Schedule: Year-round; summer hours: 5 a.m. to 9 p.m.

Maps: USGS Horsetooth Reservoir; Latitude 40° Colorado Front Range; Colorado Parks and Wildlife Pocket Trail Map #36: Lory State Park Trail Use Map (available on website)

Trail contact: Lory State Park, Bellvue; (970) 493-1623; http://www.cpw.state.co.us/placestogo/Parks/lory

Finding the trailhead: From Fort Collins, head north on US 287 until you pass mile marker 350 where US 287 veers right. Continue straight onto Larimer County Road (LCR) 54G for 2.7 miles. Turn left onto Rist Canyon Road/LCR 52E. After 1.0 mile, turn left onto LCR 23N in Bellvue. Drive 1.4 miles south and then turn right onto Lodgepole Drive/LCR 25G. Drive another 1.6 miles to the park entrance. Turn left and follow the dirt road for 0.3 mile to the Visitor Center. Pay the entrance fee and continue 0.9 mile south until you see a sign for the Well Gulch Trail/South Eltuck Picnic Area. A large parking lot sits on the left side of the road across the street from the trailhead. **GPS: N40 34.699'/W105 10.735'**

The Hike

Walk west through an open grassland community where yucca, wild plum, Boulder raspberry, and aromatic sumac thrive. Staying on the main trail, pass tall coneflower, horsemint, and a few spiderwort flowers hiding amid the grass as you head deeper into Well Gulch, a riparian corridor with an intermittent stream. Cross the creek to find Boulder raspberry and chokecherry blooming with a fragrant flourish. Pass wild rose, showy milkweed, Fremont geranium, and silvery lupine to reach a small outcrop where water pours over black rocks and impressive bushes of chokecherry and wild plum bloom.

After crossing the creek, the trail narrows, giant boulders line the path, and vegetation turns lush as you delve deeper into the forest passing currant bushes, wild rose, aromatic sumac, and purple patches of silvery lupine and Nuttall's larkspur. Gently ascend through ponderosa pines and junipers passing smooth goldenrod and prickly pear cactus to reach another crossing. Note the beautiful rock cliffs towering overhead before the trail—lined with Oregon grape, Canada violets, spring beauty, and mouse-ear chickweed—curves back toward the creek. Cross it again, climb rock steps away from the water, and find a field of Nuttall's larkspur dappled with leafy cinquefoil awaiting your arrival. Cross the cottonwood-lined brook again to enjoy more violets, chickweed, pussy toes, and Fendler's waterleaf. Hugging the south side of the creek,

Waterfall

climb a bit more to enters parser conifer forest, where golden banner, larkspur, wild rose, lanceleaf chiming bells, whiskbroom parsley, Parry's milkvetch, and mountain ninebark bloom.

Turning left at the Timber Trail intersection, leave the creek behind and climb along a more rugged section of trail offering stunning glimpses of the reservoir, Fort Collins, and plains. Spotted coralroot, an orchid with loose racemes of up to thirty flowers, whose two-lobed lower lip petal is white and spotted with purple, hides amid the pine needles and undergrowth.

Keep climbing to find lambstongue groundsel, whiskbroom parsley, Parry's milkvetch, Boulder raspberry, pussytoes, and prickly pear cactus interspersed among the pine trees. The trail gradually switchbacks upward passing tons of larkspur, chickweed, prickly pear cactus, and mountain bladder-pod and opening up to offer unfettered vistas of the giant reservoir and vast plains. The trail descends through a small grove harboring chokecherry, wild plum, wild rose, and virgin's bower clematis, creamy blossoms dispersed over a mangled mess of woody vines known for its tendency to wind and climb shrubs, trees, and fences.

Pass through the Overlook Trail junction and descend past more mountain bladderpod, whiskbroom parsley, chickweed, wallflower, lanceleaf chiming bells, four-nerve daisy, sand lilies, golden aster, rosy pussytoes, and Geyer's larkspur. A sharp left offers an excellent view to the east as you move through sweet-smelling ponderosa pine forest dappled with

Sugar bowls

aromatic sumac and mountain mahogany and teeming with yellows, purples, blues, and whites including scarlet beeblossom, prickly pear cactus, Colorado locoweed, and northern bedstraw. Periodically, death camas makes an appearance amid the undergrowth. A rocky ravine provides habitat for a plethora of shrubs including chokecherry, wild plum, wild raspberry, wild rose, and ninebark. Leveling, the trail passes rocky outcrops bursting with stonecrop, harebell, low penstemon, and sulphur flower. The trail traverses a slope above the reservoir passing silvery lupine, cinquefoil, sprawling daisy, Parry's milkvetch, locoweed, sulphur flower, and sand lily. Impressive red rock cliffs below set against striking blue water draw your gaze upward as the trail follows gentle switchbacks downward. New flowers appear at every turn, including yarrow, sugar bowls, mountain harebells, and Parry's milkvetch. Right after passing a shaded bench, turn onto the West Valley Trail traveling through lush green vegetation punctuated with Drummond's milkvetch, lupine, and larkspur and curving back toward the ravine where your journey began. Turn east (right) and pick up the spur to the trailhead.

Miles and Directions

- **0.0** Start from the Well Gulch Nature Trailhead, located across the street from the parking lot.
- **0.1** Reach the West Valley Trail junction. Cross the bridge and turn west (right) onto the main trail.
- **0.2** Arrive at a small outcrop with a falls. Immediately after, cross the creek.
- **0.3** Cross the waterway again and climb rock steps away from the water.

0.4   Hop rocks to cross the water again and climb up through the forest.

0.6   At a junction with the Timber Trail, turn southeast (left) to stay on the Well Gulch Trail.

1.0   At a signed junction with the Overlook Trail, head north (straight) on a trail that meanders downhill toward the Homestead Picnic Area.

1.5   After traversing an open slope, reach a shaded bench.

1.6   Come to a trail junction near the Homestead Picnic Area. Turn north (left) onto the West Valley Trail.

1.9   Reach a familiar junction and turn east (right) toward the trailhead.

2.0   Arrive back at the trailhead.

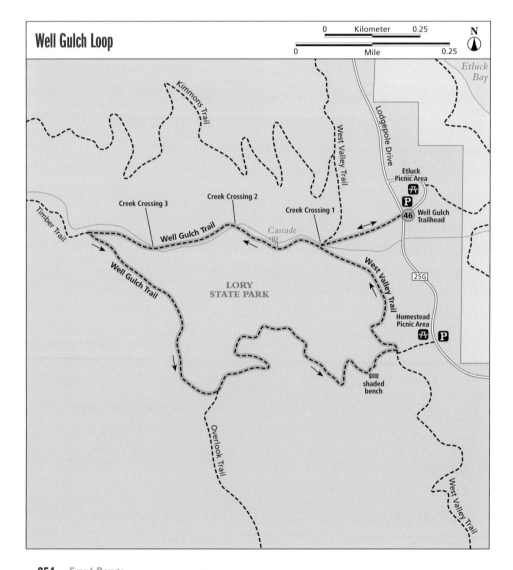

Hike information

General Information

Fort Collins Chamber of Commerce: Fort Collins; (970) 482-3746; fcchamber.org

Fort Collins Conventions & Visitors Bureau: Fort Collins; (800) 274-3678, (970) 232-3840; visitftcollins.com

Local Events/Attractions

New Belgium Brewery: 500 Linden St., Fort Collins; 888-NBB-4044, (970) 221-0524; newbelgium.com

Rocky Mountain Raptor Program: 720B East Vine Dr., Fort Collins; (970) 484-7756; rmrp.org

Clubs and Organizations

Colorado Mountain Club—Fort Collins group: (303) 279-3080, (800) 633-4417; fortcmc.org

Friends of Lory State Park: PO Box 11, Bellvue, 80512; (970) 235-2045; loryfriends.org

Volunteer at Lory State Park: (970) 493-1623; http://www.cpw.state.co.us/placestogo/Parks/lory

HONORABLE MENTIONS

Front Range

Here are three great hikes in the Front Range region that didn't make the A-list this time around but deserve recognition.

F. Mount Audubon

During summer, the Indian Peaks' Brainard Lake area is hard-hit by droves of city dwellers and tourists—but for nature lovers and wildflower enthusiasts it's worth it especially if you are willing to venture out on an 8.0-mile out-and-back climb of a thirteener. Perched above it all at 13,233 feet, Mount Audubon stands out with its open tundra and broad, sloping ridges bursting with a dazzling display of blossoms. Along the way, panoramic views of Mitchell Lake, Little Pawnee Peak (12,466 feet), and Mount Toll (12,979 feet) abound while periodic glimpses of Longs Peak (14,259 feet) and Mount Meeker (13,911 feet) reward your progress. At the summit on a clear day, you'll be greeted with visions of the vast Indian Peaks, the Never Summers, Rocky Mountain National Park, and even Pikes Peak to the south. From Hwy. 72, just north of

Ward, turn west on Brainard Lake Road. After 2.7 miles, reach the entrance station and pay the fee. Continue another 3.1 miles to the Mitchell Lake Trailhead parking lot. Information: Contact Arapaho and Roosevelt National Forests at (303) 541-2500 or www.fs.usda.gov/arp.

G. High Lonesome Loop

If you're looking for a spectacular but challenging day hike or overnight backpacking trip full of alpine lakes, unbelievable vistas, and a mind-blowing range and density of wildflowers, this 15-plus-mile loop (awesome side trip options abound) with over 3,500 feet of climbing, snaking through the Indian Peaks Wilderness and cutting across the Continental Divide, is for you. From Boulder, take Hwy. 119 through Boulder Canyon to reach Nederland. Continue south on 119 to Hwy. 130. Turn right, pass through the tiny hamlet of Eldora, and continue another 2 miles until you reach the Hessie Trailhead. Alternatively, the Hessie Trailhead offers shorter options full of flowers including a 3-mile out-and-back trip to Lost Lake. Learn more from Arapaho and Roosevelt National Forests at (303) 541-2500 or www.fs.usda.gov/arp.

H. Blue Lake

The 100-plus different wildflowers found along this very popular 10-mile out-and-back hike near Cameron Pass draw locals and visitors alike—not to mention the picturesque scenery, the lovely creeks crossing the trail, and the pristine alpine lake, which is perfect for swimming or fishing. Even getting to the trailhead involves a scenic canyon drive along the Poudre River. Take US 287 north from Fort Collins for 10 miles to CO 14. Turn left on CO 14, and travel 54 miles west to the Blue Lake Trailhead parking lot on the right, located across the highway from FR 156, Long Draw Road. Information: Arapaho and Roosevelt National Forests, (970) 295-6600 or www.fs.usda.gov/arp.

Eastern

O ften overlooked, Colorado's Eastern region rewards visitors with solitude, subtle beauty, a plethora of wildlife, historic gems, and interesting geologic features. Dominated by the Great Plains, the state's lowest point rests near the Nebraska border just east of Wray (note that at 3,337 feet, this spot still rises to great heights compared to most of the country).

North of Greeley and east of Fort Collins in the northeastern corner of the state, two mighty and unearthly buttes rise dramatically from the flatlands of Pawnee National Grasslands. Pronghorn (antelope), fox, and prolific birdlife, including many raptors who utilize the cliffs during nesting season, draw nature enthusiasts to the area.

Heading south, Castlewood Canyon State Park, a designated Colorado natural area with Cherry Creek flowing through its center, encompasses 2,303 acres of the northernmost section of the Black Forest. The Black Forest, also known as the Palmer Divide, refers to an elevated peninsula that juts eastward from the Front Range and divides the drainages of the Platte and Arkansas Rivers. Bordering Front Range foothills and plains grassland ecosystems, this unique ecological region supports a range of flora and fauna.

In the southeast, Comanche National Grassland encompasses 400,000 acres of unblemished short-grass prairie, a quickly fading environment on our continent. Comanche's grasslands and waterways, which support nearly 400 bird species, play an important role in the ecological fabric. Wild, narrow canyons like Vogel and Picket Wire wind through this rugged landscape; delve deeper to find pioneer settlements, dinosaur footprints, old missions, petroglyphs, and wildflowers aplenty.

47 Pawnee Buttes

Enjoy a peaceful meander through a unique section of Colorado's Eastern Plains to reach two giant sandcastle-like rock formations towering a few hundred feet overhead. This easy hike snakes through an unearthly badlands, sandy arroyos, and rugged cliffs carved by wind, water and, time. In spring, colorful blooms stand in stark contrast to the severe, flesh-toned landscape that supports a diversity of wildlife including raptors, eagles, pronghorn, and coyote.

Start: From the Pawnee Buttes Trailhead (5,430 feet)
Distance: 4.0 miles out and back
Hiking time: 1.5–2.5 hours
Difficulty: Easy due to gradual, smooth terrain and moderate elevation gain
Trail surface: Dirt trail
Best season: May to June
Peak bloom: mid-May to early June
Flowers commonly found: prairie ragwort, white evening primrose, narrowleaf puccoon, sand lily, prickly pear cactus, wallflower, carpet phlox, silky, Missouri, plains and Drummonds' milkvetch, slender wild parsley, Hooker's sandwort, spiked gilia, many-stem pea, mountain bladderpod, sand verbena, yucca, mat prickly phlox, wild rose, narrowleaf penstemon, mountain cat's eye, Colorado locoweed, lemon scurf-pea, large Indian bread-root, lavender-leaf sundrops, four-nerve daisy
Other trail users: Equestrians
Canine compatibility: Leashed dogs permitted; dogs under verbal control permitted
Land status: National grassland
Nearest town: Grover, Keota, Sterling, and New Raymer are the nearest towns. Ault, located on Hwy. 14, is the nearest major population center with a range of facilities.
Fees and permits: No fees or permits required for hiking, except for groups larger than 25 people
Schedule: Year-round
Maps: USGS Grover SE and Pawnee Buttes; Pawnee National Grassland Visitor Map
Trail contact: Pawnee National Grassland, Greeley; (970) 346-5000; www.fs.usda.gov/main/arp
Special considerations: Please do not disturb any hawks and falcons nesting in the rocky cliffs. The Pawnee Buttes Trail is open year-round; however, the nearby Overlook and Lip Bluff areas are closed March 1 through June 30 due to nesting hawks, eagles, and falcons. Please stay on the main trail during this time as adult birds may desert their eggs or young ones if disturbed. Rain and snow can make the roads difficult to drive, so keep an eye on the weather and approaching storms. This is a very remote area; come prepared and make sure you have a full tank of gas.

Finding the trailhead: From Fort Collins, travel east on Hwy. 14 east for 54 miles. Turn left onto CR 103, just east of mile marker 189. After 4.8 miles, turn right onto CR 103. Follow it for 6 miles until you reach CR 112. Turn right and continue for 2 miles until you reach an intersection with CR 107. Turn right onto CR 107 and then after 300 feet, turn left onto CR 112. After 2.0 miles, turn left onto FR 685 at a sign for the Pawnee Buttes Trailhead. After 1.2 miles, pass the old trailhead on the left and continue following FR 685 as it curves east and then south to reach the new trailhead complete with toilets, interpretive signs, and picnic tables. **GPS: N40 48.492' / W103 59.362'**

The Hike

A stroll through the expansive Eastern Plains rewards explorers with striking beauty and noticeable peace. Walk north on a wide dirt trail that meanders through a grassy field teeming with prairie ragwort, white evening primrose, puccoon, sand lily, and prickly pea. Note bright orange-yellow wallflower and carpet phlox before reaching the Overlook Trail junction. Continue straight to climb gently through bunches of groundsel, prairie ragwort, delicate but showy white sand lilies, and yellow trumpet-shaped puccoon rising in stark contrast to the tan soil and ragged green grass.

Crest a slight hill, pass through a wooden gate, and go straight on the main trail to drop into an alien landscape featuring flower-filled arroyos and towering rock formations reminiscent of sand castles rising from the otherwise flat terrain. Descend along a sandy, well-maintained trail to explore the canyon's depths. Lining the trail in bright pink, yellow, and white are phlox, puccoon, and wallflower accompanied by Drummonds' milkvetch, slender wild parsley, and plains milkvetch. Hooker's sandwort, known for its giant tufts of spiky, dark green leaves giving rise to tiny five-petaled flowers shaped like stars, draws your eye downward. As you progress, a number of blooms including spiked gilia, many-stem pea, mountain bladderpod, and silky and Missouri milkvetch defy the odds by bursting from dry soil. Patches of sand verbena, with a large spray of tiny but attractive white trumpet flowers clustered in a sphere, add a sweet smell that lingers in the air. Cross a series of ravines noting yucca, mat prickly phlox, wallflower, wax currant, wild rose, and narrowleaf penstemon. Impressive specimens of magenta Colorado locoweed burst forth from the earth.

Note the giant turbines of the Cedar Creek Wind Farm turning silently off to the north (left). Creamy bell-shaped nodding blossoms sway from the woody stalks of huge yucca plants while the small but bright trumpet-shaped flowers dapple the trailside in yellow. The scene opens up and West Pawnee Butte, which rises 200 to

Colorado locoweed flourishes en route to West Pawnee Butte

Sand lily

300 feet into the sky, dominates the skyline, begging the question: How did the Buttes form? In short, 70 to 90 million years ago, an uplift of the Rockies drained this inland sea and deposited sediment, which over time hardened into sandstone and siltstone to create different rock layers. Five million years ago, the whole region was again uplifted thousands of feet. Rivers grew in volume and speed, causing erosion through the sediment layers and carving a number of features, including the buttes whose tops represent ground level prior to these forceful erosion events.

Continue heading straight toward the butte, discovering mountain cat's eye, yucca, phlox, Colorado locoweed, and wallflower blooming. After a grassy ravine, tackle a short, steep set of stairs before curving toward the Lip Bluffs, giant brown sandstone cliffs shaped like tables whose hearty capstone top keeps the skinnier and softer bottom leg from eroding. Continue straight past the Lip Bluffs Trail, which is closed March 1 to June 30 to protect nesting raptors. Nearing the buttes, massive clusters of Colorado locoweed, mountain cat's eye, wallflower, groundsel, lemon scurf-pea, narrowleaf puccoon, and large Indianbreadroot adorn the route. Enjoy meandering along a stone bench in the shadow of the butte, taking time to revel in the host of magenta, purple, yellow, and white blossoms growing directly out of the rocky surface beneath your feet.

Arc all the way round to the east side of the West Butte to find fields of magenta locoweed, lavender-leaf sundrops, and four-nerve daisy making their

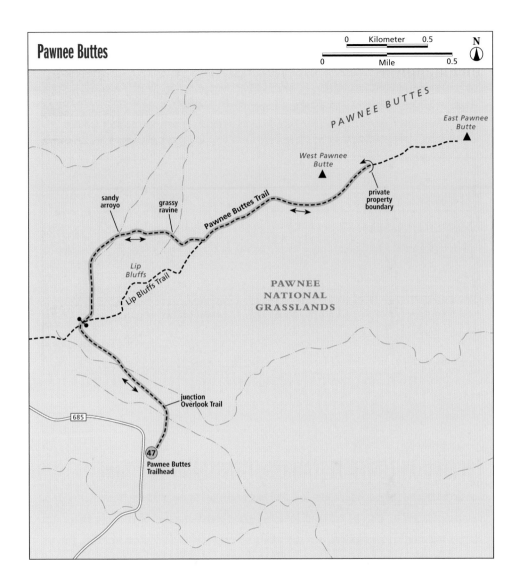

Pawnee Buttes

PAWNEE BUTTES

East Pawnee Butte

West Pawnee Butte

sandy arroyo

grassy ravine

Pawnee Buttes Trail

private property boundary

Lip Bluffs

Lip Bluffs Trail

PAWNEE NATIONAL GRASSLANDS

junction Overlook Trail

685

47

Pawnee Buttes Trailhead

0   Kilometer   0.5

0   Mile   0.5

N

debut with a flourish of yellow. Head slightly downhill to find East Butte towering ahead. Turn around at a "Private Property: Respect Owner's Rights" sign and retrace your steps.

Miles and Directions

0.0 Start on the main trail behind the interpretive sign at the Pawnee Buttes Trailhead. In 300 feet, pass through a fence with a green gate.

0.2 Continue straight past a junction with the Overlook Trail (closed March 1 to June 30).

0.5 Pass through a wooden gate to reach an intersection with a stock trail. Veer left to continue north on the main trail, which traverses the canyon rim.

1.0 Descend, cross a sandy arroyo, and enjoy a short climb out of it.

1.2 Cross a grassy ravine and climb up a series of stairs.

1.3 At a signed junction with the Lip Bluffs Trail (closed March 1 to June 30), continue east (straight) toward the buttes.

1.8 Reach the West Butte. Follow the trail around its east side.

2.0 Come to a national grasslands–private property boundary in between the West and East Buttes. Turn around and return the way you came.

4.0 Arrive back at the trailhead.

Hike information

General Information

Pawnee National Grassland: Greeley; (970) 346-5000; www.fs.usda.gov/main/arp

Local Events/Attractions

Pawnee Pioneer Trails Scenic Byway: Pawnee National Grassland, Greeley; (970) 353-5004; http://www.codot.gov/travel/scenic-byways/northeast/pawnee-pioneer-trails

Accommodations

Crow Valley Recreation Area: Pawnee National Grassland, Briggsdale; (970) 346-5000; http://www.recreation.gov/camping/crow-valley/r/campgroundDetails .do?contract Code=NRSO&park Id=73754

LOOKING AT LOWER ELEVATIONS: GRASSLAND LIFE ZONE

The Great Plains, ranging from 4,000 to 6,000 feet above sea level, dominate the eastern side of Colorado. Shaped by drought and wind, the short-grass prairie is a land of extremes where dust storms, hail, blizzards, tornadoes, and stiff winds are common. Characterized by native grasses that vary based on climate, topography, and soil, native grasslands rank among the most imperiled ecosystems in the world; only about half of the original mixed-grass and short-grass prairies survive today largely due to overgrazing, urban sprawl, and irrigation. Fortunately, Colorado has two protected areas where you can visit intact short-grass prairie: Pawnee National Grasslands in the northeast and Comanche National Grasslands in the southeast.

The short-grass prairie receives only 10 to 16 inches of precipitation per year on average—a factor that determines its character. The bulk comes between May and July bringing life to grass species like blue grama and buffalo grass and wildflowers including sand lily, stemless Easter daisy, scarlet globemallow, stemless white evening primrose, and prickly poppy, among others.

Plants here survive by developing adaptations that allow them to conserve water. Many have long taproots that can take advantage of moisture reserves deep down while others grow a series of fine rootlets near the surface that spread laterally to make use of quickly passing moisture. The Purgatoire, Arkansas, and South Platte Rivers cut across the plains to provide important riparian habitats for plants and animals. Pronghorn, coyote, black-tailed prairie dog, jackrabbit, burrowing owls, and a range of birdlife from ferruginous hawks to mountain plover dominate the grasslands.

Grasslands

48 Castlewood Canyon Loop

Meander through a healthy riparian corridor and forest dominated by scrub oak, Douglas fir, and ponderosa pines while exploring the understated wonders along this 2-mile loop that skirts the rim of Castlewood Canyon before dropping down to follow the strong waters of Cherry Creek. Views of Pikes Peak and the Front Range stretch out amid the expansive space of the high plains. Activate all your senses as you pass through a variety of habitats supporting a range of colorful blooms. Don't expect the same density or showy displays found in lusher mountain environs, but do keep looking. The subtle beauty of wildflowers thriving in this unique environment between prairie and montane communities is worth the extra effort.

Start: From the Lake Gulch Trailhead at the east entrance of Castlewood Canyon State Park (6,630 feet)

Distance: 2.0-mile loop

Hiking time: 1–1.5 hours

Difficulty: Easy due to gradual, smooth terrain and moderate elevation gain

Trail surface: Dirt trail

Best season: April to July

Peak bloom: mid-May to mid-June

Flowers commonly found: sand lily, orange paintbrush, American vetch, Drummond's milkvetch, beautiful cinquefoil, salsify, Nuttall's larkspur, Colorado locoweed, Britton skullcap, yarrow, Colorado locoweed, prairie milkvetch, scarlet globemallow, yellow stonecrop, silvery lupine, mountain bluebell, wild rose, prickly pear cactus, Onesided penstemon, cow parsnip, American yellow-rocket, Jim Hill's mustard, rosy pussytoes, wild plum, waxflower, mountain ninebark, northern bedstraw

Other trail users: Runners; mountain bikers and equestrians permitted only on the Cherry Creek Regional Trail

Canine compatibility: Leashed dogs permitted; no dogs allowed on the East Canyon Trail

Land status: State park

Nearest towns: Franktown/Castle Rock

Fees and permits: Daily fee or annual parks pass required; available at the park entrance station, the Visitor Center, or the self-service station

Schedule: Year-round, 8 a.m. to 9 p.m.

Maps: USGS Castlerock South, Russellville Gulch; Colorado Parks and Wildlife Pocket Trail Map #17: Castlewood Canyon Trail Map (available on website)

Trail contact: Castlewood Canyon State Park, Franktown, 80116; (303) 688-5242; http://www.cpw.state.co.us/placestogo/Parks/castlewoodcanyon

Special considerations: The area is day-use only. Inbound gates close an hour prior to park closure; both gates are locked promptly at 9 p.m.

Finding the trailhead: From I-25 at Castle Rock, drive 6 miles east on CO 86 to Franktown. Turn south (right) onto CO 83 (South Parker Road) for 5.0 miles to the park entrance. Follow the park road north until it curves west to the trailhead. **GPS: N39 20.005'/W104 44.691'**

The Hike

Nestled in the plains, Castlewood Canyon State Park offers a unique opportunity to explore a giant creek-carved chasm cutting through rolling grasslands in the east. From the park's northern parking lot, pick up the Lake Gulch Trail, a wide dirt path that cruises past a picnic area and through an open grassy field brightened by delicate white sand lilies, brilliant orange paintbrush, deep magenta American vetch, creamy colored Drummond's milkvetch, and shiny yellow beautiful cinquefoil. Pause for a moment and peer out at the horizon; a line of jagged peaks way off in the distance captures your eye. At your feet, salsify, Nuttall's larkspur, Colorado locoweed, and Britton's skullcap add bits of yellow, bluish purple, magenta, and grape to the scene, making these views even sweeter.

Drop down into ponderosa pines where yarrow, Colorado locoweed, prairie milkvetch, scarlet globemallow, and yellow stonecrop adorn the trail. As you descend this rocky shallow soil, note the huge rock bluffs—some resemble mushrooms with giant caps while others are sheer columns—up above on the right. Yellow stonecrop, silvery lupine, sand lilies, and mountain bluebells color the forest floor. When you reach a viewpoint where a gnarled juniper tree hangs over the edge, take a moment to absorb expansive views of the valley floor.

Cherry creek flows through the canyon

From here, the trail descends toward the water and curves along a rocky cliff edge passing wild rose, mountain bluebells, yellow stonecrop, prickly pear cactus, and Onesided penstemon. Reach Cherry Creek, a waterway lined with impressive rock slabs and giant boulders. Spend some time cherishing the sound of the rushing water before crossing a small bridge and walking a short way uphill to reach a junction. Where stairs climb left to Dam Trail, turn right to follow the Inner Canyon Trail, a path that guides

Wild plum

your magical journey through this riparian oasis. Near the creek, keep an eye out for cow parsnip, American yellow-rocket, and more mountain bluebells—all of which thrive in damper environs. Rising uphill just slightly, veer left to stay on the main path as it climbs above the water.

Cross two small bridges in succession to return near the water. Huge chunky boulders adorn the trail as do flowers like American yellow-rocket, yellow stonecrop, Jim Hill's mustard, pussytoes, and bluebells. Reach a shaded bench and rest if you'd like to take a break. When you're ready, continue climbing along the gradual trail paralleling the creek. As you ascend through this shady cool scrub oak canyon, notice how all of your senses are engaged. Catch a glimpse of bluffs rising high above off the left. Listen for frogs croaking and watch for snakes and turtles squiggling along the undergrowth. Brilliant yellows, blues, and pinks light up the forest floor. Your hands graze rough rock as you squeeze in and out of boulders that form narrow gauntlets in this riparian corridor. Fragrant wild plum flowers beckon your nose.

Continue this exploration of all the senses as youcross a much bigger bridge spanning a raging section of the creek. Walk around a tall rock pillar right in the middle of the trail. Nuttall's larkspur and mountain bluebells blossom along this section of trail lined with giant boulders. Cross an even bigger bridge to head back into

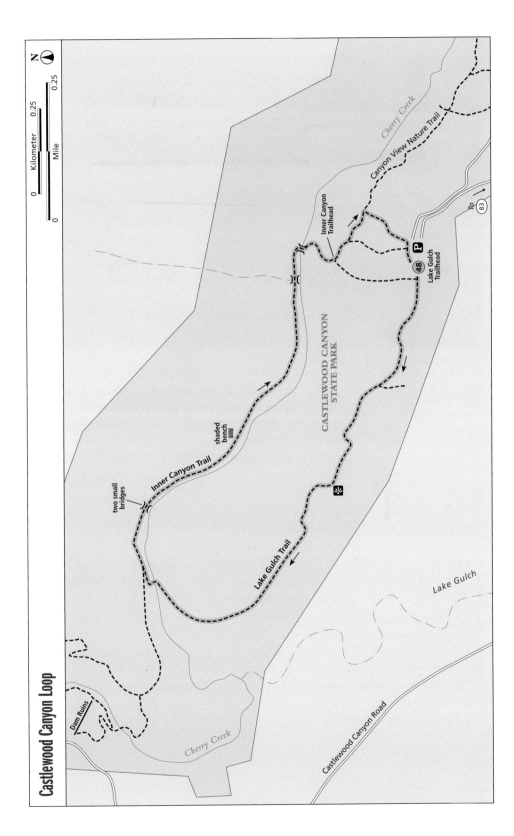

Castlewood Canyon Loop

N

Kilometer
0   0.25

Mile
0   0.25

Dam Ruins

Cherry Creek

two small
bridges

Inner Canyon Trail

shaded
bench

Lake Gulch Trail

Lake Gulch

Castlewood Canyon Road

**CASTLEWOOD CANYON
STATE PARK**

Inner Canyon
Trailhead

Cherry Creek

Canyon View Nature Trail

P

48

Lake Gulch
Trailhead

To 83

Cherry Creek flows through the canyon

the shade of the forest where scrub oak, waxflower, mountain ninebark, and northern bedstraw await. Climb steps and follow switchbacks that bring you away from the river. At the top of the hill, reach the signed trailhead for the Inner Canyon Trail. Turn southeast (left) to intersect with the Canyon View Nature Trail. Turn south (right) and arrive at the parking area.

Miles and Directions

0.0 Start from the Lake Gulch Trailhead.

0.4 Reach a viewpoint. Drop down to the creek along rocky cliffs.

0.9 Cross Cherry Creek. Turn east (right) at a junction with the Inner Canyon Trail and head uphill.

1.1 Nearing the water again, cross two bridges in succession.

1.3 Arrive at a shaded bench near the creek.

1.6 Heading east, cross a larger bridge.

1.7 Turning south, cross over an even bigger bridge leading to switchbacks climbing away from the water.

1.8 At the top of the hill, reach the Inner Canyon Trailhead. Turn southeast (left).

1.9 Turn south (right) onto the Canyon View Nature Trail.

2.0 Arrive back at the trailhead/parking area.

Hike information

General Information

Castle Rock Chamber of Commerce: (866) 441-8508; castlerock.org

Local Events/Attractions

Castle Rock Wine Fest: (303) 688-4597; castlerockculture.com/castle-rock-winefest/
Colorado Renaissance Festival and Artisan Marketplace: Larkspur; (303) 688-6010; coloradorenaissance.com

Accommodations

Chatfield State Park: 11500 North Roxborough Park Rd., Littleton; (303) 791-7275; http://www.cpw.state.co.us/placestogo/Parks/Chatfield
Jellystone Castle Rock Campground: 650 Sky View Ln., Larkspur; (720) 325-2393; jellystonelarkspur.com

Clubs and Organizations

Friends of Castlewood Canyon State Park: a nonprofit organization providing support for educational and interpretive activities at the park; Franktown; castlewood-friends.org.

49 Picket Wire Canyon

The scenery along this gentle 11-plus-mile hike through a rugged canyon dappled with grassland flowers and rimmed by pinyon-juniper forest is only surpassed by the historic, prehistoric, and archeological surprises it harbors. Go back in time as you follow the river past the ruins of an old Mexican mission, Native American rock art, and an early nineteenth-century homestead. Travel even further back as the exposed rock layers of prehistoric seabeds and ancient lakeshores reveal the largest dinosaur track site in North America containing over 1,300 prints. Explore the riverbanks to find three-toed allosaurus tracks and herds of brontosaurus prints.

Start: From the Withers Canyon Trailhead (4,650 feet)

Distance: 11.3 miles out and back

Hiking time: 5–7 hours

Difficulty: Strenuous due to distance, but with smooth terrain and minimal elevation gain

Trail surface: Dirt road, mainly double-track, sometimes rocky, with one steep section

Best season: mid-April to early June, August

Peak bloom: May, August (there is a second bloom later in summer)

Flowers commonly found: Fendler's bladderpod, western wallflower, sand aster, black-foot daisy, American vetch, Nuttall's sophora, little cryptantha, golden corydalis, blue flax, copper globemallow, long-leaved phlox, white evening primrose, whitestem blazingstar, textile onion, Chinese lanterns, greenleaf five eyes, tree cholla, prickly pear cactus, lavender-leaf sun-drops, mountain spring parsley, plains spring-parsley, four-nerve daisy, western stickseed, sprawling daisy, yellow prairie violet, dotted blazing star, spreading draba, western tansy mustard, many-stem pea, slender milkvetch, Buckley's penstemon, sidebells penstemon, Colorado rubberweed, purple prairie vervain, Carolina larkspur

Other trail users: Equestrians, mountain bikers, four-wheel drives (during Sat tours led by the Forest Service)

Canine compatibility: Dogs must be under control

Land status: National grassland

Nearest town: La Junta

Fees and permits: No fees or permits required

Schedule: Year-round, dawn to dusk

Maps: USGS Riley Canyon, Beaty Canyon, O V Mesa; US Forest Service Comanche National Grassland

Trail contact: Comanche National Grassland, La Junta; (719) 384-2181; www.fs.usda.gov/psicc

Special considerations: The canyon is day-use only, but primitive camping exists on top of the canyon near the trailhead. This is a harsh environment; searing temperatures, flash floods, and rattlesnakes are just a few of the possible dangers. Bring a lot of water and take care if you choose to cross the river, which can be high and fast, to explore the dinosaur tracks.

Finding the trailhead: From La Junta drive south on Hwy. 109 for 13 miles. At signs for Vogel and Picket Wire Canyon turn west (right) onto CR 802 (David Canyon Road) and continue for 8 miles. Turn south (left) onto CR 25 (also signed for Picket Wire Canyon) and follow it for 6 miles. Turn left at Picket Wire Corrals onto FSR 500A. Continue for 3 miles along a high-clearance, two-wheel-driveroute that often becomes impassable when wet, until you arrive at the trailhead parking area. **GPS: N37 39.586'/W103 34.255'**

The Hike

Steeped in history, the 350 feet deep Picket Wire Canyon offers an interesting adventure complete with ruins, an old mission, dinosaur tracks, and grassland wildflowers.

Begin walking on the mesa, a rocky plateau awash with spring wildflowers including sand aster, Fendler's bladderpod, western wallflower, four-nerve daisy, golden corydalis, and little cryptantha. At a junction with the Withers Canyon Trail, turn left to descend on an increasingly rugged trail dropping steeply through the rimrock of Withers Canyon past black-foot daisy, American vetch, Nuttall's sophora, western stickseed, blue flax, spreading draba, and copper globemallow. Leveling and curving east, the trail enters Purgatoire Canyon and leaves behind Withers Canyon, a tributary that dominates the view to the west (left).

Work your way through this vast canyon on a rolling trail that passes long-leaved phlox, white evening primrose, mountain spring parsley, sprawling daisy, and whitestem blazingstar. Changing direction to parallel the river, note the arrival of textile onion, Chinese lanterns, greenleaf five eyes, black-foot daisy, tree cholla, and various prickly pear cactus species.

Continue south to find ruins with stone and clay walls crumbling under a toppled frame—a reminder of settlers who grew crops and raised livestock along the river. Though this homestead is from the nineteenth century, humans have lived in the valley for as long as 11,000 years. Rock art and the remnants of dwellings, stone tools, and pottery in the canyon date back to prehistoric times. Evidence suggests that explorers from Spain first came here in the 1500s, when it was lush and teeming with wildlife. Folklore says that a group of Spanish pioneers seeking treasure died in the canyon before having their last rites administered, which led to the river's name: El Rio de las Animas Perdidas en Purgatorio (the River of Lost Souls in Purgatory). Eighteenth-century French trappers shortened it to the "Purgatoire," but when English-speaking travelers journeying along the Santa Fe Trail struggled with pronunciation, the name became corrupted into "Picket Wire."

View of Picket Wire from above

Golden corydalis

▶ **GREEN TIP—Don't take
souvenirs home with you.
This means natural materials
such as plants, rocks, shells,
and driftwood, as well as
historic artifacts such as
fossils and arrowheads.**

Undulating over rolling terrain that follows the twists of the river, the trail visits lavender-leaf sundrops, plains springparsley, yellow prairie violet, dotted blazing star, and western tansy mustard. Open grassy areas with sandy soils also support many-stem pea, sidebells penstemon, slender milkvetch, purple prairie vervain, and Buckley's penstemon. Colorado rubberweed grows on the rocky slopes of the canyon.

At a sharp oxbow, the trail turns west (right) and then south to pass old adobe buildings and the Dolores Mission ruins and cemetery. Settled in 1871 by twelve Catholic New Mexican families, this spot lacked a church until the community built one in 1898.

Travel even further back in time by continuing down canyon to the dinosaur track sight. Keep an eye out for Carolina larkspur as you meander toward the river where an interpretive sign explains the fossilized prints spread out across the largest track site in North America. Explore at will; more than 1,300 tracks in 100 separate trackways punctuate this quarter mile of riverbank. Amazing to think that right here, 150 million years ago, the enormous brontosaurus and the smaller allosaurus wandered the muddy shoreline of a lake.

Picket Wire is the only portion of the entire National Forest system with a specific mandate for the management and protection of fossil resources. Though you might not see them, there are also bones and skeletons representing as many as a hundred different animals that lived 150 million years ago. Federal law protects all cultural resources within Picket Wire. Collecting or damaging artifacts is strictly prohibited, so please take only pictures and leave only footprints. Return the way you came.

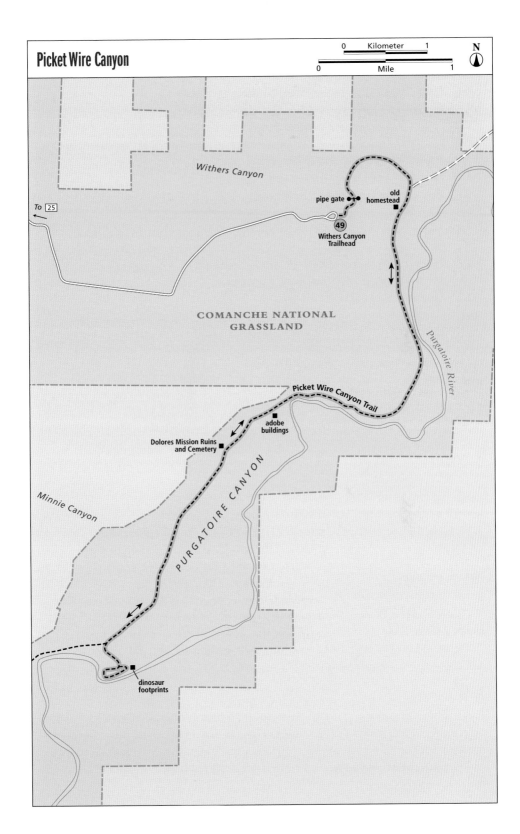

Miles and Directions

0.0   Start from the Withers Canyon Trailhead. Travel east and at the trail register, turn left onto the Picket Wire Trail.

0.2   Reach a pipe gate and walk around it.

0.9   Reach the intersection with a nonmotorized dirt road (double-track) in Purgatoire Canyon, and turn right to parallel the river.

1.1   Reach the remains of an old homestead.

3.5   Arrive at the remains of old adobe buildings.

3.8   Reach the Dolores Mission ruins and cemetery.

5.1   When the road forks, take the left road branch to reach a trail to the dinosaur track site. Turn left again.

5.5   Read the interpretive signs and then begin looking for tracks along both sides of the riverbank if you are comfortable crossing the water.

11.3   Arrive back at the trailhead.

Options: After exploring the track site to your heart's content, you can continue down canyon for another 3.4 miles to the historic Rourke Ranch, which housed a cattle operation for over a century. For a shorter hike, you can always turn around at the Dolores Mission or even earlier.

Hike information

General Information

La Junta Chamber of Commerce: La Junta; (719) 384-7411; lajuntachamber.com
    Unofficial Comanche National Grasslands website: www.visitlajunta.net/comanche.html

Local Events/Attractions

Bent's Old Fort National Historic Site: La Junta; (719) 383-5010; www.nps.gov/beol
    Koshare Indian Museum: La Junta; (719) 384-4411; kosharehistory.org
    Otero County Museum: La Junta; (719) 384-7500; oteromuseum.org

Accommodations

KOA: La Junta; (719) 384-9580, (800) 562-9501; koa.com/campgrounds/la-junta/
    Vogel Canyon Picnic Ground: camp in parking lot; Comanche National Grassland, La Junta; (719) 384-2181; www.recreation.gov (search for Vogel Canyon)
    Withers Canyon Trailhead area: Comanche National Grassland, La Junta; (719) 384-2181; www.fs.usda.gov/psicc

Hike Tours

Picket Wire Canyonlands Guided Auto Tour: La Junta; (719) 384-2181; Visit www.recreation.gov and search for Picket Wire Canyonlands. Four-wheel-drive tour to the dinosaur tracksite from the opposite direction on Saturday in May, June, September, and October. Must provide your own four-wheel-drive vehicle with high clearance (trucks and SUVs only).

50 Vogel Canyon

Carved out of sandstone by the Purgatoire River, Vogel Canyon is a unique and captivating destination nestled within the state's southeastern prairie lands, which—in wet years—can be awash in spring and summer wildflowers. Explore this hidden gem by combining the easy Overlook and Canyon Trails to create a short loop that meanders across a mesa top, over sandstone planks, through the valley bottom, and past steep cliffs. Sandy grassy landscape, delicate wildflowers, stony red rock formations, and sweeping prairie sky join to create an expansive and tantalizing scene while pinyon pine forest, Native American rock art, natural springs, and homestead ruins make a visit to Vogel worth the short drive from La Junta.

Start: From the Vogel Canyon Trailhead (4,400 feet)
Distance: 2.1-mile loop
Hiking time: 1-2 hours
Difficulty: Easy due to smooth and level terrain
Trail surface: Sandy and dirt trail
Best season: March to May
Peak bloom: May
Flowers commonly found: four-nerve daisy, prairie spiderwort, small lupine, aromatic sumac, Missouri milkvetch, blue flax, blackfoot daisy, puccoon, white evening primrose, golden corydalis, narrowleaf penstemon, copper globe-mallow, scarlet globemallow, little cryptantha, tree cholla, prickly pear cactus ssp.
Other trail users: Equestrians, mountain bikers

Canine compatibility: Dogs must be under control
Land status: National grassland
Nearest town: La Junta
Fees and permits: No fees or permits required
Schedule: Year-round
Maps: USGS La Junta SE, CO; US Forest Service Comanche National Grassland
Trail contact: Comanche National Grassland, La Junta; (719) 384-2181; www.fs.usda.gov/psicc
Special considerations: Be aware of rattlesnakes and cacti. Rock art is a sensitive and important piece of history that is protected by federal law. Please help preserve this valuable resource by taking photographs but not touching or vandalizing the petroglyphs.

Finding the trailhead: From La Junta, drive south on Hwy. 109 for 13 miles. At the Vogel Canyon sign, turn west (right) onto CR 802. Follow it for 1.5 miles, then turn south (left) onto FR 505A. Continue for 1.5 miles until you reach the parking lot. **GPS: N37 46.199'/W103 30.781'**

The Hike

Head south along the sandy but level two-track Overlook Trail. As you traverse the mesa top, find white evening primrose, narrowleaf penstemon, golden corydalis, and small lupine in the open sandy soil. Varied prickly pear cactus species and the distinct tree cholla, with distinct yellow buds, proliferate here on the plains.

At the Mesa Trail junction, continue straight to reach the cliff edge for a bird's-eye view into the canyon. Sweeping views illustrate that Vogel Canyon, which was

Vogel Canyon offers vast opportunities for exploration

carved by a tributary of the Purgatoire River, envelopes varied habitat from short-grass prairie to the pinyon-juniper ecosystem. Near the overlook, the delicate yellow buds of puccoon shine brightly against the crimson and tan canyon rim. Before dropping down, absorb how the mix of sandy grassy landscape, delicate wildflowers, stony red rock formations, and sweeping prairie sky join to create an expansive and tantalizing scene.

From the overlook, drop into the canyon by carefully navigating some steep rock steps and sandstone planks. Look for aromatic sumac, a shrub whose profusion of tiny yellow spring flowers and light green serrated leaves are followed by tight clusters of red hairy berries with a tart lemonade taste.

On the canyon bottom, the trail turns west (right) and passes Missouri milkvetch, blue flax, and black-foot daisy to hug the jagged rocky cliffs. Head west and then south across this section of wide-open canyon along the fence line to reach ruins constructed of native stone. The remnants of this corral and possible homestead harken back to the sheep and cattle ranching days of the nineteenth century. Off to the west beyond the fence, spot a spring—one of only a few springs in this canyon; this precious water supports a range of wildlife including jackrabbits, great horned owl, pronghorn, coyotes, and more. At this same spot, reach a junction with the Prairie Trail, which heads west to investigate the remnants of an old stagecoach stop built in the 1870s as part of a Santa Fe Trail spur developed by the Barlow and Sanderson Mail and Stage Line.

Instead of going that way, follow the trail curving east (left) passing spots of little cryptantha, white evening primrose, black-foot daisy, four-nerve daisy, blue flax, and copper globemallow until you reach a sign that points north (left). Turn north (left) to work back up the canyon and past another spring. Trees grow abundantly nearby.

Sandstone cliffs and walls dominate the east side of the canyon offering shelter for canyon wrens and lizards. Native Americans lived here for thousands of years and several spur trails and signposts guide you to large, vertical rock faces where you can still see some of their handiwork in the form of petroglyphs. Shallow rock overhangs display abstract designs and symbols that are faint but worth a visit. Unfortunately, people have vandalized these archeological sites, so they are no longer pristine.

White evening primrose

Continue following a sandy trail that guides you north through a small unnamed side canyon full of interesting rock formations that shelter spiderwort, scarlet globe-mallow, puccoon, black-foot daisy, and four-nerve daisy. As you walk north over smooth sandstone slickrock marked with cairns, ruins of the Depression-era Westbrook homestead come into view on the left. Aged junipers and pinyon pines provide spots of shade while you climb out of the canyon. The trail reaches a rocky plateau, flattens out, and turns into a wider sandy trail where jackrabbits and lizards roam. Make your way back to the picnic area and trailhead.

Miles and Directions

0.0 Start from the Vogel Canyon Trailhead. Walk south on the Overlook Trail.

0.3 Reach a junction with the Mesa Trail. Continue south (straight).

0.7 Travel to an overlook at the edge of a cliff face.

1.0 Reach remnants of a corral and a junction with the Prairie Trail, which heads west. Continue straight to follow the Canyon Trail southeast.

1.2 The trail curves east (left) to reach a sign pointing north (left). Turn north to work back up the canyon and past another spring.

1.3 A side trail heads east (right), guiding you to one series of petroglyphs.

1.4 Another side trail leads to a rock overhang with petroglyphs.

1.8 Pass the Westbrook homestead ruins, a Depression-era settlement.

2.1 Arrive back at the trailhead.

Options: Vogel Canyon offers four varied hiking trails that allow visitors to explore the canyon bottom and rim. Extend your journey by exploring the Mesa and/or Prairie Trails.

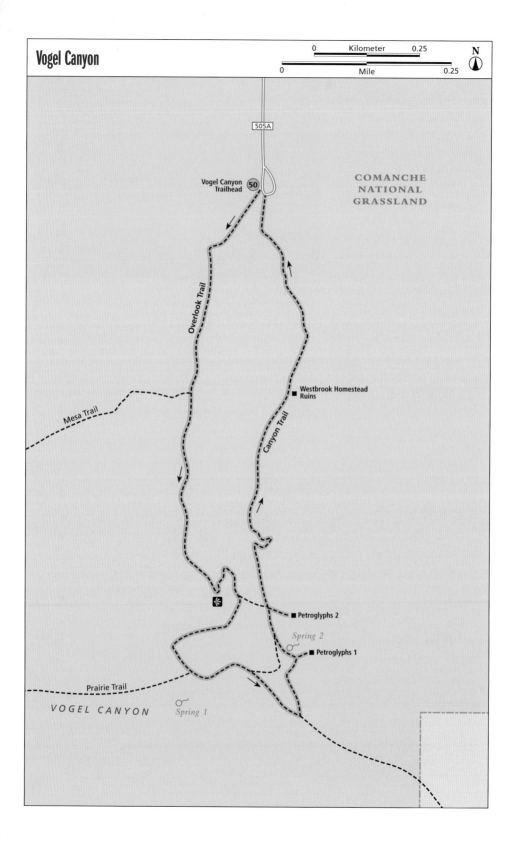

Vogel Canyon

505A

Vogel Canyon
Trailhead   50

COMANCHE
NATIONAL
GRASSLAND

Overlook Trail

Mesa Trail

Canyon Trail

Westbrook Homestead
Ruins

Petroglyphs 2

Spring 2

Petroglyphs 1

Prairie Trail

VOGEL CANYON   Spring 1

Hike information

General Information

La Junta Chamber of Commerce: La Junta; (719) 384-7411; lajuntachamber.com
Unofficial Comanche National Grasslands website: www.visitlajunta.net/comanche .html

Local Events/Attractions

Bent's Old Fort National Historic Site: La Junta; (719) 383-5010; www.nps.gov/beol
Koshare Indian Museum: La Junta; (719) 384-4411; kosharehistory.org
Otero County Museum: La Junta; (719) 384-7500; oteromuseum.org

Accommodations

KOA: La Junta; (719) 384-9580, (800) 562-9501; koa.com/campgrounds/la-junta/
Vogel Canyon Picnic Ground: camp in parking lot; Comanche National Grassland, La Junta; (719) 384-2181; www.recreation.gov (search for Vogel Canyon)
Withers Canyon Trailhead area: Comanche National Grassland, La Junta; (719) 384-2181; www.fs.usda.gov/psicc

HONORABLE MENTIONS

Eastern

Here is a great hike in the Eastern region that didn't make the A-list this time round but deserves recognition.

I. Canyon Loop at Aiken Canyon Preserve

This easy 4-mile loop at Aiken Canyon Preserve meanders through a range of habitats including pinyon-juniper and prairie scrub oak nestled in the transition zone between the plains and mountains. Interpretive signs highlight important features as you make your way through forest and wide-open meadows and past dramatic red spires and outcrops. Home to a treasure trove of plant and animal communities, you can find over a hundred bird species and fifty wildflower species that adorn the trail and hillsides most impressively in early June. From Denver, take I-25 South toward Colorado Springs. Take exit 135 (Academy Boulevard) west to CO 115. Take 115 south 11.5 miles to Turkey Canyon Ranch Road (located 0.1 mile south of milepost 32). Turn west (right) and drive 200 yards to the preserve parking. The preserve is open year-round, dawn to dusk, on Saturday, Sunday, and Monday. For more, contact The Nature Conservancy at (720) 974-7021 or visit: http://www.nature.org/ourinitiatives/regions/northamerica/unitedstates /colorado/placesweprotect/aiken-canyon-preserve.xml.

Appendix A: Common & Scientific Names of Wildflowers Mentioned

Common Name	Scientific Name
Alpine avens	*Geum rossii var. turbinatum, Syn: Acomastylis rossii ssp. turbinate*
Alpine bistort	*Bistorta vivipara, Syn: Polygonum viviparum*
Alpine chiming bells	*Mertensia alpina*
Alpine clover	*Trifolium dasyphyllum*
Alpine fireweed	*Chamaenerion latifolium, Syn: Chamerion latifolium, Chamerion subdentatum*
Alpine fleabane	*Erigeron grandiflorus*
Alpine forget-me-not	*Eritrichium nanum var. elongatum*
Alpine harebell	*Campanula uniflora*
Alpine milkvetch	*Astragalus alpinus*
Alpine paintbrush	*Castilleja puberula*
Alpine primrose (aka Fairy primrose)	*Primula angustifolia*
Alpine sandwort	*Minuartia obtusiloba, Syn: Lidia obtusiloba Areneria obtusiloba*
Alpine sorrel	*Oxyria digyna*
Alpine speedwell	*Veronica wormskjoldii variety wormskjoldii, Syn: Veronica nutans*
Alpine spring beauty	*Claytonia megarhiza, Syn: C. arctica megarhiza*
Alpine thistle	*Cirsium scopulorum*
Alpine violet	*Viola adunca var.bellidifolia*
Alplily	*Lloydia serotina*
American bistort	*Bistorta bistortoides, Syn: Polygonum bistortoides*
American smelowsky	*Smelowskia americana, Syn: Smelowskia calycina var.americana*
American speedwell	*Veronica americana*
American vetch	*Vicia americana*
American yellow-rocket	*Barbarea orthocera*
Annual sunflower	*Helianthus annuus*
Antelope-horn milkweed	*Asclepias asperula*
Arctic gentian	*Gentiana algida, Syn: Gentianodes algida*
Aromatic sumac (aka Three-leaf sumac, Lemonadeberry)	*Rhus aromatica ssp. trilobata*
Arrowleaf balsamroot	*Balsamorhiza sagittata*
Aspen sunflower	*Helianthella quinquenervis*
Baccada yucca	*Yucca baccada*
Ball head sandwort	*Eremogone congesta*

Common Name	Scientific Name
Ball head waterleaf	*Hydrophyllum capitatum*
Baneberry	*Actaea rubra ssp. arguta*
Beautiful cinquefoil	*Potentilla pulcherrima, Syn: P.gracilis var. pulcherrima*
Beautiful daisy	*Erigeron elatior*
Beautiful rockcress	*Boechera formosa*
Bitterbrush (aka Buckbrush)	*Purshia tridentata*
Black foot daisy	*Melampodium leucanthum*
Black-eyed susan	*Rudbeckia hirta*
Blackheaded daisy	*Erigeron melanocephalus*
Blacktip senecio	*Senecio atratus*
Blanketflower	*Gaillardia aristata*
Blue flax	*Linum lewisii var. lewisii*
Blue violet (aka Hook violet)	*Viola adunca*
Blueberry	*Vaccinium myrtillus*
Blueleaf cinquefoil	*Potentilla glaucophylla*
Bog pyrola (aka Pink pyrola)	*Pyrola asarifolia ssp. asarifolia, Syn: P.rotundifolia ssp.asarifolia*
Bog saxifrage	*Micranthes oregana*
Boulder raspberry	*Rubus deliciosus*
Bracted alumroot	*Heuchera bracteata*
Bracted lousewort (aka Wood betony, Fernleaf lousewort)	*Pedicularis bracteosa var. paysoniana*
Britton skullcap	*Scutellaria brittonii*
Brook saxifrage	*Micranthes odontoloma, Syn: Saxifraga odontoloma*
Brownie ladyslipper	*Cypripedium fasciculatum*
Buckley's penstemon	*Penstemon buckleyi*
Butter 'n' eggs	*Linaria dalmatica*
Canada violet	*Viola canadensis var. scopulorum, Syn: V. scopulorum*
Carolina larkspur	*Delphinium carolinianum ssp. virescens*
Carpet phlox	*Phlox canescens/hoodii?*
Case's fitweed	*Corydalis caseana ssp. brandegei*
Chinese lantern	*Quincula lobata*
Chokecherry	*Prunus virginiana*
Claret cup	*Echinocereus triglochidiatus*
Cliff fendler bush	*Fendlera rupicola, Syn: F.falcata*
Colorado columbine	*Aquilegia coerula*
Colorado locoweed	*Oxytropis lambertii*
Colorado rubberweed	*Hymenoxys richardsonii*
Colorado thistle	*Cirsium scariosum var. coloradense, Syn: C. coloradense*
Coneflower	*Ratibida columnifera*

Common Name	Scientific Name
Copper globemallow	*Sphaeralcea angustifolia*
Corn lily (aka False hellebore, Skunk cabbage)	*Veratrum californicum var californicum*, Syn: *V. tenuipetalum*
Coulter's daisy	*Erigeron coulteri*
Cow parsnip	*Heracleum maximum*, Syn: *H.sphondylium ssp. montanum, H. lanatum*
Cowbane	*Oxypolis fendleri*
Cranesbill (aka Filaree)	*Erodium ciutarium*
Creamtips	*Hymenopappus filifolius*
Crescent milkvetch	*Astragalus amphioxys*
Curly dock	*Rumex crispus*
Curly-cup gumweed	*Grindelia squarrosa*
Cushion buckwheat	*Eriogonum ovalifolium var. purpureum*
Cushion phlox (aka Alpine phlox)	*Phlox pulvinata*
Cutleaf daisy	*Erigeron pinnatisectus*, Syn: *E. compositus*
Death camas	*Anticlea elegans*
Desert dandelion	*Malacothrix sonchoides*
Desert paintbrush	*Castilleja chromosa*
Desert parsley	*Cymopterus glomeratus*
Desert trumpet	*Eriogonum inflatum*
Dogbane	*Apocynum androsaemifolium*
Dotted blazing star	*Liatris punctata*
Dotted saxifrage	*Saxifraga austromontana*, Syn: *Cilaria austromontana*
Double bladderpod	*Physaria acutifolia*
Drummond's milkvetch	*Astragalus drummondii*
Drummond's rockcress	*Boechera stricta*, Syn: *Boechera drummondii, Arabis drummondii.*
Dwarf clover	*Trofolium nanum*
Dwarf evening primrose	*Oenothera caespitosa*
Dwarf golden aster	*Heterotheca pumila*
Easter daisy	*Townsendia hookeri*
Edible valerian	*Valeriana edulis var.edulis*
Elephant heads	*Pedicularis groenlandica*
Fairy slipper	*Calypso bulbosa var. americana*
False Solomon's seal	*Maianthemum racemosum ssp. amplexicaule*, Syn: *M.amplexicaule, Smilacina racemosa*
Fendler's bladderpod	*Physaria fendleri*
Fendler's meadowrue	*Thalictrum fendleri var. fendleri*
Fireweed	*Chamaenerion angustifolium ssp. circumvagum*, Syn: *C. danielsii, Epilobium angustifolium*

Common Name	Scientific Name
Four-nerve daisy	*Tetraneuris acaulis*
Freckled milkvetch	*Astragalus lentiginosus var. palans*
Fremont geranium	*Geranium caespitosum*
Fringed gentian	*Gentianopsis thermalis, Syn: Gentiana thermalis, Gentianopsis detonsa*
Fringed sagewort	*Artemisia frigida*
Geyer's larkspur	*Delphinium geyeri*
Geyer's onion	*Allium geyeri*
Giant lousewort	*Pedicularis procera*
Glacial daisy	*Erigeron glacialis, Syn: E. peregrinus.*
Glacier lily	*Erythronium grandiflorum*
Globeflower	*Trollius laxus ssp. albiflorus, Syn: T. albiflorus*
Golden aster	*Hetherotheca pumila*
Golden aster	*Heterotheca villosa*
Golden banner	*Thermopsis montana var. montana*
Golden corydalis (Scrambled eggs)	*Corydalis aurea*
Golden currant	*Ribes aureum*
Golden draba	*Draba aurea*
Graceful buttercup	*Ranunculus inamoenus*
Grass of parnassus	*Parnassia fimbriata*
Gray's angelica	*Angelica grayi*
Green mitrewort	*Pectiantia pentandra, Syn: Mitella pentandra*
Greenflower pyrola	*Pyrola chlorantha*
Greenleaf five eyes	*Chamasaracha coronopus (Chamaesaracha arida)*
Hairy arnica	*Arnica mollis*
Hall's penstemon	*Penstemon hallii*
Heartleaf arnica	*Arnica cordifolia*
Heartleaf bittercress	*Cardamine cordifolia*
Heartleaf twistflower	*Streptanthus cordatus*
Hooker's sandwort	*Eremogone hookeri*
Horsemint	*Monarda fistulosa ssp. fistulosa var. menthifolia*
Hound's tongue	*Cynoglossum officinale*
Indian breadroot	*Pediomelum megalanthum*
Jim Hill's mustard	*Sisymbrium altissimum*
King's crown (aka Roseroot)	*Rhodiola integrifolia*
Kinnikinnick	*Arctostaphylos uva-ursi*
Lambstongue groundsel	*Senecio integerrimus*
Lanceleaf chiming Bells	*Mertensia lanceolata*
Large Indian-breadroot	*Pediomelum esculentum*
Large leaf avens	*Geum macrophyllum*
Lavenderleaf sundrops	*Oenothera lavandulifolia*
Leafy cinquefoil	*Drymocallis fissa*

Common Name	Scientific Name
Lemon scurf pea	*Ladeania lanceolata, Syn: Psoralidium lanceolatum*
Little cryptantha	*Cryptantha micrantha*
Little gentian	*Gentianella amarella ssp. acuta, Syn: G.acuta*
Littleflower penstemon	*Penstemon procerus*
Long-leaved phlox	*Phlox longifolia*
Loveroot	*Ligusticum porteri*
Low penstemon (aka Bluemist penstemon)	*Penstemon virens*
Macauley's buttercup	*Ranunculus macauleyi var. macauleyi*
Mariposa lily	*Calochortus gunnisonii*
Marsh marigold	*Caltha leptosepala*
Mat prickly phlox	*Linanthus caespitosus*
Meadow anemone	*Anemone canadensis*
Miner's candle	*Oreocarya virgata, Syn: Cryptantha virgata*
Missouri milkvetch	*Astragalus missouriensis*
Monkshood	*Aconitum columbianum*
Monument plant (aka Green gentian)	*Frasera speciosa*
Mormon tea	*Ephedra viridis*
Moss campion	*Silene acaulis var. subacaulescens*
Mountain ball cactus	*Pediocactus simpsonii*
Mountain beardstongue	*Penstemon glaber*
Mountain bladderpod	*Physaria montana*
Mountain bluebells (aka Tall chiming bells)	*Mertensia ciliata*
Mountain cats-eye	*Oreocarya cana*
Mountain currant	*Ribes montigenum*
Mountain dandelion (aka Agoseris)	*Physaria montana*
Mountain harebell	*Campanula rotundifolia*
Mountain mahogany	*Cercocarpus montanus*
Mountain ninebark	*Physocarpus monogynus*
Mountain parsley	*Cymopterus lemmonii*
Mountain pepper plant; peppergrass	*Lepidium montanum*
Mountain spring parsley	*Cymopterus montana*
Mountain thistle	*Cirsium scopulorum*
Mouse-ear chickweed	*Cerastium arvense ssp. strictum*
Mule's ears	*Wyethia amplexicaulis*
Mullein	*Verbascum thapsus*
Muttongrass	*Poa fendleriana*
Narcissus anemone	*Anemone narcissiflora var. zephyra, Syn: Anemonastrum narcissiflorum ssp. zephyrum*
Narrow-leaf penstemon	*Penstemon angustifolius*
Narrowleaf puccoon	*Lithospermum incisum*

Common Name	Scientific Name
Narrowleaf yucca	*Yucca harrimaniea*
Nettle-leaf giant-hyssop	*Agastache urticifolia*
Nodding onion	*Allium cernuum*
Northern bedstraw	*Galium boreale, Syn: G. septentrionale*
Northern goldenrod	*Solidago multiradiata*
Northern green bog orchid	*Platanthera aquilonis, Syn: Limnorchis hyperborea, Habenaria hyperborea*
Northern paintbrush	*Castilleja septentrionalis, Syn: C. sulphurea*
Northern sweetvetch	*Hedysarum boreale*
Nuttall's gilia	*Linanthastrum nuttalli*
Nuttall's larkspur	*Delphinium nuttallianum*
Nuttall's sophora	*Sophora nuttalliana*
Old man of the mountain	*Hymenoxys grandiflora, Syn: Rydbergia grandiflora, Tetraneuris grandiflora*
Onesided penstemon	*Penstemon unilateralis, Syn: P.virgatus ssp.asa-grayi*
One-sided wintergreen	*Orthilia secunda, Syn: O.obtustata, Pyrola secunda*
Orange paintbrush	*Castilleja integra*
Orange sneezeweed	*Hymenoxys hoopesii, Syn: Dugaldia hoopesii, Helenium hoopesii*
Oregon grape	*Mahonia repens, Syn: Berberis repens*
Parrot's beak (aka Rams horn lousewort)	*Pedicularis racemosa ssp. alba*
Parry arnica	*Arnica parryi*
Parry clover	*Trifolium parryi*
Parry gentian	*Gentiana parryi, Syn: Pneumonanthe parryi*
Parry primrose	*Primula parryi*
Parry's harebell	*Campanula parryi*
Parry's lousewort (aka Alpine lousewort)	*Pedicularis parryi*
Parry's milkvetch	*Astragalus parryi*
Pasqueflower	*Pulsatilla patens ssp. Multifada*
Pearly everlasting	*Anaphalis margaritacea*
Peavine	*Lathyrus lanszwertii var. leucanthus*
Perky Sue	*Tetraneuris ivesiana*
Pinedrops	*Pterospora andromedea*
Plains larkspur	*Delphinium carolinianum*
Plains milkvetch	*Astragalus gilviflorus*
Plains paintbrush	*Castilleja sessiliflora*
plains springparsley	*Cymopterus acaulis*
Plantain-leaf buttercup	*Ranunculus alismifolius variety montanus*
Poison hemlock	*Conium maculatum*

Common Name	Scientific Name
Pond lily	*Nuphar polysepala, Syn: N. lutea ssp. polysepala*
Prairie milkvetch	*Astragalus laxmannii*
Prairie ragwort	*Packera plattensis*
Prairie smoke	*Geum triflorum var. triflorum, Syn: Erythrocoma triflora*
Prickly pear	*Opuntia spp.*
Prickly poppy	*Argemone polyanthemos*
Purple prairie vervain	*Glandularia bipinnatifida v. bipinnatifida*
Pygmy bitterroot	*Lewisia pygmaea, Syn: Oreobroma pygmaeum*
Pygmy gentian	*Gentiana prostrata, Syn: Chondrophylla prostrata*
Queen's crown	*Rhodiola rhodantha*
Rattlesnake plantain orchid	*Goodyera oblongifolia*
Red clover	*Trifolium pratense*
Red columbine	*Aquilegia elegantula*
Red elderberry	*Sambucus racemosa*
Richardson's geranium	*Geranium richardsonii*
Rimrock milkvetch	*Astragalus desperatus*
Rock clematis	*Clematis occidentalis, Syn: Atragene occidentalis*
Rocky Mountain loco	*Oxytropis sericea*
Rocky Mountain penstemon	*Penstemon strictus*
Rocky Mountain pussytoes	*Antennaria parvifolia*
Rocky Mountain trifolium	*Trifolium attenuatum*
Rosy paintbrush	*Castilleja rhexifolia*
Rosy pussytoes	*Antennaria rosea, Syn: A. microphylla*
Rydberg's penstemon	*Penstemon rydbergii*
Sagebrush buttercup	*Ranunculus glaberrimus var. ellipticus*
Salsify	*Tragopogon dubius*
Sand aster	*Chaetopappa ericoides*
Sand lily	*Leucocrinum montanum*
Sand verbena	*Abronia fragrans*
Scarlet bee blossom	*Oenothera suffrutescens*
Scarlet gilia	*Ipomopsis aggregata*
Scarlet globemallow	*Sphaeralcea coccinea*
Scarlet paintbrush	*Castilleja miniata*
Scorpionweed	*Phacelia heterophylla*
Serviceberry	*Amelanchier alnifolia*
Shooting star	*Dodecatheon pulchellum ssp. pulchellum*
Short's milkvetch	*Astragalus shortianus*
Showy daisy	*Erigeron speciosus*
Showy goldeneye	*Heliomeris multiflora*
Showy locoweed	*Oxytropis splendens*
Showy milkweed	*Asclepias speciosa*

Common Name	Scientific Name
Showy ragwort	*Senecio amplectens variety amplectens*
Shrubby cinquefoil	*Dasiphora fruticosa ssp. floribunda, Syn: Pentaphylloides floribunda, D. floribunda*
Sidebells penstemon	*Penstemon secundiflorus*
Silky milkvetch	*Astragalus sericoleucus*
Silky phacelia	*Phacelia sericea*
Silverleaf phacelia (aka Silverleaf scorpionweed)	*Phacelia hastata*
Silverweed cinquefoil	*Potentilla anserina*
Silvery cinquefoil	*Potentilla hippiana*
Silvery lupine	*Lupinus argentus*
Single delight	*Moneses uniflora, Syn: Pyrola uniflora*
Sky pilot	*Polemonium viscosum*
Slender cryptantha	*Cryptantha gracilis*
Slender milkvetch	*Astragalus gracilis*
Slender wild parsley	*Musineon tenuifolium*
Slender-tubed phlox (aka Nuttall's gilia)	*Leptosiphon nuttallii ssp.nuttallii, Syn: Linanthus nuttallii, Linanthastrum nuttallii*
Small lupine	*Lupinus pusillus*
Small-flowered alyssum	*Alyssum parviflorum*
Smooth goldenrod	*Solidago missouriensis*
Smooth woodland star	*Lithophragma glabrum*
Snow buttercup	*Ranunculus adoneus*
Snowball saxifrage	*Micranthes rhomboidea, Syn: Saxifraga rhomboidea*
Snowlover	*Chionophila jamesii*
Spiderwort	*Tradescantia occidentalis*
Spiked gilia	*Ipomopsis spicata*
Spotted coralroot orchid	*Corallorhiza maculata*
Sprawling daisy	*Erigeron divergens*
Spreading draba	*Draba reptans*
Spring beauty	*Claytonia lanceolata*
Squashberry	*Viburnum edule*
Star gentian	*Swertia perennis*
Star solomonplume	*Maianthemum stellatum, Syn: Smilacina stellata*
Stemless Easter daisy	*Townsendia exscapa*
Stemless Easter daisy	*Townsendia exscapa*
Stemless evening primrose	*Oneothera caespitosa ssp. macroglottis*
Sticky geranium	*Geranium viscosissimum*
Stinging nettle	*Urtica dioica ssp.gracili, Syn: Urtica gracilis*
Stinking milkvetch	*Astragalus praelongus*
Straggling milkvetch	*Astragalus lentiginosus*
Strawberry blite	*Chenopodium capitatum*

Common Name	Scientific Name
Subalpine arnica	*Arnica rydbergii*
Subalpine buttercup	*Ranunculus eschscholtzii*
Subalpine Jacob's ladder	*Polemonium pulcherrimum ssp. delicatum, Syn: P. delicatum*
Sugar bowls	*Clematis hirsutissima var. hirsutissima, Syn: Coriflora hirsutissima*
Sulphur flower	*Eriogonum umbellatum*
Tall coneflower	*Rudbeckia ampla*
Tall larkspur (aka Subalpine larkspur)	*Delphinium barbeyi*
Tall ragwort	*Senecio serra*
Textile onion	*Allium textile*
Thickbract senecio	*Senecio crassulus*
Thick-leaf ragwort	*Senecio crassulus*
Thimbleberry	*Rubus parviflorus*
Three-tooth groundsel	*Packera thurberi*
Thrifty goldenweed	*Stenotus armerioides*
Towering Jacob's ladder	*Polemonium foliosissimum var. foliosissimum*
Townsend's daisy	*Townsendia incana*
Tree cholla	*Cylindropuntia imbricata*
Triangularleaf senecio	*Senecio triangularis*
Tuber starwort	*Pseudostellaria jamesiana, Syn: Stellaria jamesiana.*
Twinberry	*Lonicera involucrate, Syn: Distegia involucrata*
Twinflower	*Linnaea borealis*
Twisted stalk	*Streptopus amplexifolius*
Valerian	*Valeriana acutiloba var. acutiloba, Syn: Valeriana capitata ssp. acutiloba*
Virgin's bower clematis	*Clematis ligusticifolia*
Wax currant	*Ribes cereum*
Waxflower	*Jamesia americana*
Western stickseed	*Lappula occidentalis*
Western tansy mustard	*Descurainia pinnata*
Western wallflower	*Erysimum capitatum*
Western yellow paintbrush	*Castilleja occidentalis*
Western chainpod	*Hedysarum occidentale*
Westwater tumble-mustard	*Thelypodiopsis elegans*
Whiplash daisy	*Erigeron flagellaris*
Whipple's penstemon	*Penstemon whippleanus*
Whiskbroom parsley	*Harbouria trachypleura*
White bog orchid	*Piperia dilatata var. albiflora, Syn: Limnorchis dilatata ssp. albiflora, Habenaria dilatata*

Common Name	Scientific Name
White clover	*Trifolium repens*
White evening primrose	*Oenothera albicaulis*
White fairy trumpets	*Ipomopsis aggregata ssp. candida*
White penstemon	*Penstemon albidus*
Whitestem blazingstar	*Mentzelia albicaulis*
Wild candytuft	*Noccaea fendleri ssp. glauca, Syn: N.montana, Thlaspi montanum*
Wild iris	*Iris missouriensis*
Wild licorice	*Glycyrrhiza lepidota*
Wild plum	*Prunus americana*
Wild raspberry	*Rubus idaeus*
Wild rose	*Rosa woodsii*
Wild strawberry	*Fragaria virginiana*
Wolf's currant	*Ribes wolfii*
Woolly locoweed	*Astragalus mollissimus var. thompsoniae*
Wyoming paintbrush (aka Narrowleaf paintbrush)	*Castilleja linariifolia*
Yarrow	*Achillea millefolium, Syn: A. lanulosa*
Yellow avens	*Geum aleppicum*
Yellow cryptantha	*Oreocarya flava, Syn: Cryptantha flava*
Yellow monkeyflower	*Mimulus guttatus*
Yellow prairie violet	*Viola nuttallii*
Yellow stonecrop	*Sedum lanceolatum ssp. lanceolatum, Syn: Amerosedum lanceolatum*
Yellow violet	*Viola purpurea*
Yellow-eye cryptantha	*Oreocarya flavoculata, Syn: Cryptantha flavoculata*
Yucca	*Yucca glauca*

Appendix B: Wildflower Resources

Ackerfield, Jennifer. 2015. *Flora of Colorado*. Botanical Research Institute of Texas.

Allred, Kelly. 2012. *Flora Neomexicana: Volume II: Glossarium Nominum*, 2nd ed. Lulu Enterprises.

Allred, Kelly and Robert DeWitt Ivey. 2012. *Flora Neomexicana: Volume III: An Illustrated Identification Manual*, 1st ed. Lulu Enterprises.

Anderson, Berta. 1976. *Wildflower Name Tales*. Colorado Springs, Colo.: Century One Press.

Carter, Jack L. 1988. *Trees and Shrubs of Colorado*. Boulder, Colo.: Johnson Books.

Coffey, Timothy. 1994. *The History and Folklore of North American Wildflowers*. Boston, Mass.: Houghton Mifflin.

Colorado Native Plant Society. 1997. *Rare Plants of Colorado,* Revised edition. Estes Park, Colo.: Rocky Mountain Nature Association; Helena, Mont.: Falcon.

Craighead, John J., Frank C. Craighead and Ray J. Davis. 1987. *A Field Guide to Rocky Mountain Wildflowers: Northern Arizona and New Mexico to British Columbia*. Boston: Houghton Mifflin.

Cronquist, Alfred. *Intermountain Flora, Vol. 1–8*. New York: New York Botanical Garden Press Dept.

Dahms, David. 1999. *Rocky Mountain Wildflowers Pocket Guide*. Windsor, CO: Paragon Press.

Duft, Joseph F. and Robert K. Mosely. 1989. *Alpine Wildflowers of the Rocky Mountains*. Missoula, Mont.: Mountain Press.

Elmore, Francis H. 1972. *Ethnobotany of the Navajo*. Albuquerque, NM: University of New Mexico Press.

Guennel, G. K. 1995. *Guide to Colorado Wildflowers: Mountains*. Englewood, Colo.: Westcliffe Publishers.

Harrington, Harold D. 1954. *Manual of the Plants of Colorado*. Denver, Colo.: Sage Books.

Kassar, Chris and Leigh Robertson. 2015. *Southern Rocky Mountain Wildflowers: A Field Guide to Wildflowers in the Southern Rocky Mountains, Including Rocky Mountain National Park,* 2nd ed. Guilford, Conn.: FalconGuides, an Imprint of Globe Pequot Press.

Kershaw, Linda. 2000. *Edible & Medicinal Plants of the Rockies*. Edmonton: Lone Pine.

Kershaw, Linda, Andy MacKinnon, and Jim Pojar. 1998. *Plants of the Rocky Mountains*. Grand Rapids, Mich.: Lone Pine.

Moerman, Daniel E. 1986. *Medicinal Plants of Native America*. Museum of Anthropology, University of Michigan.

Mutel, Cornelia F. and John C. Emerick. 1984. *From Grassland to Glacier*. Boulder, Colo.: Johnson Books.

Nelson, Ruth A., revised by Roger L. Williams.1992. *Handbook of Rocky Mountain Plants.* Denver, Colo.: Denver Museum of Natural History; Niwot, Colo.: Roberts Rinehart Publishers.

Pesman, M. W., revised by Dan Johnson. 2012. *Meet the Natives: A Field Guide to Rocky Mountain Wildflowers, Trees, and Shrubs: Bridging the Gap between Trail and Garden,* 11th ed. Boulder, Colo.: Johnson Books.

Spellenberg, Richard. 2001. *Audubon Society Field Guide to North American Wildflowers, Western Region,* Revised edition. New York: Alfred A. Knopf.

Weber, William A. and Ronald C. Wittmann. 2012. *Colorado Flora: Western Slope,* 4th ed. Niwot, Colo.: University Press of Colorado.

Willard, Beatrice E. and Michael T. Smithson. 1988. *Alpine Wildflowers of the Rocky Mountains.* Estes Park, Colo.: Rocky Mountain Nature Association.

Wingate, Janet L. and Loraine Yeatts. 2013. *Alpine Flower Finder: The Key to Rocky Mountain Wildflowers Found Above Timberline.* Wingate Consulting.

Online and/or Electronic Resources

Biota of North America Program (BONAP): Searchable, comprehensive, up-to-date database providing in-depth information on the taxonomy of the entire vascular flora of North America (excluding Mexico). http://www.bonap.org/

Colorado Rocky Mountain Wildflowers App: Developed by Al. Schneider and Whitney Til for phones and tablets, Apple and Android. Contains several thousand photos of 600 species from the foothills to the alpine zone. http://www.highcountryapps.com/

Eastern Colorado Wildflowers: A site with fantastic photos and bloom season information. www.easterncoloradowildflowers.com

Flora of North America: This vast, 30-volume work in progress provides one comprehensive resource for information on the names, taxonomic relationships, continent-wide distributions, and morphological characteristics of all plants native and naturalized found in North America, north of Mexico. http://www.floranorthamerica.org/ and www.efloras.org

Native American Ethnobotany: A searchable database of plants used as drugs, foods, dyes, fibers, and more by native peoples of North America. http://www.herb.umd.umich.edu/

Southwest Colorado Wildflowers: A comprehensive site covering the more common flowers seen in the Four Corners Area. Full of great photos and extremely informative details about plants, their names, and the botanists who discovered them. www.swcoloradowildflowers.com

Synthesis of the Flora of North America, The: This DVD "database on the taxonomy, nomenclature, phytogeography, and biological attributes of [all] North American vascular flora" is the culmination of forty years of work by John Kartesz.

These DVDs provide over 150,000 photographs, plant descriptions, and county-by-county records of every plant in North America.

USDA Plants Database: This searchable datatbase provides "standardized information about the vascular plants, mosses, liverworts, hornworts, and lichens of the United States and its territories." Includes synonyms, images, species information, and distribution maps. www.plants.usda.gov/java/

Hike Index

About the Author

Chris Kassar is a conservation biologist, guide, and writer with a reverence for nature, a thirst for adventure, and a desire to leave the world a little bit better. She gained extensive knowledge about wildflowers and plants through various field courses, formal studies in pursuit of her master's degree in Wildlife Biology at Utah State, and through her work as a biologist, guide, environmental educator, and interpreter in various National Forests and parks across the west, including Rocky Mountain, Denali, Arches, and Canyonlands.

Over the past few years, Chris has also turned her attention to using words and imagery to document various adventures, bring attention to important issues, and advocate for environmental change. Chris works as senior editor of *Elevation Outdoors Magazine* and as a freelance writer with published works in numerous publications, including *Climbing*, *Mother Jones*, the *Boston Globe Magazine*, *National Geographic Adventure*, and *Southern Rocky Mountain Wildflowers*. Chris, who is most at peace in the outdoors and considers a successful year one where she spends more nights sleeping under the stars than under a ceiling, lives in Salida, Colorado.